The Ironist's Cage

The Ironist's Cage

Memory,
Trauma,
and the
Construction of History

Michael S. Roth

Columbia University Press • New York

Columbia University Press
New York   Chichester, West Sussex
Copyright © 1995 Columbia University Press

Library of Congress Cataloging-in-Publication Data

Roth, Michael S.
    The ironist's cage : memory, trauma, and the construction
of history / Michael S. Roth
        p.   cm.
    Includes bibliographical references and index.
    ISBN 0-231-10244-5 — ISBN 0-231-10245-3 (pbk.)
    1. History—Philosophy.   2. Historiography.   I. Title.
D16.8.R847   1995
901—dc20   95-5816
                                                    CIP

⊗

Casebound editions of Columbia
University Press books are printed
on permanent and durable
acid-free paper.

Printed in the United States
of America
c 10 9 8 7 6 5 4 3 2 1

For Kari

Contents

Acknowledgments

I have been blessed with wonderful teachers, including some of those whom I have written about in *The Ironist's Cage:* Michel Foucault, Richard Rorty, Carl Schorske, Hayden White. It gives me enormous pleasure to acknowledge the continual influence their teaching has had on my approaches to the past. Most of the essays in this book were written while I was working with students at various levels in Claremont, California. I owe a lot to the students who critically responded to many of the ideas contained here. Scripps College supported this project with research grants and staff assistance, for which I am very grateful. I completed the preparation of this manuscript as a Getty Scholar at the Getty Center for the History of Art and the Humanities, and I am grateful to the Getty Trust for its support.

Several colleagues and friends read earlier versions of these papers, and I am grateful for having had their input. They include Elazar Barkan, Jan Goldstein, Victor Gourevitch, Dominick LaCapra, Harry Liebersohn, William McGrath, Allan Megill, Elizabeth Minnich, Anson Rabinbach, Charles Salas, Tracy Strong, and Kari Weil. Robert Dawidoff, whose work as a historian and community-based scholar has inspired colleagues, students, and friends, gave me the initial push to form my interest in contemporary history and memory into a book. His support, criticism, and friendship have enriched this book and my life.

How is it possible to be connected to the past without being overwhelmed by it? This is a question that is at the center of this book, and of my thinking about history and memory. Jeremy and Max offer me a continual source of information on this topic, a series of experiments in which they give me many chances. And Kari Weil does the most amazing thing of all: she simply shows me that it is possible. Voilà.

The Ironist's Cage

Introduction

When I wrote the earliest essay in this book in 1983, I was completing a study of the appropriation of Hegel in French intellectual life from the 1930s through the postwar period.[1] The rise and fall of Hegelianism in France was an index to the changing status of the historical as a resource for making meaning in the world. When in 1993 I completed the most recent essay collected here, I was working on a project on the conceptualization of memory disorders in nineteenth-century France.[2] The identification of memory disorders required the development of criteria for defining the normal connection between present and past. The question that connects these projects and all the essays collected in this book is "what does it mean to claim to have a reasonable, legitimate, or worthwhile connection between the present and the past?" Over the last ten years I have been interested in the resources that history as a discipline and as a genre might contain to help one answer this question. The essays in *The Ironist's Cage* are an expression of this interest.

Although few of the following chapters are properly historical, history is the problem of these essays. How do we make meaning and find direction from change over time, and for what purposes? The historians I examine in part 1 address the problem of history very differently from the philosophers or theorists discussed in part 2, and from the writers and filmmakers I explore in the final section of the book. Despite the different registers in which they work, however, all the authors confront the problem of constructing a meaningful connection to the past. The essays in *The Ironist's Cage* assess the changing status of historical consciousness within the discipline of history itself and explore how the various ways of making sense of the world and its representations have appropriated history.

By the early 1980s historical consciousness was seen by many as an ineffective, ideological, and unsophisticated mode of apprehending the world. The humanities seemed to have moved far away from any claim to orient inquiry through an appeal to the meaning and direction of change over time. Within the discipline of history itself, a crisis of confidence had shaken many of the most theoretically minded practitioners, as it became unclear what contribution the organized study of the past could make to the conversation of our culture. By the early 1990s much had changed. Scholars in a variety of fields were turning to the historical again as an area from which they could learn lessons essential to their disciplines (or to their attacks on their disciplines). Now historians themselves often evince a confidence in their practice by identifying "culture" as their object of study or identifying their techniques of studying the past as "culturalist."[3] In this way many historians are able to use some of the reflexive work done by literary critics on the very terms of literary criticism and by anthropologists on the possibilities for understanding the meaning systems of others. The *new* cultural history flourishes both by announcing (like the "new" social history in the 1960s) its difference from *old* ways of investigating the past and by using its affinities with other disciplines' strategies for making sense of the ways people generate, comprehend, and disseminate meaning. If intellectual history in the early 1980s was "agitated" by the "invasion of new theoretical perspectives and research practices from Europe," cultural history in the early 1990s brims with the (parochial, professional) confidence that "we are . . . entering a new phase when the other human sciences (including especially literary studies but also anthropology and sociology) are discovering us [historians] anew."[4] The difference between being invaded and being discovered marks the changes in this decade in the self-perception of historians concerned with the dynamics of cultural change. This difference in self-perception has not grown out of any theoretical advances or empirical discoveries. Despite the increased interest in historical studies or in cultural studies with a historical dimension, questions about the basic value of historical consciousness or historical knowing remain open and vital. The essays in this book pursue these questions in relation to historiography, political theory, philosophy, psychoanalysis, and film.

Throughout the modern period a key current of Enlightenment thought coded participation in tradition as a kind of slavery, whereas historical consciousness was keyed as a royal road to freedom. As Hegel said, history is the consciousness of the progress of freedom. In the contemporary period the link between historical consciousness and freedom became an object of criticism or derision. Without this link questions about the *point* of historical consciousness became embarrassingly difficult to answer. The defense against such questions became an increasingly sophisticated discourse in which the questions themselves were redescribed in ironic terms. The trap of this move to irony (the metamove) worked all too well, cutting off possibilities of reconnecting historical consciousness to any public discourse at all. Ironic sophistication marks the distance that some intellectuals have been able to take on political issues outside the academic realm, even as the impoverishment of contemporary political life has been a leitmotif of innovative work (so often called "radical") in the human sciences. The ironic form of that innovative work has often been a symptom, not a critique of that impoverishment.

Part 1 of this book focuses on problems that historians have considered central to their effort at representing the past: objectivity, contextualism, and realism. In the first three chapters, through an examination of books by Peter Novick, H. Stuart Hughes, and Carl E. Schorske, I raise questions about the professional strategies available to historians in their efforts to situate themselves in relation to their recounting of the past. All three authors share a problem that is perhaps common to *any* attempt to represent what is past: *What to do about fragmentation?* All historians encounter fragmentation as a feature of evidence as trace. For some the move to "it all fits together" comes quickly and even unconsciously. This is not the case for the three authors considered here.

Novick's concern is not with the fragmentation of evidence that the individual historian encounters but with the state of the discipline generally.[5] For Novick, fragmentation in the historical profession has resulted, in part, from the decline of its guiding myth of objectivity. The proliferation of topics, methodologies, and forms of representation has resulted in the loss of "discourse across the discipline." Novick details how the unity in the profession that had existed was often based on the most narrow prejudice, practices of exclusion, and intellectual mystification. The loss of *this* unity is not to be lamented and instead Novick places himself in ironic relation to it; that is, he writes for the profession as a whole as he denies that the profession is a whole, and his ironic stance allows him the sophisticate's luxury of knowingly recognizing unsatisfactory conditions while having to propose nothing at all to change them. This ironic stance, typical of much contemporary work in the humanities, will be examined in detail in part 2.

H. Stuart Hughes conceived the problem of fragmentation very differently from Novick, for he saw history as a means to forge new unities among increasingly isolated forms of discourse. By the early twentieth century the strands of social theory were pulling apart, as separate methodologies and concerns made it increasingly difficult for philosophers, economists, sociologists, psychologists, and novelists to speak to one another. The intellectual historian was able to tie these strands back together, showing connections of which the thinkers themselves were unaware. Hughes's narratives aimed to overcome fragmentation by enclosing the disparate elements into new syntheses. The intellectual/social context created by the historian allowed the reader to stand in a position from which fragmentation dissolved. History restored wholeness through contextualization.

Carl E. Schorske's response to fragmentation differs from both Novick's ironic and Hughes's synoptic modes of reconfiguring the past. Schorske is concerned with the fragmentation of sociocultural life in postwar America, a condition that has important affinities with the modernist antihistoricism that ran deep in Vienna at the turn of the century. His *Fin-de-Siècle Vienna* confronts modernist fragmentation with historical consciousness, but it does not enclose modernism within a synoptic historical narrative. The modernist rejection of historicism is historicized but never rejected. The tension between the historian's object of study (modernist antihistoricism) and his strategies for making sense of it (historical contextualization) is never dissolved. In fact, the tension is at the core of Schorske's own modernist contextualization of the past.

In part 2, Uses and Abuses, the essays move away from the profession of history to a consideration of recent attempts to assess the significance and construction of historical knowledge and sometimes to put it to work in the present. Fragmentation remains an issue for the philosophers and theorists considered in this section, but they respond to this issue in very different ways. For Foucault fragmentation is not something to be overcome through the construction of historical contexts that make connections among diverse phenomena. The tendency to use history in this way is instead exposed by Foucault as an effort to control discontinuity and to inhibit change.

Foucault writes his histories of the present to confront us with the fragmentation, the instability, that conventional historical narratives often conceal. In seeing the instability, the shifting ground on which we stand, we can begin to "think otherwise," to imagine that our pasts do not necessarily lead to a future that will validate some meaning and direction in our lives or our culture. In this regard Foucault's project has certain affinities with Richard Rorty's use of the past. Rorty, too, turns to history as a disruptive force, as a reservoir of stories that can underscore contingency, multiplicity, and possibility rather than necessity, homogeneity, and limitation. For both, history can be used to delegitimate any firm convictions we have about how we have come to be who we are. For Rorty, however, history is also something that can be used to construct forms of solidarity and the energy that comes from social hope. Unlike Foucault, Rorty is committed to use history to find new stories that will legitimate our practices and beliefs, not just undermine them. Whereas Foucault often writes as if he thinks history *in fact really is* discontinuous, Rorty seems committed to the position that history can be narrated so as to support an emphasis on discontinuity and fragmentation or an emphasis on continuity and wholeness. It all depends on what you want to *do* with history.

In this regard Rorty's position is not that different from Hayden White's. White's rhetorics of history shows how the past is constructed into a diversity of stories to achieve various ends. The emplotment of the past is a rhetorical molding of material according to patterns that can be analyzed through the grid of formalist literary theory. Recognizing the constructedness of any historical account can lead one to an ironic position vis-à-vis the significance of the past. If the past can be made to mean anything at all, one way to cope with this relativism is by taking ironic distance from it or by simply celebrating the meaninglessness of the past. White refuses these alternatives for moral or political reasons, and attempts to make room for a rejection of naive realism that does not fall prey to the nihilistic relativism of much of contemporary cultural theory.

Foucault, Rorty, and White are all "undoers," to use Ian Hacking's word;[6] that is, all of them want to undo the narrative knots into which the past has been tied, so as to make new (and less tight) combinations possible. Rorty and White are very concerned with controlling the combinations that may emerge after their work of undoing. Rorty would like to confine the celebration of contingency and reconfiguration to the private realm, where the human damage of having the past continually destabilized is kept to a minimum (or simply confined to those who have the taste for that sort of thing). For Rorty, the narrative knot we have about our own public past may need some slight attention now and then, but it seems to be holding together pretty well, thank you. White has been trying to limit the range of plot structures "suitable" to certain events in response to the pressure that the appearance of holocaust revisionists has put on his relativism. The disjunction between fact and emplotment (that one cannot simply judge the latter by the former) seems to have become too painful in light of the events of our century, and White has attempted to find some boundaries on the kinds of stories that can legitimately be told about particular events in the past.[7]

The attempt to limit the range in which the past can legitimately be used has been a crucial feature of post-Hegelian historicism. Without such limitation, historical knowing seems to be little more than a form of self-congratulation, the winners getting to construct their histories so as to validate their victories. The fact that in our own time losers are extremely interested in constructing their histories so as to validate their status as victims does not alter the problem of how to separate a legitimate use from an abuse of history. Hegel thought he had solved this problem by showing that the essential meaning of historical development had already been revealed and by creating a philosophical system that provided the logical structure of this meaning (and its revelation). As history seemed to continue, however, post-Hegelian thinkers were left to grapple again with making sense of the past from their new and changing present. Hegel's borders on the rational use of the past were crossed as subsequent thinkers believed they had to construct a new past from the new vantage point of their (changing) present.

Alexandre Kojève reinstalled the Hegelian limitations on the construction of history by claiming that History had already come to an end and that from the universal perspective provided by that end one could make sense of the whole. History (and its representations) was no longer plagued by multiplicity or fragmentation. It was one, unique and coherent: it provided knowledge not just stories. In Kojève's debate with Leo Strauss, discussed in chapter 5, we can see the universalist alternative to the fragmentation of the historical field with which the other figures in the book contend. Strauss argued that only a philosophy of nature that would generate criteria of judgment would allow one to begin to contend with the multiplicity of historical change. Kojève argued that a philosophy of History, possible only when History, properly so-called, had run its course, provided one with stable (and enforceable) criteria of judgment. In his recent reflections on the end of History, discussed in chapter 9, Francis Fukuyama attempts to play the realist card (with Kojève) in claiming that History ends with us and to play the idealist card (with Strauss) in condemning the ending of History for which most people seem willing to settle. Even if History is limited to a single (universal) story, Fukuyama can still find some comfort in condemning the mediocrity of the tale. Of course, this move is meant to elevate the critic above this mediocrity.

Strauss and Kojève, and hence Fukuyama, attempt to come to terms with historical change from somewhere beyond historical change. Strauss makes no claim to know the stable, unchanging realm that orders thinking about the unstable, changing world we live in; he offers only the recognition that such a realm is necessary for philosophical knowledge, rightly conceived. Kojève escapes the fragmentation of historical change by writing from a position where essential change (change that affects the meaning of History) no longer takes place. These thinkers agree on an essential point: escape from the unstable, fragmented, multiplicitous world of history is necessary for genuine knowledge.

By contrast, Foucault, Rorty, and White do not think that such escape is possible, and they question the idea of genuine knowledge to which Kojève and Strauss are committed. Foucault, Rorty, and White certainly share the view that all knowledge is constrained by the paradigm, *epistēmē,* or simply, the culture of the knower. This is no more than saying that knowledge is constrained by, since it is expressed in, language or that it is dependent on the knower's historical context. The dream of escaping from this constraint into a "genuine" knowledge is one of the objects of their critical perspectives on modern philosophy and theory. However, the acceptance of the constraints of one's own historical situation becomes increasingly problematic as one becomes more critical of one's own historical situation—that is, as one regards these constraints as illegitimate (but from where does one regard them?). Thus the acceptance of these constraints is more of a problem for Foucault (at least when he is in a radical mood) than it is for Rorty (at least when he is in a patriotic mood). In contemporary cultural criticism this problem results in what I call the ironist's cage, the prison of cultural critics who realize that they have no position from which to make their criticism. The desire to be politically radical and still be intellectually sophisticated has lead many contemporary critics into the ironist's cage. Paul de Man perhaps knew the contours of this confinement better than most:

> Irony divides the flow of temporal experience into a past that is pure mystification and a future that remains harassed forever by a relapse into the inauthentic. It can know this unauthenticity but can never overcome it. It can only restate and repeat it on an increasingly conscious level, but it remains endlessly caught in the impossibility of making this knowledge applicable to the empirical world. It dissolves in the narrowing spiral of a linguistic sign that becomes more and more remote from its meaning, and it can find no escape from this spiral.[8]

Irony, de Man emphasizes, reveals a "truly temporal predicament." One can, like de Man, relish this seemingly complex spiral, this "permanent parabasis." But the effort to display one's knowledge of it (to show that one is on an "increasingly conscious level") while still connecting to the political world leads much of contemporary cultural criticism to rattle the bars of the ironist's cage.

The essays in part 3 of the book are all concerned with the intersection of trauma, its remembrance, and the possibilities for overcoming it. Memory has become a cultural obsession for Americans in our fin de siècle, much like it was for Europeans a century ago. There is much to discuss about memory because very little is certain about it. Despite the enormous amount of ongoing research, our knowledge about the basic neurophysiology, about forgetting, and about the effects of trauma on memory formation remains rudimentary. Talk about memory has become the language through which we address some of our most pressing concerns. This is because in modernity memory is the key to personal and collective identity. With the demise of religious notions of an essential soul as self, and with the decline in the powers of groups to designate communal missions or the identities of individual members, personal memory has come to be seen as that which defines who we are. Memory in modernity is seen less as a public, collective function than as a private, psychological faculty: it is imagined by philosophers and doctors from the eighteenth century on as being internal to each of us, at the core of the psychological self. We are what we remember, and this is one of the reasons why forgetting (and sudden recall) arouses so much anxiety and excitement. But the psychologization of memory makes it extremely difficult for people to share the past, for them to have confidence that they have a collective connection to what has gone before.

Memory seems to promise immediacy, a kind of certainty about the existence of particular events in the past. It also enables people to believe in the persistence of the past: as long as people are remembered, they are, we are often told, still alive. In *Telling the Truth About History,* Joyce Appleby, Lynn Hunt, and Margaret Jacob have gone so far as to base the possibility of historical knowledge on our existential dependence on memory.[9] In recent years, however, we have encountered an extraordinary array of challenges to our notions of the stability of memory. The popular media delight in showing cases of recovered memories, false memories, and implanted memories. It is clear that memory can be manipulated, and that the persistence of the personal past is dependent on the needs of the person remembering in the present. So it would seem that memory, like history, is always constructed in or is a response to the present. And we have seen in recent years that any particular recounting of the past may well be a violation of someone else's memory of it. What is the connection of this popular interest in memory with recent debates about historical thinking?

One of the key works exploring the connection of memory and history is Yosef Yerushalmi's *Zakhor,* which is the subject of chapter 10. Yerushalmi explored the tensions between memory and history for European Jewry, and showed how the latter did not become important for Jewish communities until the former began to slip away; that is, the past can be embodied in many "vessels" in traditional communities, and history writing only assumed an important function for Jews after the stable structures of these communities began to disappear. Without the apparent stability of traditional sources of legitimation, history writing began to play a critical role in relation to the past: evaluating what is important and assigning relative significance to particular elements as they are given a place in some narrative emplotment. But Yerushalmi, and now several other scholars, have shown that history writing is a sign of forgetting because it indicates that collective memory is in the process of disappearing.

Here we see one of the most important tensions between history and memory. On the one hand, history writing appears as the traditional forms for containing the past are disappearing. However, once these forms are gone and collective memory has lost access to important aspects of the past, history writing is one of the crucial vehicles for reconstructing or reimagining a community's connection to its traditions. This is especially true for groups who have been excluded from the mainstream national histories that have dominated Western historiography, and who have suffered a weakening of group memory as part of their experience of modernity. These groups are not only rewriting their own pasts but are challenging the dominant narratives that have been told about modernization and progress. As a substitute for collective memory, history writing since the nineteenth century has assumed the function of creating a past with which a group of people can live, but in our own time the criteria for establishing a particular history as legitimate have become extremely unstable.

The greatest obstacle to creating a usable past is the existence of trauma. Trauma may also be what gives the greatest urgency to this task because it may seem that we cannot go on living without some way of "integrating" the traumatic moment with the rest of our lives. Yerushalmi is skeptical about history's capacity to turn the past into something that sustains a community over time. He sees historical writing less as a community's response to trauma than as a symptom of a community's disintegration. The strength of history lies in its capacity to critically evaluate claims about change over time; although the genre of monumental history has retained a certain viability, modern history writing until recently thrived on its powers of demystification. In the last several years many historians have offered a strange combination of demystification and hagiography. The critical perspective is aimed at the dominant culture; the hagiography is devoted to showing how a particular group can claim a legacy of oppression (and often resistance) within the dominant culture.

Claiming a legacy of oppression establishes what moral philosophers call a "we-group," people with whom one identifies and with whom one feels connected. Establishing a we-group can be a source of comfort, of defense, and of pleasure. This is the dimension of solidarity that Rorty emphasizes in contradistinction to irony. In addition to establishing a we-group, claiming a legacy of oppression can enable individuals to work through the traumas of their collective and personal histories. The avoidance of a painful past or the failure to recognize its lasting effects often creates disabling patterns of behavior that only cause further pain. Our literary scene is flooded with self-help books that lead one to discover the pain in one's past, but their triviality should not obscure the deep dilemmas of which they are symptoms. Judith Herman's important study, *Trauma and Recovery,* details how an escape from patterns of suffering is often dependent on recognizing them as part of one's history.[10] Herman shows in a very powerful and sometimes subtle way that recognizing and giving voice to one's suffering is a necessary stage in moving past that suffering. Recent history writing, especially in its effort to "give voice to" the oppressed of the past, is responding to some of the same issues that Herman's feminist psychiatry addresses.

Claiming a legacy of oppression has come to be used not only as a tool to escape the past, however, but as a vehicle for maintaining one's connection to and even identification with it. In attaching oneself to a legacy of oppression one may reach for a moral superiority that our culture often awards to victims (that it recognizes as such). This award of moral superiority is no real substitute for justice, but it can be a powerful balm in a world of continued economic, social, and political inequality. Universities and the media have become specialists in providing people with feelings of moral superiority instead of intelligent responses to demands for real social change. In these cultural arenas recognized marginality has become a moral high ground, the latest opiate of the people.

In some ways this may be perfectly reasonable. After all, victims do have a different claim on our moral and political responsibilities than do those who profit from victimizing others. But this claim can be easily abused by individuals, groups, or institutions who appropriate a collective memory of oppression to legitimate irresponsibility and violence. The most dramatic recent cases of this tendency on the world scene are in the former Yugoslavia and in Rwanda. The construction of a historical memory that portrays the Serbs or the Hutus as victims of History allows for genocidal policies without obvious guilt. No matter what the victims do, they are only defending themselves, or at least aiming for justice through the destruction of (even potential) oppressors. Serbia and Rwanda may be the most obvious cases of this dynamic at the level of international relations, but we can all too easily find many examples of the same phenomenon: from Bensonhurst to Jerusalem, from Belfast to Beverly Hills and into our own family rooms. Memory of trauma in the past is constructed in the present as a *cause* of abhorrent behavior or as a reason for political or military strategies that would otherwise clearly be morally repugnant.

There is already a backlash against the use of memory to construct one's identity as a victim, and much of it sounds like the denial of bad news rather than thoughtful criticism. The whipping boys of "political correctness" and "false memory syndrome" may only be nasty full-employment programs for journalists. There are, of course, legacies of oppression whose effects continue, even though some claim these legacies in ways that can be rejected on scientific, moral, or political grounds. This means that we have to pay attention both to the forces that engender these claims and to the content of the claims themselves. We must examine memory historically, and try to understand why claims to remember how one has been oppressed have extraordinary power at particular times for particular purposes. This will be true whether those who claim this kind of past do so to validate their ethnic, religious, or gender identity or to protest against the continued exploitation of this identity by others.

The cultivation of traumatic memory can lead to a harvest of hatred and violence. On the other hand, memory—even of the most painful kind—can be used to expand that group of people who count for us, those who we do not consider merely strangers. The difficulty lies in seeing how these two offspring of memory are related and have developed together over time; how the irresponsibility and violence that are legitimated by reference to the past are linked to the solidarity that a common past can be used to promote.[11]

In chapter 11 I examine how Freud came to develop psychoanalysis as a mode of interpretation that would create a past with which one could live. Psychoanalysis emerges out of mourning, out of the work that enables a person to detach him- or herself from the past even while retaining some (narrative) connection to it. The talking cure demands that one situate oneself (or one's desires) in relation to the past, not that one reconstruct the *actual* past in the present. The role of trauma has been of decisive significance in the history of psychoanalysis, and as Freud emerged from mourning for his father he also radically altered the place of childhood trauma in the theory of hysteria. This has led some writers to claim that Freud was either fleeing from an insight into the persecution of children (especially female), that he was covering over his and his friend Fliess's gross incompetence, or that he was protecting his own abusive father. I do not attempt to evaluate these claims here, only to show how Freud created psychoanalysis as a mode for connecting and representing the past with important affinities to mourning, in contradistinction to neurosis. He developed a hermeneutics of memory rather than a tool for some unmediated expression of the past (whatever that might be) which would pretend to get free of it; that is, Freud developed psychoanalysis as a way of using the past rather than revolting against it.

The final two chapters in the book are also concerned with the question of developing a past with which one can live, and they examine it in relation to two films, *Hiroshima Mon Amour* and *Shoah*. In the former, a Resnais/Duras film, the ambivalent response to trauma's claims on an individual is incisively explored. Letting go of the painful past ("recognizing and giving voice to one's suffering is an necessary stage in moving past that suffering," as I summarized Herman above) is also being unfaithful to the past, to (at least) the person who suffered back then. When does fidelity to the past become a poison, or simply an avoidance of the present? How does one come to ask oneself, or someone else, this question?

We might say that *Hiroshima Mon Amour* takes very seriously Nietzsche's view that happiness is impossible without forgetting. The challenge of this film is to represent forgetting, and to underline the ways in which conventional, narrative memory necessarily forgets in order to remember. Narrative memory, like history, is constructed or configured by emphasizing some things and leaving others out. The voices of the past never simply appear in the present—unless of course one has lost one's temporal bearings in madness, as we are shown in *Hiroshima*. The past is necessarily violated in narrative memory and in history writing, and so the very act of remembering can seem like an act of infidelity. *Hiroshima Mon Amour* is not ironic about this necessary infidelity; the film remains at the level of ambivalence. That which is unforgettable is that which cannot be remembered, cannot be recounted.

The recognition that any particular recounting of the past may well be a violation of someone's memory of it underscores that every representation of the past (whether in memory or in history) takes place in a particular (present) context, not in the removal of all contextual distortion through methodology. This brings us back to the problematics discussed in chapter 5 in relation to Hayden White's rhetorics of history. White is concerned with the formal mapping of the rhetorical strategies we use to recount the past. In the final section of this book I am interested in particular contextual and existential pressures on the use of the past. For example, the historical approach to tradition, discussed in chapter 10, raises problems of judgment that are beyond the scope of any particular form of tradition. These are problems of what Jürgen Habermas has discussed as "the public use of history":

> The inevitable pluralism of readings, which is by no means un-monitored but on the contrary rendered transparent, only reflects the structure of open societies. It provides an opportunity to clarify one's own identity-forming traditions in their ambivalences. This is precisely what is needed for the critical appropriation of ambiguous traditions, that is, for the development of a historical consciousness that is equally incompatible with closed images of history that have a secondary quasi-natural character and with all forms of convention-al, that is, uniformly and prereflexively *shared* identity.[12]

One might say that Freud, too, is concerned with the "critical appropriation of ambiguous traditions," both on the personal and the collective levels. The possibilities for change opened by the historical consciousness psychoanalysis aims to provide is the capacity for such critical appropriation (rather than unconscious repetition or refusal).

Personal or collective trauma certainly interrupts the critical appropriation of the past, although it may also heighten the importance of such appropriation. This has been especially clear in the Historians' Debate in Germany, as the evaluation of the Nazi period in relation to German history generally has fed concerns about an adequate remembrance of the victims of Nazi genocidal policies. Discussions of these issues and others surrounding the fiftieth anniversaries of the ending of World War II have made clear that there is no consensus (or formula for generating one) about what "adequate remembrance" would be, just as there is no consensus (or formula for generating one) about the proper historical weight to assign to this period in the history of modernity. The absence of agreement and of criteria for achieving it generates opposite reactions: both an ironic disengagement from the past that leans on relativism about historical representation generally, and an urgency to affect what representations will be made (whatever their empirical validity) since these will continue to have important effects on collective identity.

In the context of these difficulties in adjudicating claims about the discovery and portrayal of the past as it really was, many historians have recently become extremely interested in questions about memory and commemoration. As Patrick Hutton has suggested, this probably stems from the recognition that there is no way to recover the past, and that the best one can do is to explore efforts that others have made to recover it.

> Places of memory, viewed as wellsprings by the memorialists of the nineteenth century, are regarded by historians today as mirrors in which people once tried to see themselves. In other words, the places of memory are self-referential for those who had recourse to them. In their attempts to reckon with their own heritage, they invented them in order to assign a meaning to the past that accorded with their contemporary concerns. Yesterday's places of memory, therefore, are today's place markers for historians mapping the many ways in which the past was once imagined.[13]

By concentrating on the ways the past was imagined, historians distance themselves from simple empiricism without disconnecting themselves entirely from the effort to remember. The past becomes something that other people longed for, fought over, strove to make vivid. In our present, knowing that these desires cannot be satisfied, we can watch with fascination (and sometimes with ironic sophistication) as other people vainly act on them. But why do we continue to care about the practices of commemoration if we have no ability (or need) to connect with the past?

Pierre Nora has emphasized the individual's interiorization of the relation to the past as the collective milieux of memory disappear.[14] The psychologization of memory and the doubts about the possibilities for objective history have combined to create an attitude that lets each person have his or her own history. What may appear to be a benign pluralism (or multiculturalism), however, can actually be another symptom of the continuing privatization (or ghettoization) of our relationship to the past. This form of social amnesia depends on a superficial relativism in which one has no investment in the past that one might share with another. Without such an investment, one has no real ties to other persons or groups and no possibilities for progressive collective action.

If memory is the core of identity, the attention given to studying it is a sign of our own troubled sense of who we are in relation to who we have been. But the study of memory should not merely be a continuation of its privatization, its disconnection from public, political life. The study of the past and its representations, especially those aspects of the past "that will not pass" should do more than provide us with examples of naive dreams or dirty scandals from which we can take our distance.

In the final chapter of this book I explore contemporary connections between history and memory in two very different registers. On the one hand I consider why I have been drawn to these issues of historical representation in my own work, and on the other I discuss how Claude Lanzmann's film *Shoah* grows out of and responds to these issues. In considering these different registers I think we can see two fundamental dimensions of historical investigation and representation: the empirical and the pragmatic. The former is the effort to "get the past right," to provide an interpretation of something in the past that is recognized as *of* that thing. The latter is the effort to find or create a usable past, something that can be put in the service of a particular goal. The tension between the empirical and the pragmatic investments in the past has been crucial for modern historical work, and it may be that no complex representation of the past is possible without both components.

In "*Shoah* as Shivah" I discuss a third fundamental dimension of historical work that plays an important role in Lanzmann's film and in my own approach to the past. I call this the dimension of piety. By *piety* I mean the placing of oneself in relation to the past in its otherness and potential connection to oneself. Piety may be linked with the effort to render the past as it really was, or, in the popular metaphor, in its own voice; that is, it may be linked with an empirical stance in relation to the past. Piety may also be linked with the effort to make the past usable or relevant in the present; that is, it may be linked with the pragmatic. But piety is not reducible to either the empirical or the pragmatic. Piety is the turning of oneself so as to be in relation to the past, to experience oneself as coming after (perhaps emerging out of or against) the past. This is the attempt at fidelity to (not correspondence with) the past. We do not encounter the past only in order to understand it correctly (although this may be important), nor only to extract lessons from it (although this too is often crucial). When the dimension of piety is powerful in our historical work, we encounter the past by acknowledging its absence, its having been. Living with this absence but not overcoming it is an expression of our piety in relation to the past.

Through the dimension of piety, we acknowledge the importance of something in the past, and we acknowledge the claim that that thing has on us. The object that we acknowledge in this way is certainly *for us,* but piety is our refusal simply to *use* the object or to forget it. We give it an authority, but the fact that *we* give it this claim on us does not reduce the claim. Our cultivation of the persistence of that claim without the empirical and pragmatic dimensions is blind, but the cultivation of these more familiar dimensions of historical perspective without piety is empty.

Piety in relation to the past has at best an awkward place in contemporary thinking about history. We are accustomed to work in terms of the tension between the empirical and the pragmatic, but the dimension of piety reminds us of why we turn to (and stay with) the past at all. Of course in an age that privileges irony, this dimension will be weak or may be present only as the target of techniques for sophisticated disengagement. But in the effort to think *with* history as well as about it, we must reconsider our attachments to the past, not only our capacity to distance ourselves from it. The essays in *The Ironist's Cage* consider history as a problem and a resource as they explore various distances from which attachments to the past can inform our present.

NOTES

1. Revised and published as *Knowing and History: Appropriations of Hegel in Twentieth-Century France* (Ithaca: Cornell University Press, 1988).

2. See "Remembering Forgetting: Maladies de la Mémoire in 19th-Century France," *Representations* 26 (1989): 49–68; "Dying of the Past: Medical Studies of Nostalgia in Nineteenth-Century France," *History and Memory* 3, no. 1 (1991): 5–29. Reprinted as "Returning to Nostalgia," in *Home and Its Dislocations in Nineteenth-Century France,* ed. Suzanne Nash (Albany: State University of New York Press, 1993), 25–43; "The Time of Nostalgia: Medicine, History and Normality in Nineteenth-Century France," *Time and Society* 1, no. 2 (1992): 271–86.

3. As Marilyn Strathern has put it, "The nice thing about culture is that we know that everyone, regardless of time or place, has it." See her review of *The New Cultural History,* in *Annals of Scholarship* 9, nos. 1/2 (1992): 199–208.

4. Dominick LaCapra and Stephen L. Kaplan, eds. *Modern European Intellectual History: Reappraisals and New Perspectives* (Ithaca: Cornell University Press, 1982), 7; Lynn Hunt, ed.,

The New Cultural History (Berkeley: University of California Press, 1989), 22. The extraordinary difference in tone between these two volumes, especially in regard to professional confidence (no doubt influenced by the decline of quantitative social history in the 1980s) is striking.

5. See Allan Megill, "Fragmentation and the Future of Historiography" *American Historical Review,* 96, no. 3 (1991): 693–98.

6. Ian Hacking, "History and Philosophy," in *History and . . . : Histories within the Human Sciences,* ed. Ralph Cohen and Michael S. Roth (Charlottesville: University of Virginia Press, 1995), 296–318.

7. See Wulf Kansteiner, "Hayden White's Critique of the Writing of History," *History and Theory* 32, 3 (1993): 273–95.

8. Paul de Man, *Allegories of Reading: Figural Language in Rousseau, Nietzsche, Rilke and Proust* (New Haven: Yale University Press, 1979), 118.

9. Joyce Appleby, Lynn Hunt, and Margaret Jacob, *Telling the Truth about History* (New York: Norton, 1994), 258–59, 270.

10. Judith Herman, *Trauma and Recovery* (New York: Basic Books, 1993).

11. I have discussed some of these issues in the magazine *Tikkun.* See my essays "Victims, Memory, History" (March/April 1994): 59–60, 95, and "Education for Democracy" (July/August, 1994): 51–52.

12. Jürgen Habermas, *The New Conservatism: Cultural Criticism and the Historians' Debate,* ed. and trans. Shierry Weber Nicholsen (Cambridge, Mass.: MIT Press, 1989), 226–27. See also the essay "On the Public Use of History" in the same volume.

13. Patrick Hutton, *History as an Art of Memory* (Burlington: University of Vermont Press, 1993), 10.

14. See, for example, "Between Memory and History: *Les Lieux de Mémoire,*" *Representations* 26 (1989): 14–15.

PART I

Objectivity and the Construction
Of Historical Context

• 1 •

Unsettling the Past: Objectivity, Irony, and History

The publication in 1988 of Peter Novick's *That Noble Dream: The "Objectivity Question" and the American Historical Profession* was an *event* for those with a stake in the writing and teaching of history in the United States. *That Noble Dream* provokes. It is a challenge to how we consider history as a way of thinking and writing and as a profession. But well before its appearance, historians, philosophers, and literary critics had been challenging the pretensions of professional history writing to objectivity, even to referentiality. There has been a growing sense of uncertainty about the purpose of historical writing and historical thinking in contemporary culture, as there have been serious theoretical and practical questions raised about the value of professional history in American society. In the *longue durée* of history writing and doubts about it, how can one assess the importance of Peter Novick's event?

That Noble Dream "explores the fortunes of the idea of objectivity among American professional historians over the last century" (1). Novick traces the use and abuse of this idea for historical writing: how it served to legitimize the consolidation of the profession; how it was used to stimulate contempt for those who did not embrace it as a goal or foundation for their research; and how at certain periods in the twentieth century major professional historians abandoned the idea without giving up their claims to be historians. In other words, Novick tells the story of how the American historical profession defined itself in relation to the idea of objectivity, and how the profession has changed as the idea no longer sustained a good many working historians.

That Noble Dream is divided into four major sections. The first shows how ideas about objectivity and realism were appropriated from a European context and used in the United States to promote professionalization and scientific legitimation. By the early decades of the twentieth century, historical inquiry was seen as something in which one could become an expert. A key element in the path to that expertise was the acquisition of a method to guarantee a high standard of objectivity. The second section of the book explores the initial wave of reactions against the ideal of objectivity. In times of crisis, politics and history acted as partners, but this compromised professional historians' claims to distance and neutrality. The experience of historians in both world wars disrupted their understandings of, and in some cases their commitments to, objectivity. The third section deals with the aftermath of World War II and the early stages of the cold war, when the ideal of detached truth-telling was reinvigorated as a defining feature of historical professionalism, at least in the "free world." Politicizations of history were then seen as departures from a rigorous and sophisticated method characteristic of open societies and of modern sciences. The fourth and last section examines the collapse of "normal history" in the face of the disruption of the homogeneous composition of the historical community, and as new subjects and methodologies competed for legitimacy in the contested terrain of academic scholarship.

During the latter part of the nineteenth century, American scholars in what we now call the humanities sailed to Germany in search of something for which many today fly to Paris: sophistication through method. German historical seminars provided a scientific baptism for Americans who wanted to channel their curiosity about the past into a form of learning that could be taught and built upon. At least that's what the Americans wanted from these seminars; so that's what they found. Novick recounts the American appropriation of Ranke as the apogee of scientific detachment, sobriety, and empiricism. "All German historians saw Ranke as the antithesis of a non-philosophical empiricism," Novick shows, "while American historians venerated him for being precisely what he was not" (28). American historians wanted a scientist, and they found one; they craved European legitimation for what they hoped would be a science of history, and they came back from Germany with it.

How was historical investigation and writing to be turned into a science? The first task was to discover primary facts, basic and indisputable elements of any historical explanation. German *Quellenkritik* was the rigorous determination of source material. It allowed one to be sure of the facts at one's disposal. Reliable facts based on primary sources "when justly arranged interpret themselves" (39). The personality, imagination, and politics of the historian were irrelevant here. One could be trained in *the method,* and this guaranteed that the results of one's inquiry would be unbiased, detached, objective.

With training and method in hand a profession could readily be formed. Unity, stability, and continuity were key elements in historical representations deemed objective, and although these elements had no necessary connection with evidence, they were said to be necessary to any professional historical account of the past. An important goal in the early years of the American Historical Association was the creation of a national history, one based on a broad consensus not beholden to local concerns. The major rift to overcome, of course, was that between Northerners and Southerners, and the great conflict to be avoided was in regard to their respective views on the Civil War and Reconstruction. Novick expertly traces the process through which they came to a consensus: slavery was wrong and secession unconstitutional but reconstruction was an outrage against fellow Americans: "Through some give-and-take, a nationalist and racist historiographical consensus, which demonstrated historians' impartiality and objectivity, was achieved on the 'middle period' of the nineteenth century" (77). Southern historians were brought into the fold and the value of objectivity was enhanced. "What better way for northern historians to show their fairness and impartiality," Novick writes, "than by bending over backward to appease the southerners" (80).

In the early years of the new century, a consensus about historical methodology and about the usefulness of history writing in the present held together. The homogeneous collection of professional historians differed about specific political issues and about some historical explanations, but they were committed to a notion of historical knowledge that overcame whatever differences they had. The Progressives challenged pieties about the American founding and about the aggressive use of historical knowledge in the present, but they shared an allegiance to the general professional commitments of their more conservative colleagues. As Novick notes, "Before the war, optimism was the great solvent of doubt in the epistemological as in the ideological realm" (105). We might contrast this with contemporary intellectual culture in which pessimism, often justified with sophisticated theoretical frameworks, functions as a solvent of conceptual consensus and professional solidarity.

The theoretical and practical consensus among historians was undermined by their experience of World War I. First, the route of legitimation via German science was broken as nationalism and xenophobia infected the historical profession. Whereas detachment and cosmopolitanism were the values that once were crucial to the ethos of those who "loved the past for its own sake," suddenly historians were anxious to prove that they could be counted on as strong patriots ready to *act* on behalf of their country. And historical writing came to be accepted as a mode of action. Second, if the war swept away the possibility of detachment, the peace overturned the various degrees of progressive optimism characteristic of the profession in the early part of the century. Listen to the progressive historians Becker and Robinson:

> [The war] was as a whole the most futile and aimless, the most desolating and repulsive exhibition of human power and cruelty without compensating advantage that has ever been on earth. This is the result of some thousands of years of what men like to speak of as "political, economic, intellectual and moral Progress . . . " (130)[1]

> History does not seem to stop any more. All the historian can do nowadays is to leave off, with a full conviction that he may have played up merely specious occurrences and have overlooked vital ones. . . . It is as difficult to tell where to start as where to stop. . . . I have come to think that no such thing as objective history is possible.
> (131)[2]

Before World War I the subjective perspective of the historian was thought to be overcome by dedication to a method and participation in a profession. The experience of the war showed that the method of historical inquiry could be put in the service of the political aims of one's country. Most historians did not conclude from this that the ideal of objectivity was false or that it should be given up. There was, however, an important group of historians who, emphasizing the present-mindedness of all historical investigation, came to think that all historical knowledge was relative to the "frame of reference" of the historian. Borrowing from new understandings

of science developed during the interwar years, they understood all knowledge as influenced by the environment in which it was discovered. This
influence was not a condition of subjectivism to be left behind through
the application of a rigorous method but a condition of living and thinking (166).

As the rifts in the profession's understanding of historical knowledge
became more important, consensus about the interpretation of specific
historical events also broke down. The great sign of professional and scientific convergence in the 1890s and early twentieth century was the civil
and racist agreement about the causes and meaning of the Civil War; this
consensus collapsed in the interwar period. Historians armed with what
seemed to be the same information arrived at sharply opposed conclusions.
Thus historians came to appreciate what the "relativists" had been arguing
for some time: that the study of the past supported ideas and values held
independently of the study itself. This was true whether one concentrated
on the selection of what would count as facts or on the influences on an
individual's interpretation. The notion that the profession as a whole was
closing in on stable truths about the past was belied by the sharp divergence among historians about some of the most pressing and well-
studied subjects in fairly recent history (238–39).

Although Novick rehearses some of the arguments for and against so-
called historical relativism in the 1930s, he is not really concerned with
whose position is right (even from our present-day "frame of reference").
Instead he delights in the rhetoric of attack and defense, as he shows the
nervousness with which conservative historians greeted the "new" ideas
that became popular during this period. He writes of the sociology and
politics of objectivity, and although this leads him through some philosophical gardens, he does not stop long to smell the roses. He is, however,
eager to show the variety of *uses* to which ideas are put: how the profession
managed to suffer through a period in which there were grave doubts
about objectivity and consensus, and to emerge after World War II with a
reconstructed version of objectivity aimed to satisfy both professional and
political agendas.

Part of the postwar consensus about objectivity came from the identification of relativism with defeatism, isolationism, and with the general
failure to be willing to risk one's life to protect one's values. In other words,
relativism became a bogeyman: a doctrine that would make one incapable

of standing up to Hitler. This portrait was useful to those on both the Left and the Right. The reconstructed version of objectivity fit in nicely with the concerns of the cold war: science in the "free world" was empirical and nonideological, whereas science in totalitarian societies was subordinated to ideological concerns. A key facet of "our" science was its tendency to move toward consensus. We could expect to see minor changes in historical descriptions of important events, but in a value-free atmosphere that recognized complexity, historical reinterpretation would develop slowly, continuously.

Novick describes historical inquiry within a "convergent culture," and within a profession that more or less ignored the antiobjectivist questions posed a generation earlier. Perhaps these questions were important to philosophers but real, *working* historians could afford to pass them by. When pressed, historians would acknowledge that they did not believe in an old positivist approach to facts and to description. They would even acknowledge that the past did not speak for itself and that history owed much to literature. But in the late 1950s and early 1960s historians in the center of the profession still believed that if you went "deep into the context" or "spent enough time in the archives" or "waded your way through the mass of documents," you would emerge with a story similar to that of anyone else who had had the same experience. Oscar Handlin said that "historians had learned to live with relativism"; Novick describes this in a wonderful phrase as "rejection by partial incorporation" (410). The same phenomenon continues, especially among established historians anxious to show that they are as interested as the next humanist in complexity and tough questions.

The culture of convergence, and the professional consensus that went along with it, split apart of course in the mid 1960s. During this period oppositional tendencies in the profession developed for the first time (417), and in battles between different interpretations of the "same events," often nobody seemed to be thinking about the possibility of a compromise that would unite all but the most extreme partisans of each side. It is interesting that in such debates often the only thing participants had in common was a commitment to some version of the ideal of objectivity. Even the overtly politicized histories written on the Left, which seemed to reject many professional conventions, claimed an objectivity that would serve, rather than compromise, political engagement. But without convergence and consensus to guarantee objectivity, how could these claims be taken seriously outside the community of one's friends?

At least since World War I the profession did not have a single unifying methodology, but it did have an *ethos,* a commitment to comity, convergence, and continuity in scientific knowledge that united its practitioners. This ethos has been deeply eroded in the past twenty years. The recognition in the 1960s of the politicization of history and the radical shifts in focus stemming from new methodologies (especially, though not exclusively, in social history) have made ideas of consensus of merely historical interest. Moreover, as women and minority group members have become major participants in the profession, the basis for civil consensus has been challenged, since, as Novick repeatedly shows, that basis was often comprised by shared anti-Semitism, conservatism, sexism, and racism. Indeed the word *metanarrative* has replaced *consensus* as pointing to that story which dominant members of the profession believe. And one rarely hears talk by younger historians of improving, shifting, or correcting the metanarrative. Instead they want to see it "undermined" or "deconstructed."

Novick charts this development, examining what he calls the fragmentation of the profession. Part of the "refocusing" that makes up this fragmentation comes from the introduction of new subjects for historians. Novick discusses the growth of women's history and black history in some detail, and charts the proliferation of accounts under the rubric of "every group its own historian." The changes in subject often result in changes in method, as new sources are explored in novel ways. But what tied these studies together? What made them all histories as opposed to anthropologies, sociologies, or—horror of horrors—fictions? Literary theorists and antiepistemologists offered only cold comfort as they pointed out that historians were really no worse off than any other investigators anxious to turn their claims into well-founded truths.

> Ideological disarray replaced the consensus on which ideas of objectivity had always depended so heavily. The resurgence of particularist tendencies further undercut the objectivist vision of a convergent past. Various "post-modern" intellectual currents worked together to chip away at the philosophical foundations of the objectivist posture.   (573)

There were still loud and confident calls that if we just immersed ourselves in the documents, everything would be all right, but now these calls received a mixed reception: for some the epistemological lullaby provoked sighs of relief, whereas for others it merely stimulated nasty snickers. "Discourse across the discipline," Novick writes about the 1980s, "had effectively collapsed" (592).

In keeping with the detached tone of *That Noble Dream,* Novick never presents an argument that "discourse across the discipline" is a good thing. He makes no claim that a consensus is important for historical research or writing nor that the proliferation of subfields within the profession is progress or corruption. It is important to see, however, that *That Noble Dream* is aimed precisely at the discipline of history, no, the profession of history, as a whole.[3] His book *is* a "discourse across the discipline." Novick has written a traditional historical account of the development of a profession in relation to its ideals. He shows us how the ideals were constructed within a specific context to satisfy particular needs. He then recounts how the ideals failed to be true guides given changing historical realities. Altered political and social circumstances undermined the original faith in the ideals, and so reformers came along to refurbish the ideals to make them fit more readily into new circumstances. However, the pace of change soon outran those aiming at reconstruction, and before long nothing was holding the profession as a whole together. This does not mean that there are no ideals *within* the profession. Each group has its own set of them.

Novick's story, then, is one of consolidation, crisis, reconstitution, and finally fragmentation. The story ties various facts together in a totality; Novick's narrative itself unites the various groups into a coherent whole. What's the point of the story? Does *That Noble Dream* have a political, moral, or aesthetic lesson to teach? In fact, the book does not contain a brief for any particular political perspective. But Novick does show that politics has played a role throughout the development of professional history writing in America, not least of all when the writers claimed to be value-neutral in their approach to the past. Nor does the book have a moral agenda, although its author seems to delight in his discovery of the moral failings of well-known historians in hiring and promotion decisions. He usually reports these findings without much comment, counting on our easy pleasures (or sad surprises) in seeing some of the more established members of the profession nodding into racism, sexism, and pettiness, as the gossipers had always suggested.

The mode of the study is ironic, and in some ways this form is its defining feature. The irony stems from a tension between the book's form and its content: we are shown that historians usually write with a moral or political agenda, and that the idea of objectivity guiding their work is usually a smokescreen for other concerns. But the study that reveals these facts claims to have no moral or political agenda, and to have no concerns with which to instruct the profession. The author is careful to say at the end of *That Noble Dream* that he makes no predictions for the future. The book claims that the discipline of history has ceased to exist and yet it is aimed at members of the discipline. What is the connection between the claims of the book and those to whom the claims are addressed?

I make this point about the tension between the form and the content of Novick's book not as a criticism of it. Novick is well aware that he has used the tools of the tradition to undermine the tradition all the more effectively.[4] Novick is not a historical objectivist nor a relativist but a historical ironist, and it is irony, not objectivity, that gives him a distance on the history he has to tell. Like Rorty's ironists inclined to philosophize, ironists inclined to historicize "play the new off against the old" in order to show the foundationlessness of any choice of vocabulary (or of method or of style).[5] Ironists may arise when doubts about the foundations of any set of practices become widespread. As Hayden White has noted:

> Ironic styles have generally predominated during periods of wars against superstition, whether the superstitions in question be identified as naive religious faith, the power of the monarchy, the privileges of the aristocracy, or the self-satisfaction of the bourgeoisie. Irony represents the passage of the age of heroes and of capacity to believe in heroism.[6]

The "superstition" Novick is after is the historian's belief in objectivity, and the "self-satisfaction" he aims to undermine is the status that comes with professionalization. The historical ironist deflates the lofty dream said to hold the profession together.

Why do it? The Enlightenment attack on religion was motivated by a deep commitment to science, and attacks on the aristocracy and bourgeoisie grew out of a faith that it was not necessary for people to live under certain forms of oppression. What motivates the strategy of *That Noble Dream*? Why should one want to awaken others from the dream of objectivity; to what does one awaken them?

The aim of the book, Novick states explicitly in the introduction and concluding paragraph (and implicitly throughout), "was to provoke my fellow historians to greater self-consciousness about the nature of our activity, to stimulate alternative ways of thinking about works of history and the claims made on their behalf" (628–29). Novick means to further, then, a more open-ended, pluralist profession. This is the kind of profession he sees emerging in the 1970s and 1980s. There are times in his description of the fragmentation of the profession that he worries about the inability of various groups to speak to one another. This should not be understood as a nostalgia for the days of civility and racism or the longing for some unifying master narrative. Novick worries, instead, about the incapacity of many historians to tolerate a multiplicity of redescriptions of the past. The increased self-consciousness he wants to provoke through redescription— that is, through narratives rather than through theory—would enable historians to have sympathy for and to explore "alternative ways of thinking about works of history." And the alternative ways of thinking do not have to fit together, although we might also tolerate redescriptions that look for such fits. This does not mean that the historical ironist must welcome with open arms any description of the past. There will still be failures to meet accepted canons of accuracy, of logical reasoning, and of political or moral values. A sense of tolerance, as American pragmatists have been arguing for more than a hundred years now, does not make it impossible to stand up for what you believe.[7]

White may be right to suggest that irony appears when the capacity to believe in heroes vanishes.[8] *That Noble Dream* certainly contains no recommendations for new historian-heroes on the horizon, but the author wants the horizon to remain as open as possible. This opening is achieved by forcing professional historians, through the use of their own methods and sources, to acknowledge the messy and fitful development of the ways of their tribe, alongside their own typically self-congratulatory description of this same development. Novick is a member of the tribe of historians, and his ironic interpretation of its central professional myth is not meant to break his solidarity with it but to point to a more open, pluralistic form of belonging. "When the work of interpretation has been completed," Freud wrote, "we perceive that a dream is the fulfillment of a wish."[9] Novick's powerful event is meant to awaken us from the noble dream of cumulative, objective knowledge about stable sets of problems, but also to stimulate the wish for enhanced self-consciousness through historical redescription.

NOTES

1. Novick quotes a letter of June 17, 1920, from Charles Becker to William E. Dodd.

2. James Harvey Robinson, "After Twenty Years," *Survey* 53 (1924): 18–21, quote at 18–19.

3. James T. Kloppenberg makes a related point in "Objectivity and Historicism: A Century of American Historical Writing" (review article on Novick, *That Noble Dream*), *American Historical Review* 94 (1989): 1011–30, at 1014.

4. This was clear in Novick's response to papers on *That Noble Dream* presented at the December 1990 meeting of the American Historical Association in New York City; see Peter Novick, "My Correct Views on Everything," *American Historical Review* 96 (1991): 699–703.

5. Richard Rorty, *Contingency, Irony, and Solidarity* (New York: Cambridge University Press, 1989), 73.

6. Hayden White, *Metahistory: The Historical Imagination in Nineteenth-Century Europe* (Baltimore: Johns Hopkins University Press, 1973), 232.

7. See Rorty's *Contingency, Irony, and Solidarity,* and my review of it in *History and Theory* 3 (1990): 340–57; Kloppenberg's review of Novick cited above; and Kloppenberg's *Uncertain Victory: Social Democracy and Progressivism in European and American Thought, 1870–1920* (New York: Oxford University Press, 1986), passim. See also Robert B. Westbrook, *John Dewey and Democracy* (Ithaca: Cornell University Press, 1991).

8. It is interesting to note, however, that Novick's ironic account of objectivity in history has been taken as comfort by Mormon historians fighting against a secular or naturalistic historical establishment. See Louis Midgley, "The Myth of Objectivity: Some Lessons for Latter Day Saints," *Sunstone: Mormon Experience, Scholarship, Issues and Art* 14, no. 4 (1990): 54–56. (I am grateful to Wayne Sandholtz for making this article available to me.) Ironic delegitimation can go in any direction.

9. Sigmund Freud, *The Interpretation of Dreams* in *The Standard Edition of the Complete Psychological Works of Sigmund Freud,* ed. and trans. James Strachey (London: Hogarth Press, 1953), 4:121.

• 2 •

Narrative as Enclosure:
The Contextual Histories of H. Stuart Hughes

The only fitting attitude is that of the cosmopolitan, detached intellectual.
—H. Stuart Hughes, *Consciousness and Society*

In 1987 Wesleyan University Press reissued two important works by one of the most influential writers and teachers of modern European intellectual history. As sequels to H. Stuart Hughes's *Consciousness and Society* (1958), *The Obstructed Path* (1968) and *The Sea Change* (1975) have now been combined in a volume entitled *Between Commitment and Disillusion*. In 1988 Harvard University Press published Hughes's latest study of contemporary intellectual life in Europe, *Sophisticated Rebels: The Political Culture of European Dissent*. The time seems right for taking another look at Hughes's approach to intellectual history and for considering it in relation to contemporary trends in the field.[1]

In his introduction to the Wesleyan edition of his work Hughes situates his approach to history "between two others which have focused primarily on textual analysis," those associated with Lovejoy on the one hand and "Parisian structuralism and deconstruction" on the other. Whereas Hughes and his cohorts "laid heavy stress on context," the textualisms of his predecessors and successors have been more concerned with "precision of method" (ix). The school with which Hughes identifies depends less on philosophy and literary theory than it does on "general speculation on the role of human beings in the societies that have formed them and that they in turn have altered" (x). How is the use of this "general speculation" related to the relative neglect—perhaps even suspicions about—methodology? And how is the knowledge produced (or the desires satisfied) by his narratives of historical context related to the knowledge produced (or the desires satisfied) by intellectual histories that focus primarily on textual analysis?

In trying to speak to these questions I do not mean to contribute to the ongoing "debate" between textualists and contextualists, a debate in which much ink can be spilled as long as there remains a confusion of terms and aims.[2] It is sometimes entertaining and sometimes tiresome to make a "theoretical" case for or against contextual intellectual history,[3] or to invoke—after the appropriate moves to show one's theoretical sophistication—the irreducibility of "lived experience" (readers kick the stone!). Rather than trying to turn linguistically or to plead for a re-turn to stuff more substantial than mere texts, I want here to examine how an important historian constructed specific narrative contexts. As Richard Harvey Brown has noted, "the methods one uses to gain agreement about a phenomenon depend . . . on the kind of explanation one chooses to seek."[4] In order to understand better how contextual intellectual history creates agreement, how it satisfies, in this essay I shall examine some of the important works by one of its most successful practitioners.

The two volumes contained in *Between Commitment and Disillusion* continue the exploration of the tensions in modern European intellectual life that provided the drama for *Consciousness and Society*. In the earlier work Hughes showed how a "cluster of geniuses" developed in the early twentieth century, and how these thinkers strove to connect their investigation of the subjective life of the individual with an analysis of the social and historical sphere. The tension between the internal and the external, the subjective and the objective, the psychological and the social, would be at the center of Hughes's concerns as a historian. Indeed he seemed to feel that the historian was in an exceptional position to understand these dynamic oppositions. Whereas through much of the nineteenth century philosophy was a form of thought that embraced these tensions, by the end of the century specific fields were developing to focus on only a single dimension. History was the form of inquiry that existed not only between art and science but that could embrace both in a single account of their development over time.[5]

These oppositions reappear in *The Obstructed Path,* the first half of *Between Commitment and Disillusion.* The entire book is structured by the tension between intuition and reason, which is mirrored by the conflict between a parochial French classicism and the challenges presented by contemporary history that called for a new cosmopolitanism. Hughes fits his figures into this particular intellectual context, and he judges them by their willingness

not simply to leave their tradition behind (what would that mean?) but by
their capacity to open to the wider world while retaining their specific
qualities as French thinkers. Insofar as the path of French intellectual life
was obstructed, it was because it could not resolve the tensions between
intuition and reason, between provincialism and cosmopolitanism.

We can see these conflicts in the case of Marc Bloch and Georges
Lefebvre, whom Hughes describes in the second chapter of *The Obstructed
Path*. According to Hughes, Lefebvre had his roots deep in the soil of
France; he had his *pays*. He approached the past with passion, and his writings benefited from his subjective connections to the material. Bloch, on
the other hand, came from the city, a cosmopolitan, rational Jew. His analytic skills gave his histories a force that made his findings relevant to anyone concerned with societies in the past. Lefebvre and Bloch comple-
mented one another nicely, and the history writing they fostered combined
some of the virtues of each man. They never arrived at a synthesis of their
different approaches to the past, however, and, according to Hughes, their
failure to do so resulted in confusion for subsequent generations of *an-
nalistes*. For the successors of Bloch and Lefebvre the path of intellectual
development was obstructed by the tendency to choose between the
strengths of each man, rather than to combine them in a new opening to
the world beyond France.

The French intellectual of this period whom one might expect to escape
from the inability to connect the virtues of French intellectual traditions
with an openness to the wider world is Jean-Paul Sartre. After all, Sartre's
existentialism drew heavily on German thought, and his politics and ideas
extended well beyond the borders of his homeland. Yet Sartre was unde-
niably French, both in his commitment to a certain form of thinking—
sometimes called Cartesian—and in his political engagement as an intellectual. Still, Hughes shows how despite appearances, Sartre was a sign of,
and not an exception to, France's cultural isolation. For example, the historian fits Sartre into the frame of obstruction by reducing the philosopher's
politics to a psychological tic:

> The conclusion seems inescapable [this rhetorical move betrays the
> lack of evidence]: Sartre's relation to Communism and revolution
> was inspired by an inner need for atonement—a need to take upon
> himself the sins of the French bourgeoisie. Whether one chooses to

call this attitude heroic or masochistic is immaterial: the evidence of self-punishment remains.[6]

Sartre's politics led him away from "disinterested inquiry" and from the "purity of literature." In the end, "the fact that the most powerful and original among the French thinkers of the mid-century chose to pursue so eccentric a course could not fail to retard the efforts of his countrymen to break out of their self-imposed confinement."[7] Biography, or rather psychology, is the link between Sartre's written work and the context Hughes wants to construct. Thus a putative desire for self-punishment figures as an emblem for a cultural trend that rejects the resources of the progressive world.

In Hughes's narrative, then, it is the scientific Lévi-Strauss, not the politically engaged Sartre, who found the "way out" of the obstructed path. Lévi-Strauss mediated not only between the agendas of the generations of the 1930s and the 1950s, he served to connect important traditions within French intellectual life with developments in social science on a world scale: "He broke out of his countrymen's cultural confinement while remaining authentically and recognizably French."[8] If as an *intellectual* historian Hughes admires the achievement of the structuralist anthropologist, as an intellectual *historian* he has serious reservations about the implications of that achievement. Lévi-Strauss developed a method to dig beneath the surface of events and expressions in order to get at their essential, formal characteristics. Although Hughes is ready to acknowledge the importance of this project, he also saw its threat to the narrative historian who strove to make sense of the surface rather than to consider it mere appearance:

> By training and temperament historians were more concerned with the content than with the formal characteristics of their subject. They were similarly inclined to take the values they studied "straight"— rather than trying to convert them into an abstract and universal code. What Lévi-Strauss was after was precisely the opposite.[9]

Taking values straight evidently means to Hughes integrating them into a coherent and recognizable context. It also means critically judging these values. The value relativism that he sees in structuralism is anathema to Hughes.

But we have just seen that Hughes criticizes Sartre for abandoning "disinterested inquiry." How, then, can he take aim at Lévi-Strauss's value-neutral relativism? What values inform the disinterested inquiry of the historian's narrative? We might say that it is liberalism which lies "between commitment and disillusion." It is a liberal project that goes hand in hand with this narrativizing strategy in intellectual history. The major principle of this strategy is enclosure. The historian should be able to make sense of a real diversity of expressions, to see why they developed the way they did, and then to integrate them—to enclose them—into a coherent story. In order to do so he or she must see the ideas "on their own terms"—the equivalent to the liberal notion of seeing the world from the other person's point of view—but this does not mean that intellectual criticism must be forever postponed. On the contrary, the ideas can be evaluated according to the values that inform the narrative itself: tolerance, cosmopolitanism, and antifanaticism without relativism.

The Sea Change comprises the second half of *Between Commitment and Disillusion*. Here Hughes examines how living in America affected the thinking of some of the major intellectuals in the second half of the twentieth century. How did these thinkers deny, accept, or integrate their new context in relation to the native development of their ideas? The continuities are strong between *The Sea Change* and *The Obstructed Path*. In the earlier book the guiding issue was how each thinker managed to hold on to his specifically French tradition while opening up to a contemporary cosmopolitanism. In the later work the central question concerns the capacity of each intellectual to make use of the experience of emigration. The way out of the obstructed path was to remain "authentically French" while being truly cosmopolitan; successfully negotiating the sea change was to remain true to your original identity while remaining open to the experiences of the new world.

The main body of *The Sea Change* begins with what Hughes calls "a philosophical prologue in England." This is odd, for it is unclear what this chapter on Wittgenstein has to do with the rest of the book. What is clear is Hughes's sympathy for the displaced philosopher, whose effort to combat "the contemptuous attitudes towards the particular case" has affinities with Hughes's brand of intellectual history. Furthermore, Wittgenstein's legacy might help to put "back into a single intellectual universe the styles of thinking that had split apart in the 1920s."[10] The construction of such a universe through the enclosure of these styles of thinking into a single narrative is a major goal of Hughes's intellectual history.

Despite its tangential relation to the content of much of the rest of the book, Hughes's treatment of Wittgenstein is in many ways typical of the strengths and weaknesses of his historical approach. The context provided by the historian does make it easier to approach the issues of the philosopher, and Hughes opens Wittgenstein to intellectual sympathy and human understanding. This is an important achievement. We get a picture of Wittgenstein from a distance: musical, troubled, intense, eccentric, brilliant. Hughes provides some facts and establishes some continuities in Wittgenstein's works. But the chapter is riddled with clichés, and neither the social analysis nor the psychological probing is pushed very hard.[11] Hughes seems to want to stay as close as possible to the surface of the philosopher's ideas and life. Although this is surely necessary for a philosopher like Wittgenstein (for to miss the surface here would be to miss much), it is not nearly sufficient.[12] How were the philosopher's concerns with privacy and intimacy connected with his social and sexual experiences in Austria and England? How were the forms in which he wrote connected with his ideas about the "human 'urge to thrust against the limits of language'?"[13] About these questions, and many others, Hughes's chapter has almost nothing to say.

The problems with Hughes's treatment of Wittgenstein should not, then, only be described as stemming from a failure to pay close attention to the *Investigations*. His aim is not to open a text to *dialogue, problematization,* or *tropological analysis*. Hughes's history does not try to "gain agreement" according to these terms. Instead it makes meaning out of the past by linking (con)texts together in a coherent narrative. But the price of making Wittgenstein "fit" into this narrative is extremely high, even from the perspective of contextualism. For successful enclosure, both life and work must be trimmed down to almost standard size.

The models of a successful sea change are provided by Franz Neumann and Heinz Hartmann. Hughes knew Neumann well, and saw up close how his postwar work profited from his experience as an immigrant to North America. Indeed Hughes himself is an heir to Neumann's legacy: helping to redefine intellectual history away from a concentration on great thoughts as protagonists, and toward "setting those thoughts in the full context of historical circumstance out of which their creators had given them form."[14]

Hartmann, too, profited immensely from a sea change that he certainly did not choose. The dilemma of emigrant psychoanalysts was of "reconciling loyalty to their common master with what they discovered on their own."[15] One might say that they, like many who are faced with great changes, strove to remain loyal to their own identities without closing off the possibilities of genuine growth. Hartmann, according to Hughes, seems to have accomplished this. And his personal accomplishment is mirrored in his theoretical work. After all, one of the major parts of Hartmann's work was to set the maintenance of identity as the ego's crucial task. He remained loyal to his own identity even as he theorized how such loyalty was not only an ethical commitment but a psychological function indicative of health.

Hartmann's ego psychology mirrors the central values in Hughes's approach to intellectual history. The historian appreciates the analyst's plain style[16] well as his commitment to objectivity. Unfortunately Hughes also mirrors his subject here in setting up a "conflict-free sphere." Hartmann's understanding of psychoanalysis was in stark opposition to that of one of the other figures Hughes writes about in this book, Herbert Marcuse.[17] Hughes does not allow for a confrontation between the two emigrés. The shallowness and superficiality often associated with the sanitized psychoanalysis represented by ego psychology goes unnoticed by the historian. Instead these qualities seem to have infected his own description of how Hartmann:

> grounded his ego in the instinctual substratum of the psyche while allowing for its almost infinite elaboration at the conscious level. Those who knew him best found it "by no means accidental" that he had hit on the concept of the conflict-free: it reflected his own self-confidence and "cheerful tranquility."[18]

A cheerful, optimistic Hartmann fits neatly into Hughes's narrative as someone who combines Old World insight with New World methods and experience. With his "conflict-free sphere" the analyst and the historian make tolerance, and open-minded cosmopolitanism, part of the healthy mind.[19]

One should not get the idea that in *The Sea Change* Hughes shrinks from criticizing his subjects' ideas. On the contrary, he takes to task those writers who fail to exemplify the virtues embodied by Hartmann. Hannah Arendt represents the most striking case in this regard. Here the failure to provide an analysis of either life or work is most striking. Arendt's vehement denunciation of communism as a form of totalitarianism fails Hughes's implicit test of tolerance, and, perhaps because she is a woman, her criticisms are described as "overwrought, highly colored" and "striving for shock effect."[20] Hughes is forced to cut Arendt pretty thin in order to fit her into his narrative about critiques of fascism between Neumann and "radicalism of the Right." Her idea of *totalitarianism* is isolated from earlier uses of the term in Germany and elsewhere, and her writing in this regard is never considered in relation to the broad sweep of her life and work. This is striking, in part, because it is so uncharacteristic of Hughes's context construction, his method of gaining agreement. But in the case of Arendt, even a superficial consideration of her political philosophy and the place of the idea of totalitarianism within it would have made it impossible to fit her into the narrative of Hughes's chapter. Such a consideration would have to pay attention not only to the cold war use of the term *totalitarian,* but to Arendt's critique of modern political life generally, and to her understanding of the place of the political in the human condition. In order to enclose her in *The Sea Change* she must be made to fit the book's narrative line. Once again, the price is high.

In the sections on Wittgenstein and on Arendt one can see the weaknesses of Hughes's approach to historical contextualization. One misses an analysis of their ideas on their own terms and not in relation to either a biographical sketch of their authors or some "general speculation on the role of human beings in the societies that have formed them and that they in turn have altered."[21] Of course I may be indulging in the historian's old (always true, always trivial) complaint: "Things are more complicated than that." Hughes does not, after all, aim at a concentrated study of ideas but at a panoramic view of a generation of thinkers. But what to do about a thinker whose ideas cannot be easily ignored, but who does not fit in easily with "her" generation and who does not blend into the smooth surface of the historian's narrative?

If the republication of two of Hughes's earlier works as *Between Commitment and Disillusion* reminds us of the breadth of the historian's learning and the expanse of his intellectual sympathy, the publication of *Sophisticated Re-*

bels recalls some of the reasons why contextual intellectual history became such a popular target for both textualists and culturalists.[22] The essays collected in that work resemble a series of newspaper articles on topics of interest to the author. It is not at all clear how the subjects treated—for example, foreign workers, Solidarity, the Greens—might represent the "political culture" mentioned in the book's subtitle or even how they might have been tied together through a set of common themes.

One expects that Hughes would weave a "context" that would link his various figures together. Here this would not be a context in terms of a shared language, experience, or social position, but the context that would be created by the historian himself. He would have to make the connections explicitly in his own voice.[23] But there is no strong narrative point of view in this volume. The chapters are like snapshots of a recent trip through the contemporary Europe section of the library. And the essays have the virtues and vices of snapshots. Sometimes Hughes catches something that claims our attention and stimulates our curiosity. But if the question "what is this picture doing here?" arises, the limits of this book have already been surpassed.

Sophisticated Rebels does exemplify the liberal spirit that also animated Hughes's earlier works. He is, after all, writing about dissenters, exploring some of the tracks that nonconformism has taken since 1968. Like good highbrow journalism, some of Hughes's efforts at paraphrase introduce readers to figures they might otherwise ignore. But unlike, let's say, Janet Malcom's essays in *The New Yorker,* Hughes avoids any rhetorical sophistication or even playfulness in favor of a direct, plain style. And he appreciates that style in his subjects. When he writes about Michel Tournier, who also aimed "to slip . . . into a form as traditional . . . and reassuring as possible, matter having none of these qualities," this approach works well.[24] However, it leaves the historian with almost nothing of interest to say about writers such as Milan Kundera and Jürgen Habermas. *Sophisticated Rebels* is another example of this historian's tendency to make few demands on his readers, but it also sacrifices any serious discussion of other writers who make such demands. Hughes has little patience for modernist experimentation or postmodern playfulness. When writing about contemporary European culture, this impatience leads him to quick and easy dismissals of thinkers who demand more careful, and critical, attention.

But one might respond that careful, critical attention is not a goal that contextual intellectual history sets for itself. Instead the historian aims at "structuring" his or her material in such a way as to create "an initial order" that may lead either to explanations or to insights into patterns of thought.[25] The creation of a narrative context opens one kind of cultural production to another so as to create dialogue among diverse but interrelatable subjects. When we understand Croce, Adorno, and Hartmann in relation to one another our capacity to gain insight from their texts and lives is enriched. The intellectual historian, to use a metaphor of some current popularity, creates the conditions of conversation among various cultural products, and we readers get to listen in. When this works we are surprised and delighted to find an interesting conversation going on over time among people who we might have thought had nothing to say to one another. In these lively discussions we can almost forget who is speaking. For the narrative trick of this genre of history (like so many others) is for the distinctive voice of the historian to vanish. The hand that does the structuring and ordering should be light, if not invisible.

Of course we know better. We know the conversation is created, not relayed, by the historian. So what? So we must be aware of how cultural products are being formed into shapes that work in the narrative. We saw this above with Arendt. Insofar as her political philosophy was treated at all, it was reduced to a symptom of a more general misunderstanding. To use another contemporary term, her *voice* was *denied.* Such denial is necessary in any kind of representation, but the form it takes in this type of narrative history is different from its form in what Hughes called the textualism that preceded and succeeded his generation. In other words, in Lovejoy's history of ideas the hand of the historian was anything but invisible. With a pretension to systematicity, he organized ideas so as to make specific philosophical claims. In more recent examples of intellectual history, the historian organizes a text or texts so as to develop (or deconstruct) specific theoretical claims. The reader asks less "what happens next?" than "how can she or he *say* that?!" When White finds a structure of four or LaCapra the carnavalesque, we are reminded of the historian's choice of the filter through which the past is heard. When Hughes paraphrases Lévi-Strauss's position in relation to Sartre's, the simplicity of the rhetoric may help us forget the enormous amount of invention involved.

This forgetting of the historian's invention is one of the signs of success that Hughes sets for his historical contextualization. As he noted in *History as Art and as Science:*

> Hence the historian's supreme technical virtuosity lies in fusing the new method of social and psychological analysis with his traditional storytelling function. . . . The trick is to follow now one, now another, of the aspects of experience . . . until finally all the streams of interpretation converge. The point of convergence is, of course, of the historian's own choosing, but there are some points well chosen and others that are not. The sign that it is a good choice is when the whole broad range of the original narrative or analysis, the multiple streams that the historian has been coaxing along, come together effortlessly and as though without prior design.[26]

The model here is clearly nineteenth-century realism: a good storyteller makes you forget you are only reading a story. Hughes weds this realism to contextualism, *but there is no necessary connection.* The opposition "text versus context" is simply not relevant here. Textual approaches to the past can use this realist mode, as contextual histories can make use of more modernist strategies that call attention to their own forms of invention, that provoke reflexive modes of reading which will call attention to the historicalness of their own ways of making sense of the past.[27] It is certainly the case that these modernist narrative strategies do not make for effortless reading, but to claim that any departure from the plain style and realism detracts from the aesthetic and pedagogic power of a text would be to cut history writing off from the major developments in European culture since the middle of the nineteenth century.[28]

Hughes's rhetoric of effortless convergence may explain, at least in part, his suspicion about, even animosity toward, more overtly theoretical work in the humanities.[29] Such work acknowledges the role of the narrator, the historian, in relation to the texts he or she examines. When intellectual history relies on paraphrase and on the "effortless convergence" strategy, as Hughes's work does, it depends on the absence of this acknowledgement.[30] But his enclosing narratives make ideas and lives fit together only by obscuring the criteria according to which they are given shape as part of a historical context. Hughes, as we have seen, rejects value neutrality or detached objectivity; he is no positivist. To be sure, history written from the perspective of a positivist confidence in methodology also obscures authorial construction, not behind a plain style or an open-minded liberal cosmopolitanism but behind the guise of scientific objectivity. Contemporary textual intellectual history shares none of this confidence. Instead it often uses "theory" to undermine any approach to the past that would result in obscuring the goals in the service of which the past is being used.

There are diverse ways of showing how one's history is a history of the present, just as there are degrees of political, moral, and aesthetic involvement with the past. I am not suggesting that historians must provide a detailed account of their own procedures, nor that they should wear their theories or their values on their sleeves. I am paying attention to the ways in which Hughes's rhetoric aims at a transparency that obscures its own criteria of judgment. This attention should be some indication of the kinds of judgments being made in this essay. Paying attention to narrative as enclosure should not be confused with a critique of narrative or of contextualism; it should point to the tension between a certain style of narration and a reflexive mode of historical reading and thinking.

Contextual intellectual history in the hands of so gifted a practitioner as H. Stuart Hughes allows us to listen to a conversation among thinkers who might otherwise remain inaccessible to us. The openings to ideas provided by his narratives remain a crucial achievement of contextual intellectual history, whose strong practitioners' contribution has never been to make difficult concepts easy, but to show why cultural productions from the past *matter,* what is at stake in their production and (continuing) reception.[31] By enclosing his writers into a coherent narrative, Hughes shows us connections that might have otherwise remained obscure. Hughes should not be criticized for his failure to be a theoretician when he writes intellectual history. It is important for the success of his narratives that they do not overtly promote a set of concepts or a specific style of reading dear to the historian; but the price of their success is that the functions of these concepts and styles are obscured in favor of rhetorical transparency. In his intellectual histories discussed in this essay the ideas of the individuals treated are "relativized" in relation to the demands of narrative continuity.[32] This process can result not only in the enhancement of ideas by a disclosure of their interconnections, it can also result in all but the erasure of the concepts being relativized. This is, as Robert Dawidoff has pointed out, a risk in *any* historical representation: the danger of the loss always connected with the effort to make present in intelligible form some aspect of the past.[33] The historical and theoretical reflexivity that is the condition of some of the best work being produced in the human sciences today is not an innoculation against this danger but an acknowledgment of it.

Hughes's intellectual histories can satisfy our desire to understand diverse collections of difficult ideas in relation to one another. He provides ready access to his narrative enclosures. This access has been an important contribution to our understanding of ideas, lives, and history. However, we can also see that such access obscures the ways in which the enclosures had been constructed, and for what purpose. The result is an intellectual history that "lets us in" to the conversation of intellectuals only by insuring that we remain unconscious about the price of admission, for them and for us. However, it is only by acknowledging the relation of the historical narrativizing to the form and the content of the ideas examined that intellectual and cultural history can continue to make a rich contribution to our understanding of the past in relation to ourselves.

NOTES

1. In this essay I shall limit myself to a consideration of these recent publications and shall mention *Consciousness and Society* (New York: Vintage Books, 1958, 1977), and some of Hughes's other work, only in passing.

2. By now the necessary note is getting quite long. Some of the most interesting recent interventions are John Toews, "Intellectual History After the Linguistic Turn: The Autonomy of Meaning and the Irreducibility of Experience," *American Historical Review* 92, no. 4 (1987): 879–907; Donald R. Kelley, "Horizons of Intellectual History: Retrospect, Circumspect, Prospect," *Journal of the History of Ideas* 48, no. 1 (1987): 143–69; David Harlan, "Intellectual History and the Return of Literature," David Hollinger, "The Return of the Prodigal: The Persistence of Historical Knowing," and Harlan, "Response to David Hollinger," all in *The American Historical Review* 94, no. 3 (1989): 581–626; James Kloppenberg, "Deconstruction and Hermeneutic Strategies for Intellectual History: The Recent Work of Dominick LaCapra and David Hollinger," *Intellectual History Newsletter* 9 (1987): 3–22; Dominick LaCapra, "Of Lumpers and Readers," *Intellectual History Newsletter* 10 (1988): 3–10.

3. But as David Hollinger has rightly noted, the "case" against contextual intellectual history should be made against history writing more generally. Why is it not?

4. Brown, "Positivism, Relativism, and Narrative in the Logic of the Historical Sciences," *American Historical Review* 92, no. 4 (1987): 915. On judging a historical narrative according to the criteria it sets for itself see Allan Megill, "Recounting the Past: 'Description,' Explanation, and Narrative in Historiography," *American Historical Review* 94, no. 3 (1989): 627.

5. See *Consciousness and Society: The Reorientation of European Social Thought, 1890–1930* (New York: Vintage Books, 1958, 1977), 25: "The alternative to social science was litera-

ture: the two aspects of speculative thought that philosophy had once held together were now condemned to part." Hughes's book, of course, was supposed to bring them back together. See also, H. Stuart Hughes, *History as Art and as Science* (New York: Harper and Row, 1964), passim.

6. *The Obstructed Path: French Social Thought in the Years of Desperation, 1930–1960* (New York: Harper and Row, 1968). I cite the republication in *Between Commitment and Disillusion* (Middletown: Wesleyan University Press, 1987), 225.

7. Ibid., 226.

8. Ibid., 264, 287.

9. Ibid., 285.

10. *The Sea Change: The Migration of Social Thought* (New York: Harper and Row, 1975), I cite the republication in *Between Commitment and Disillusion,* 67.

11. For example, the following: "Like so many other leading twentieth-century intellectuals, Wittgenstein could well have had recourse to psychoanalytic therapy. It might have mitigated his personal torment and enabled him to come to terms with the dark side of his nature" ibid., 63.

12. On this point (and many others) see Louis O. Mink's review of *The Sea Change:* "How difficult it is to probe to the bottom, and how easy it is to believe that one has understood it [émigrée experience] when in fact one hasn't" ("The End of an Era?" *The Virginia Quarterly* 51 [1975]: 464).

13. *The Sea Change,* 61.

14. *The Sea Change,* 116.

15. Ibid., 233.

16. Ibid., 270.

17. Herbert Marcuse, *Eros and Civilization: A Philosophical Inquiry into Freud* (Boston: Beacon 1955, 1974), especially the "Critique of Neo-Freudian Revisionism," 238–74.

18. Ibid., 215. Hughes here quotes K. R. Eissler.

19. In addition to Marcuse, see the important criticism of this move in Russell Jacoby, *Social Amnesia: A Critique of Conformist Psychology from Adler to Laing* (Boston: Beacon Press, 1975), 40–41.

20. Ibid., 123.

21. *Between Commitment and Disillusion,* x.

22. For an interesting collection of essays emphasizing cultures as the appropriate object for "intellectual" history see Lynn Hunt, ed., *The New Cultural History* (Berkeley: University of California Press, 1989).

23. Of course the context is always created by historians. One of the effects (perhaps crucial to what Barthes called the "reality effect" of the discourse of history) of the narrative of contextual intellectual history is the disappearance of the author's voice. In this way the construction of the context appears as discovery.

24. *Sophisticated Rebels* (Cambridge: Harvard University Press, 1988), 26.

25. Hughes refers to this structuring in *Consciousness and Society,* 8. On the historian's contribution of an "initial order" see Hughes, "The Historian and the Social Scientist," *American Historical Review* 66, no. 1 (1960): 46.

26. Hughes, *History as Art and as Science: Twin Vistas on the Past* (Chicago: University of Chicago Press, 1964). This passage should be compared to Hayden White's "The Burden of History" (1968), reprinted in *Tropics of Discourse* (Baltimore: Johns Hopkins University Press, 1978), 27–50.

27. See my comments in "Performing History: Modernist Contextualism in Carl E. Schorske's *Fin-de-Siècle Vienna,*" Chapter 3 in this collection.

28. In this regard see Paul Robinson's appreciation of Hughes. It is the plain style that Robinson defends against the "excesses" that intellectual history has fallen into in the 1970s and 1980s. Anti-intellectualism here hides behind a call to return to the intellectual community represented by the readership of *The New York Review of Books* ("H. Stuart Hughes and Intellectual History: Reflections on the State of the Discipline," *Intellectual History Newsletter* 9 [1987]: 29–35).

29. See Hughes's comments in the new preface to *Between Commitment and Disillusion* and *Sophisticated Rebels,* 15–19, 146–47.

30. At the beginning of *Consciousness and Society,* Hughes does offer a page explaining "where I am coming from," so as "not to palm off his own prejudices in surreptitious form under the guise of 'objectivity.'" But his account of his "educational influences and ethical values" ends with the hope that they make up "some sort of intellectual balance," "cosmo-politan and detached" (26). Once the balance is described in the "preliminary observa-tions" to the book, the main body of the narrative can begin.

31. In Hughes's own areas of interest, see the recent work of Jan Goldstein, Peter Jelavich, Lloyd Kramer, Harry Liebersohn, Jerrold Seigel, and Debora Silverman.

32. Carl E. Schorske, "History and the Study of Culture," in *History and . . . : Histories Within the Human Sciences,* ed. Ralph Cohen and Michael S. Roth (Charlottesville: Univer-sity Press of Virginia, 1995), 382–95.

33. Robert Dawidoff, "History . . . But," ibid., 370–81.

• 3 •

Performing History: Modernist Contextualism
in Carl E. Schorske's *Fin-de-Siècle Vienna*

*But if one were to strike through the masks of historicity that concealed modern man,
what would one find?*
—Carl E. Schorske

It is difficult for historians to imagine a topic that a priori would be off-limits to them. Some people or events or institutions are not naturally more historical than others. Inquiry in the present renders any object historical by configuring its meaning (at least in part) in relation to its development over time. Only convention delimits the range of what can be so configured. Over the last few decades, these conventions have been changing greatly, as historians (particularly those from groups hitherto underrepresented in the profession) have created and developed topics that would have seemed excessively marginal to their former graduate advisers. The proliferation of topics and of approaches to them is one of the reasons for the sense (bemoaned or celebrated) that the center will not hold, that we lack a unifying narrative of our past, or as Peter Novick has put it, that there is no king in Israel.[1]

When historians think about the new topics and methodologies, they usually consider social or, more recently, cultural history as the engine of innovation. Intellectual history, on the other hand, has recently played an important role in bringing theoretical discussions into the historical profession, but it is not usually associated with the proliferation of topics and methodologies. After all, intellectual history until a short time ago (when it was refitted as cultural history) has concentrated on mining the canon, not particularly on undermining it or adding new works to it. According to almost any set of professional criteria, Carl E. Schorske's *Fin-de-Siècle Vienna: Politics and Culture* (1980) would be called a strong example of intellectual history. It focuses on figures who defined culture and politics for turn-of-the-century Vienna and, in some cases, for the West in the twentieth century. The book is a magisterial historicization of these figures, showing how each of them retreats from politics and society—from history as the field on which meaning and direction can be created. In addition to the informative and elegant essays on these fin-de-siècle modernists, Schorske's book presents us with a problem: how to historicize but not merely reject the development of antihistoricism. This is a problem that remains critical for historians concerned with the limits and possibilities of their ways of making meaning from the past. Modernism and postmodernism confront historians with new challenges. How can these be addressed within historical writing (in contradistinction to and perhaps in addition to being addressed in criticism or theory about historical writing), and how might they affect the forms of historical expression? Schorske's text asks us to consider the power and the danger that come with the rejection of history, and it helps us to consider these within historical narratives. Of course this is not the manifest content of *Fin-de-Siècle Vienna*. In this essay, however, I shall show that it is a deeply reflexive book, with form and content interacting in complex ways for specific purposes. From the aesthetics of the book itself to the substance of its specific arguments, Schorske's work helps us to consider how historical thinking can acknowledge its own capacities and limitations. Thus *Fin-de-Siècle Vienna* remains an important text for those interested in the development of self-critical, reflexive forms of history writing. After briefly explicating the principal themes of the book, I shall situate it in relation to discussions about the value of historical knowledge in the humanities. Schorske's reflexive reenactment of the confrontation of modernism and historicism in *Fin-de-Siècle Vienna* constructs a new context for acknowledging our own connection to historical understanding.

The book consists of seven essays on the intersection of politics and culture in Vienna during the last decades of the nineteenth century and the first decades of the twentieth. "How are politics and the psyche related?" Schorske asks in the first essay on Arthur Schnitzler and Hugo von Hoffmannsthal. The connection between (and separation of) psychological exploration and political engagement is one of the recurring themes of the book. The tension between politics and the psyche becomes an important issue in Vienna after the fragile ascendancy of a liberal culture, when the

satisfactions offered by liberal power and aristocratic aestheticism were felt
to be inadequate. Schnitzler diagnosed this situation with extraordinary
acumen, and Schorske admires his insight. But the Austrian writer could
not see his way past disillusionment; he could unmask the pretensions of
society's values and the actions they inspired but was unable to generate
any values of his own: "Schnitzler was a prophet without wrath. The scientist in him avenged itself on both the moralist and the artist. As social ob-
server and psychologist he drew the world he saw as necessitous, but
not—like the true tragedian—as justified . . . Schnitzler could neither
condone nor condemn."[2]

How does historical science avenge itself on the moral and artistic concerns that bring one to the past in the first place? Is the price of understanding a culture the inability to judge or at least to participate fully in it?[3]
Hofmannsthal shared many of Schnitzler's insights into the psychological
crises of modern man but attempted to imagine an art that would offer a
communal possibility beyond these crises rather than only describe them.
"Engagement in life, Hofmannsthal felt, demands the capacity to resolve,
to will. This capacity implies commitment to the irrational, in which alone
resolution and will are grounded. Thus affirmation of the instinctual re-
opened for the aesthete the door to the life of action and society."[4]

The dive into the psyche could still affect the surface of politics. It certainly affected the environment in which politics took place, as Schorske
shows in the second essay of the book. There he examines the birth of
urban modernism in the contrasting careers of Camillo Sitte and Otto
Wagner. Sitte built his critique of urban life on an appeal to the past, while
Wagner espoused a modernist, functionalist approach to the city. Both rejected the rationalist historicist synthesis of late nineteenth-century liberalism, Sitte in the name of an archaic community and Wagner in the name
of a fluid utilitarianism. Sitte saw himself as the spokesman for the ancients
in their battle against the moderns, aiming for the spatial freedom and
spontaneity of premodern cities and against the systematic grids of the
new urban centers. Wagner, by contrast, wanted to liberate architects
from a dependence on the past and to "revitalize the aesthetic function of
the architect through his service to utility as a good."[5] In ways akin to
those of Schnitzler and Hofmannsthal, "both fed a new aesthetic of city
building in which social aims were influenced by psychological considerations."[6] In the end, however, these psychological considerations and the

aesthetics connected with them only led these urbanists to become more isolated from modern political life and the cities in which it was centered. In the case of these architects, the descent into psychology did not reconnect understanding and action.

In the third essay, Schorske turns to the realm of fin-de-siècle politics, examining the new "keys" of antiliberal political engagement explored by Georg von Schönerer, Karl Lueger, and Theodor Herzl. Schönerer led the German nationalists into a radical and violently anti-Semitic party that brought violent discourse and action into mainstream politics. Lueger succeeded in bringing this potent force into political power when his election as mayor of Vienna was ratified by the emperor in 1897. Treating the first two men, important influences on Adolf Hitler, in the same key as the father of Zionism surprised many readers, but for Schorske the three were "pioneers in post-rational politics."[7] Crucial to their politics was a turn to the depths of psychology and to aesthetics as vehicles for the manipulation of deep and often violent passions. Why should politics aim at rationality, they asked, when there was so much power to be tapped from hidden desires and fears? "Each in his own way," Schorske writes, "utilized aristocratic style, gesture, or pretension to mobilize a mass of followers still hungry for a leadership that based its authority on something older and deeper than the power of rational argument and empirical evidence."[8] Schorske is fond of quoting Hofmannsthal in this regard: "Politics is magic. He who knows how to summon the forces from the deep, him will they follow."[9]

At the core of Fin-de-Siècle Vienna is the question of how art and politics were changed by the turn to the forces of the psyche. Schorske acknowledges the power and the attraction of these forces, but he also insists on their political dangers. What happens to liberalism when its key figures begin to see the psychological as the most potent source of power and meaning? Indeed how can the historian pursue these questions about the postrational or the instinctive, given history's own reliance on rationality? Does the pursuit of these questions—giving them a sort of analytic primacy—imply participation in the same movement toward the psyche? Moreover, who will be the guide in the depths?

At the center of the book is an essay on Sigmund Freud, one that uses psychoanalytic categories and strategies of interpretation to probe the historical boundaries and limitations of psychoanalysis. Schorske uncovers what he calls "the counterpolitical ingredient in the origins of psychoanalysis."[10] Faced with an intractable Viennese establishment, Freud retreated from overt political activity into a world of subversive intellection. The famous epigraph to the *Interpretation of Dreams* reads: "If I cannot shake the higher powers, I will stir up the depths." Freud gave up his political aspirations and, according to Schorske, through psychoanalytic work made politics itself epiphenomenal. "Having exhumed his own political past through dream analysis, he had overcome it by identifying his political obligations and impulses with his father, explaining them away as attributes of his father's ghost."[11] This "explaining away" was Freud's letting go of his past and the political desires that had helped define it. Like many of his generation in Vienna, the founder of psychoanalysis was in retreat from history: "Freud gave his fellow liberals an ahistorical theory of man and society that could make bearable a political world spun out of orbit and beyond control."[12] Psychoanalysis in this view was compensation for political impotence. In its displacement of concrete political problems, the science of the depths was conformist in relation to the status quo.[13] There was a political wish at the beginnings of psychoanalysis, but that wish was given up in the face of reality. The retreat from the political in favor of either the psychological or the aesthetic is characteristic of the figures Schorske treats in the rest of the book. His comment on Freud is applicable to the other figures he discusses. All "resolve the pain of general history by translating it into personal history."[14] For all, generational and political conflict are represented in private terms or are imagined as inevitable Oedipal combat.

By weaving the stories of his culture makers back into an account emphasizing their "formative political-cultural experiences," Schorske shows how a multilayered contextual history can help us make sense not only of the personal pain of these figures but also of the cultural conditions we have inherited from them. In his hands, history fights back against modernist psychologization and aestheticization to claim legitimacy for itself as a mode of making meaning out of the radical crises of modernity. And history fights back with the tools of psychology and aesthetics, showing that even the modernist retreat from the historical can become a fertile field of reflection for the historian. Thus *Fin-de-Siècle Vienna* presents modernist contextual histories that reenact the confrontation of modernism and historicism.

If Freud's response to political frustration was creativity in science,

Gustav Klimt's response to political rejection was stylized innovation in an aesthetics divorced from social reality. Both figures focused on the instinctual as more fundamental than the historical. In his early work Klimt confronted the establishment with images from the realm of instinct. After 1901 aestheticism and withdrawal reigned for an artist who had been spurned by a generation of patrons wanting to protect ideals of rationalism and progress. "From nature to stylized culture, from direct presentation of psychophysical experience to formal symbolization: thus the journey ran."[15] That journey became an important part of the experience of a generation frustrated with liberal culture and politics. Klimt "had passed irrevocably from the realm of history, time and struggle to that of aesthetic abstraction and social resignation."[16] By 1907–1908, portraits of the Viennese haute monde are a key component of Klimt's work: art embraces decoration. Despite Schorske's emphasis on the political costs of this journey, he makes no attempt to minimize the achievements made possible by the resignation to political impotence. Just as there was no reduction in Freud's ambitions and capacity to fulfill them when he turned away from politics, there was no artistic decline in Klimt's turn to pleasing portraiture.[17] If Freud translated the pain of general history into personal terms, Klimt shifted from "public ethos to private pathos." Schorske configures the elements that comprised these shifts so he can judge them critically, but he also pays close attention to, and conveys enormous admiration for, the insights and creations to which they led.

The penultimate essay in the book presents these elements and shifts on a broader chronological scale. By looking at how Adalbert Stifter, Ferdinand von Saar, and Hugo von Hofmannsthal use the metaphor of the garden throughout the nineteenth century, Schorske is able to recognize an increasingly sharp separation of the personal and social functions of art. In a culture in which art had assumed a central place by the late nineteenth century, the cultivation of aestheticism and inwardness occurred at the expense of engagement in politics. Narcissism took over as the ability to imagine effective change retreated. "By the very fact of standing for life, art separates us from it. That is why, when art became detached from other values and became a value in itself, it produced in its devotees that sense of eternal spectatorship which in turn nourished introversion . . . . [D]e-socialization accompanied internalization."[18] Hofmannsthal acutely felt the separation of art from life and believed that poetry had the function of establishing relationships between the disparate phenomena of the social and the instinctual. He imagined poetry and perhaps the other arts redeeming society, not just fleeing from its constraints. But, Schorske notes, "the rifts in the body social had proceeded too far."[19] The image of the garden would not suggest redemption, comfort, or harmony in the early twentieth century. Instead it would be used as the scene for an explosion of forceful and fearsome dissonance.

The final essay of *Fin-de-Siècle Vienna* examines that explosion and dissonance in the work of Oskar Kokoschka and Arnold Schoenberg. The retreat from the social and political that had marked the modernism of late nineteenth-century Vienna became the substance of their art. In their prewar painting and music, they displayed a profound alienation from the bourgeois world around them, and they destabilized the conventions of that world in powerful, direct explorations of the instinctual and psychological territories they had come to inhabit. Kokoschka's expressionist portraits developed a "desublimated psychological realism" in which the body manifested the inner tensions stirring beneath conscious life. Schoenberg created a new musical language that organized in sound the wilderness of the psyche.[20] As they appropriated and then exploded the garden as the image of order, they also appropriated and then exploded the ideals of liberal, cosmopolitan Viennese culture. The retreat to inwardness that led to a decorous aestheticism in Klimt became in his artistic successors the cultivation of alienation as the vehicle for liberating the artist from the hypocrisy of a civilized life divorced from the powers of the depths.

There is no conclusion to *Fin-de-Siècle Vienna*. With Kokoschka and Schoenberg, the journey from the political to the psychological became a new form of engagement; the *voyage intérieur* became a struggle to express the truths of the instincts without the mediations required by society. Indeed the modernist artists gazing inward gave up on society and its history as fields from which meaning could be made. However, the modernist politicians who cut their teeth on the unstable liberalism of late nineteenth-century Vienna were prepared to use the powers of the depths not only to shake up surface society but to control it, to construct the meaning of its past and to direct its future. The lessons the "new key" leaders such as Schönerer, Lueger, and Herzl learned about the powers of the passions were not confined to the psychological but would change the face of politics for the twentieth century. Meanwhile, the artists and intellectuals were looking elsewhere.

Historical understanding in the humanities has taken various forms over the last fifty years. Between the two world wars, history was seen as a key to the sophisticated understanding of art, literature, and the social sciences. The value of historical understanding was often linked with the value of progress; as faith in progress declined, so did the prominence of history. By the mid-1950s the comprehension of where we had been had come to seem irrelevant to where we were going (in science, in art, in politics), and historical understanding took a back seat to conceptually well-tooled synchronic analysis. Even within the discipline of history itself, new modes of systematic investigation displaced efforts to weave continuity and change into narrative forms. The notions of continuity and change themselves had come under attack from a variety of sources in linguistics, anthropology, and philosophy. The critics suggested that in constructing historical continuities (especially in narrative forms) the historian was not confronting social structures and functions. At least since Friedrich Nietzsche, historical understanding had already come under heavy fire as privileging continuity, progress, and conservatism. In the 1950s and 1960s Nietzschean suspicions about historical consciousness were linked to social scientific complaints about the superficiality and fuzziness of historical thinking. With the decline of the idea of progress and concomitant rise of modernism's emphasis on the autonomy of particular modes of representation, faith in a general account of the meaning and direction of change over time was deeply shaken. The notion that understanding was achieved through an account of how things were and how they had changed faded in a culture that no longer assumed that changes were moving in the same direction.[21] What was the point of understanding how things had changed if this understanding bore no relation to how we might alter our own lives?

Schorske has described his project on fin-de-siècle Vienna as the product of his resolve "to explore the historical genesis of modern cultural consciousness, with its deliberate rejection of history."[22] Vienna provided the combination of a circumscribed historical context with many examples of diverse and powerful emerging cultural expressions. "The modern mind has been growing indifferent to history," Schorske writes, "because history, conceived as a continuous nourishing tradition, has become useless to it."[23] This is the central theme of *Fin-de-Siècle Vienna*. Schorske is the historian of dehistoricization. On the one hand he has deep respect for some of the ideas and productions created in the struggle to be free from history, but on the other he also believes this struggle to be dangerous and perhaps futile. Thus, in the essay on Freud, Schorske uses psychoanalysis to understand the founder of the discipline. In the essay on Klimt, the painter's retreat from social confrontation in favor of the cultivation of style inspires the most elegant and powerful writing in the book. Schorske shows how the painter's artistic development was conditioned by social failure and political resignation, but the paintings do not lose their power for Schorske because of the history from which they emerge. They are not mere symptoms of the failure to pass some political litmus test. We see that political disengagement does not necessarily make for artistic decline. Neither Freud, Klimt, nor any culture maker in the book is reduced to the conditions out of which his works are seen to develop. By weaving a history around the modern retreat from the historical, Schorske has been able to fashion meaning anew from modernism while simultaneously displaying the riches of historical consciousness.

The context for the display of these riches had changed dramatically between the time Schorske began working on *Vienna* in the 1950s and the time the book appeared in 1980. The value of history as a mode of knowledge or as a resource for artistic innovation had come upon new challenges during these years. In the United States from the 1940s through the 1960s, discussions by philosophers of the value of history were discussions about the quality of historical knowledge as a science. As the star of pragmatism waned, the dominant model for testing the scientific value of a discipline was taken from logical positivism. Historical writing, Carl Hempel had argued in an article that set a paradigm lasting twenty years, must yield general laws if history was a science.[24] Indeed, as Louis Mink remarked, "it could be said without exaggeration that until about 1965 the critical philosophy of history *was* the controversy over the covering-law model."[25] In the late 1960s, however, more interest developed in understanding what historians did when they wrote about the past and less effort was made to tell them what they must do to behave like real scientists. Philosophers began to look again at the "autonomy of historical understanding" and thus at the forms in which that understanding was expressed. Rather than concentrating on history as a form of knowledge, scholars shifted to a focus on history as a kind of writing. Even analytic philosophy of history can be said to have taken a "linguistic turn" during this period.[26]

Yet analytic philosophy was not the field that would have the greatest impact on the development of the humanities and intellectual history. It was French antihumanism that challenged conventional notions of history under the rubric of "theory." In the 1940s Hegelian Marxism had had a crucial effect on thinking about the connections between history and knowing. For the Hegelians History was the reservoir of all truths and values; as dramatic pragmatists they saw in History the court of world judgment. By the end of the decade Hegelian historicizing declined with the loss of faith in the meaningfulness of history. Contemporary events made a mockery of the idea of history as a reservoir of significance and direction, and the development of sophisticated methodologies of the synchronic in linguistics, anthropology, and cybernetics legitimated a retreat from the historical.[27]

Perhaps the most famous attack on historicizing came with Claude Lévi-Strauss's critique of Jean-Paul Sartre in *The Savage Mind* (1962). For the structural anthropologist, as for the logical positivist, historical narratives might not do any harm but seemed to have little to commend them as forms of knowledge. However, as structuralism's scientific pretensions were themselves made objects of criticism by thinkers we have come to call poststructuralists, history could be and was recuperated: not as a form of knowledge but as a text, a kind of writing.

Of course these French and American stories are not unrelated. For example, a writer on history whose work responds to both the French and American contexts is Hayden White. White's "rhetorics of history" aims to show how historical writing achieves what Roland Barthes called the "reality effect." By bracketing the question of correspondence, and by examining the rhetoric of the great historians and philosophers of history, White showed that the criteria for distinguishing between texts (or actions) could not be found in an appeal to history. Despite his distance from Jacques Derrida, White was a true "deconstructor," or what Ian Hacking has called an "undoer."[28] Beginning with "The Burden of History" in 1968 and reaching a crescendo in *Metahistory* in 1978, White demolished the notion that history can be a neutral testing ground for judgment by showing that historical writings create criteria of realism that themselves cannot be judged *according to history.*[29]

Major developments in the critical philosophy of history and in post-structuralist literary theory seemed to agree in the undoing of history as a kind of knowledge to be set off against texts or to be easily distinguished from writing or discourse.[30] No longer were we to ask about the meaning and direction of History, but instead we were to puzzle out how histories were put together, how they worked. In an intellectual world cheerfully removing privileged places as quickly as it shook up foundations, historical understanding came to be seen not as a neutral or necessary context but as a trope to be used, a literary device to be employed for proper (or subversive) effect. More recently, even the New Historicism's effort to return to history (or to histories) presupposed the linguistic turn just described; that is, it presupposed a necessary if not arbitrary connectedness that allows the historical to be read in much the same way as literary texts. By the time *Fin-de-Siècle Vienna* was published, the linguistic turn in regard to the historical had provided a deep but also very narrow understanding of the ways in which the discourse of history performs, how the "history machine" runs. Questions remained, however, about why we turn to history in the first place. What do we want from the past, and what shall we do with our history once we understand that it cannot function as a neutral court of appeal?

One of the most important uses of history in the late 1950s and 1960s was as a tool of social criticism or ideology critique. Historical understanding could be used to legitimate a certain mode of action or thinking as progressive or to undermine modes that were reactionary.[31] The linguistic turn in the humanities and the antihumanism and antihistoricism that often went with it, made this use of history much more problematic than it had been. The theoretical developments of structuralism and poststructuralism exposed (again) the tenuous grounds on which political historicism had made its judgments, as they emphasized the ways in which we are always already constrained by the conventions of the discourse that we have no choice but to speak. Those thinkers who wanted to continue to speak critically were left in an ironic position once they acknowledged being locked within the discourse they meant to subvert. Michel Foucault is probably the best example. His genealogical works undermined the idea of progress by showing that attempts at increased freedom and tolerance—in mental illness, punishment, sexuality—have actually led to ever greater constraints. But he also insisted that all forms of knowledge (including his own) were bound by the discursive constraints of what he variously called an *epistēmē,* an archive, or what we might call a paradigm. This insistence forced him into an essentially ironic position in regard to the historical because of a combination of two factors: his recognition that his own approach was bound by the discursive constraints of the present and his desire to contribute through his work to destroying these constraints. Thus, like many postmodern social critics, Foucault is locked within what I have called the "ironist's cage." From this position, sophisticated social criticism no longer laments its disconnection from effective political change, it recognizes this disconnection as the proper condition of discourse—even when it retains the aroma of radicalism.[32]

I first approached this reinscription of antihistoricism into history with strong theoretical interests. Having studied with Louis Mink and Hayden White, I had come to graduate school at Princeton to rethink intellectual history with Carl Schorske, one of the masters of the discipline. Knowing little about the profession and the alliances and disputes within it, I was stunned by Schorske's strong opposition to what I took to be the most exciting theoretical trends in the field. He seemed much more interested in continuing to practice intellectual history rather than to rethink it in any theoretical terms. But how, I wondered, could one continue to write intellectual history without facing up to the dilemmas so forcefully articulated by White, Dominick LaCapra, and others?

There was a great deal of excitement among history students at Princeton as the publication of *Fin-de-Siècle Vienna* neared. The book had been anticipated since the 1960s, and some of us hoped that in it we would finally have Schorske's response to the theoretical ferment that had become part of our own intellectual histories. As part of Schorske's seminar I had taken the task of making a presentation on his work in intellectual history. Imagine my excitement when he offered me the galleys of the introduction to what we all called "the Vienna book." Finally, I thought, I could see the theory behind the extraordinarily well-crafted essays already published on fin-de-siècle culture. I expected the introduction to reveal not merely the methodology of the book but Schorske's understanding of the basic issues of intellectual history in our time.

Of course *Fin-de-Siècle Vienna* did not explicitly address the theoretical debates reshaping intellectual history in the 1970s, nor did it explicitly acknowledge the critical distance postmodernists had already taken from the "move to the depths." Even Schorske's introduction to the several essays enters into no theoretical discussion and never moves to a metahistorical level to explain the diverse investigations that are to follow. Instead, Schorske sketches a brief history of how he came to the problems at the core of the book by locating his inquiry in the context of changes within the academic disciplines and changes within the political landscape of the United States in the decade following World War II. In other words, he does not choose theory as the context or ground of the historical narratives of the essays, nor does he take an ironic stance about the possibilities of multiple contextualizations. Instead he offers another narrative as a possible context for the historical interpretations that he has constructed as *Fin-de-Siècle Vienna*. This is part of the reflexive dimension essential to the entire text. Throughout the book Schorske employs the methods he is historicizing. Even as he explains the move to the psychological depths as a retreat from the political, he applies the insights gained in the course of this retreat to significant political and cultural figures in turn-of-the-century Vienna. The form of the book appropriates the aesthetic sensibility of the moderns Schorske reinscribes in history. Indeed the book's design and the collage effect of its essays owes much to the modernist struggle for autonomy from historicism. As Schorske wrote of Hofmannsthal, "Thus the poet, rather like the historian, accepts the multiplicity of things in their uniqueness and reveals the unity in their dynamic interrelationship. He brings the discordant into harmony through form."[33] The form of *Fin-de-Siècle Vienna* should work like a song cycle, in which "the central idea will act to establish a coherent field in which the several parts can cast their light upon each other to illuminate the larger whole."[34]

The larger whole illuminated by the particular studies of *Fin-de-Siècle Vienna* includes Vienna, Austrian culture, and the interaction of politics and culture, but the crucial subject of this text (and its proper intellectual context) is the confrontation of modernity and history. In reconfiguring this confrontation the book addresses on its own terms some of the issues raised by theoretical intellectual historians and by postmodern social critics. Schorske describes in his introduction how his generation experienced the confrontation of modernity and history in the interaction of politics and culture in the United States after World War II. There was a shift during this period "from Promethean to Epimethean culture heroes," seen most strikingly in the turn many intellectuals took from Karl Marx to Sigmund Freud. The psychological became privileged terrain as the possibilities of genuine changes in society and politics seemed ever more remote. During the 1950s and 1960s Schoenberg, Gustav Mahler, Klimt, Egon Schiele, and Kokoschka achieved new prominence on the American scene. As Schorske notes:

> Of course America made its cultural borrowings with little sense of the problems and experiences of that "other age" in which the ideas and art that attracted it were shaped. This naturally stimulated my interest in exploring within its political social context the thought which drew my contemporaries . . . [H]istorical analysis could at least reveal the characteristics with which history had endowed that culture [Vienna] at its conception and birth. Illuminating the genesis, meaning and limitations of ideas in their own time, we might better understand the implications and significance of our affinities for them in our time.[35]

Thus Schorske's work did not aim at making available to readers a wealth of cultural delights or timeless insights. Nor did it pretend to satisfy a longing for theoretical closure on the limitations of modernism or to provide sophisticated ironic distance from aestheticism and historicism. Instead it provided readers with a history of the present, showing how a contemporary desire to divorce from history could deepen connections with dangerous historical developments and patterns. These connections warn us of the costs of political resignation. Historical analysis, like psychoanalysis, allows one to diagnose one's connections to the past in order to facilitate change and escape repetition. The historian, like the psychoanalyst, helps to bring disparate elements of the past to mind and thus construct a history with which one can live. The history constructed is not a totalistic, homogeneous whole. How could it be after the "ubiquitous fragmentation" and the "ruthless centrifuge of change" of post-Nietzschean European high culture?[36] Heterogeneity could not be ironed away by a historian wanting to understand the specificity of the diverse fields of modernist cultural production.[37]

Here we can see a crucial difference between Schorske's practice of intellectual history and that of H. Stuart Hughes, despite the fact that many (including Hughes himself) see them sharing a generation's commitment to "contextual" approaches to their subjects.[38] Hughes's books develop narratives in which his figures could be enclosed and judged. His model of representation is clearly nineteenth-century realism; a good storyteller makes you forget that you are only reading a story, and the traces of invention are minimized. In *Fin-de-Siècle Vienna,* on the other hand, the historian's invention, his effort to construct the narratives as works of art, is lavishly displayed. And whereas Hughes passes judgment on the cosmopolitan capacities of the figures he examines, Schorske's book offers no criteria of judgment as such. Rather it displays a confrontation—between modernity and history, between modernism and its pasts—in which we may still find ourselves. And since we still find ourselves within this confrontation, the book makes no attempt to stand outside its subject. That is key to its reflexive dimension. Schorske does not choose between politics and culture or between society and the psyche; indeed he often seems torn between his admiration for psychological exploration and his concern for political responsibility. He explains how the tensions between these terms take different forms in different times and places. Schorske not only describes that tension and how it changed in fin-de-siècle Vienna, he *performs* the tension in *Fin-de-Siècle Vienna: Politics and Culture.*

The performative dimension of Schorske's book has been largely overlooked by commentators on it, even by readers usually sensitive to the reflexive aspects of historical writing. This sensitivity is easy to find in older examples of history writing (for instance, those by Thucydides, Jules Michelet, or Jacob Burkhardt), but for some reason it is hard to discover in more recent studies (unless they are explicitly theoretical and wear their reflexivity on their sleeves). Critics seem to be more blind in this regard when a study is written in their own area of expertise. Here the disciplinary (and transferential) reflex is to point out what is missing in the study, to show how it has not accomplished what it might have. "Where is Wittgenstein or the Vienna Circle?" some critics ask of *Fin-de-Siècle Vienna,* as if there were any pretension in Schorske's collage to present a historical picture of Vienna as a whole. Thus while we would no longer raise such questions about Burckhardt, one can, I suppose, imagine his colleagues' despair over not finding their own subjects treated adequately by *The Civilization of the Renaissance in Italy* (1860). Perhaps they even complained of the aestheticizing tendencies of the book. Burckhardt has been important for Schorske, as he has for many who have admired the Swiss historian's extraordinary writing and tried to understand it in relation to his political and social stance toward Basel and modern Europe.[39] Burckhardt's historical study of the Renaissance shows that the separation of art and politics can have enormous benefits for cultural production. Schorske is well aware of the explosion of innovation that aestheticism can bring. But he configures the aestheticism of late nineteenth-century Vienna within a political horizon. He privileges this horizon not because politics is more fundamental or more real. There is no indication in the text of such a naïve view of culture or of historical representation. Nor is there a naïve faith in the powers of theory to make a case for the politics one prefers. Instead the introduction includes a brief account of how the author came to the problem of his study. Schorske tells us that politics is his horizon because of his own history and his own concerns about the crisis in American political life during the decade after 1947, a "revolution of falling political expectations."[40] He makes no attempt to step outside the historical to a metalevel to explain what he is doing. That is for the critics, not the performer.

One of the most stimulating critics of historical writing in the United States is Dominick LaCapra, who has repeatedly emphasized the transferential aspects of our relation to the past and has been deeply concerned with the dialogic elements of complex and often critical texts. It is all the more striking, then, that his comments on *Fin-de-Siècle Vienna* have missed these aspects of the book.[41] LaCapra complains that Schorske's approach is an "unstable combination of guarded formalism and contextualist historicism,"[42] and he worries that Schorske's interpretations of artifacts or texts reduce them to merely symptomatic responses to a larger context. This methodological concern is married to a more straightforwardly empirical one (an unstable combination itself): how can there have been a crisis in liberalism in Vienna when liberalism was not yet firmly entrenched there at the end of the nineteenth century? Is this crisis not a projection on the part of a historian concerned with the fate of liberalism in postwar America?

Both these criticisms have to do with context but in very different ways. The crisis Schorske sees in Vienna *is* in part based on a projection from the historian's present. He tells us so in the introduction to avoid any simplistic misunderstandings of claims to objectivity. He presents impressions of Vienna animated by concerns about an increasingly dehistoricized high culture. These concerns are tested against the case of Vienna, but the concerns remain presentist, not positivist.[43] The intellectual context in which the (never fully successful) encounter with the past takes place is, as I suggested above, the confrontation of modernity and history. And *Fin-de-Siècle Vienna* continues the confrontation rather than describing it "from the outside." I do not find this resulting in the symptomatic, reductive reading LaCapra sees, but this may be less a question of methodology or theory than a question of taste. Be that as it may. The cultural products are not presented merely as symptoms of an a priori Viennese historical context. The Vienna that we are given in this book is constructed for us in good modernist form: no totality, no grand synoptic vision of the city as a unified whole. Schorske proposes no metanarrative to provide neat closure. The contexts created by the historian intersect and overlap, but they do not form a series of unit ideas or a Zeitgeist. Schorske knows well what Peter Gay views as an important criticism of the book: that there was no FINDESIECLEVIENNA, and this is not merely because of the particularities of the city.[44] Contexts are *always* constructed by the historian, their boundaries determined and drawn in the present in order to illuminate a problem in relation to the past. This does not in any way preclude (or guarantee) heuristic force, just as the commonsense realist view of the context did not guarantee (or preclude) it.

Pointing out that Schorske's Vienna is a historical construction does not, of course, render that construction immune from criticism. LaCapra has raised important questions about whether Schorske's insistence on the modernist move from politics to the psyche obscures the political possibilities of psychological investigation. Critical dimensions of modernism may be flattened out by repeating that its aestheticizing tendencies are necessarily antihistorical.[45] Subtle forms of historical and political critique can certainly be found in modernism by critics with concerns different from Schorske's, just as a historian posing different questions would explore other dimensions of the cultural politics of the city. Schorske's concentration on the turn away from the historical and its links with the fate of liberalism allows him to configure a wide range of material, but it may also blind him to other important dimensions of both modernism and historicism.

There has been a tendency among historians to assume a connection between textual strategies of reading and antirealist modes of presentation. Similarly contextual strategies of reading are often too quickly assimilated to simple realist modes of presentation. As I have discussed in regard to Hughes, however, textual approaches to the past can use a realist mode, just as contextual histories can use more modernist strategies of presentation.[46] These modernist strategies have a crucial reflexive dimension, calling attention to the historicity of their own ways of making sense of the past. This is precisely what we have seen Schorske doing in *Fin-de-Siècle Vienna*. LaCapra, usually without peer at picking up on these strategies in old texts or in texts from other disciplines, altogether misses the complexity of Schorske's book. He does mention a "paradoxical mirror image on a stylistic level" but goes on:

> An almost Viennese flair for the elaborate elegance of a nicely turned phrase and a butterflylike delicacy in moving from *topos* to *topos* ("post-holing" in Schorske's own deceptively down-to-earth metaphor) engender an enchanting world of words that at times seems as much to reflect off one another as to refer to Viennese "reality."[47]

The words do reflect off one another and off the images carefully chosen for the book. There *is* an attempt to make use of the "elaborate elegance" (note that even LaCapra is moved to alliteration when trying to describe the form of the book) associated with Vienna. This is not merely ornamental but part of the reflexive dimension of the book, part of the construction of Vienna as the scene where an important problem (a problem for us) can be worked through. Although we are more accustomed to finding such reflexivity in explicitly theoretical historians, it is worthwhile to be alert for it in Schorske's mode of intellectual history. In this regard it is helpful in thinking about Schorske's work to recall *Discipline and Punish,* in which Michel Foucault stated:

> I would like to write the history of this prison, with all the political investments of the body that it gathers together in its closed architecture. Why? Simply because I am interested in the past? No, if one means by that writing a history of the past in terms of the present. Yes, if one means writing the history of the present.[48]

Unlike Foucault, Schorske does not offer a theoretical discussion of why he writes history (or genealogy) in the way he does. He does not step outside (or above) the historical to describe it. Instead he offers a brief account of how *he came to write this particular project,* that is, he provides another story, another history. He continues to reenact a history in which the status of the historical is validated by being opened to question. Thus *Fin-de-Siècle Vienna* contributes to a history of the present by confronting this present with its attraction to those who abandoned the historical as a field in which meaning and direction could be constructed.

In the debate between those who think they are talking about real, lived experience and those who think they are talking about texts (as if this were a viable contrast), there is often the supposition on both sides that contextual intellectual history must be tied to commonsense realism. Schorske's work on Vienna can help dissolve this neat little distinction and make problematic the simplistic use of text and context, cultural artifact and unifying narrative. Neither the arrogance of formalist methodology nor the naïveté of commonsense realism can create a complex dialogue between mutually implicated past and present.[49] When read not as a window (more or less clear) on a cultural hothouse but as a confrontation between modernism and historical consciousness, Schorske's book has enormous importance for helping us think about the *forms* of history in relation to the *forms* of modernism. Such thinking is crucial if we are to come to terms with the postmodern construction of the historical as a field from which items can be appropriated. What are the possibilities for historicist reenactment or performance that would appropriate aspects of (post)modernism for its own, perhaps changing, purposes? What are the possibilities for (post)modernist reenactment or performance that would appropriate aspects of historicism for its own, certainly changing, purposes? Responses to these questions would lead us from reflections on modernist fin-de-siècle Vienna to considerations about what may be our own fin-de-siècle postmodernism. As we attempt to formulate such responses, Carl Schorske's book can be an important text to take with us.

If history has no real data or concepts exclusively its own but is continually poaching on other disciplines, nothing can be excluded in principle from a historian's embrace.[50] This may raise fears of annexation, of intellectual imperialism, or of being forced into a story that is not one's own. From a Schorskean perspective, however, history can be made into the field on which we find ways to talk and listen to one another. No longer tied to the narrative of progress or to any other *particular* narrative, history can be seen as the quintessential talking cure. This kind of history does not aim at closure or at a synoptic vision of the whole, nor does it settle for ironic sophistication. Instead it constructs meaning out of the connections it can establish among the diverse discourses and practices that have defined our lives and cultures over time.

NOTES

1. Peter Novick, *That Noble Dream: The "Objectivity Question" and the American Historical Profession* (New York: Cambridge University Press, 1988), 573–629. See my comments in "Unsettling the Past: Objectivity, Irony, and History," chapter 1 in this collection.

2. Carl E. Schorske, *Fin-de-Siècle Vienna: Politics and Culture* (New York: Knopf, 1980), 14.

3. On this question, see Robert Dawidoff, "History . . . But," in *History and . . . : Histories Within the Human Sciences,* ed. Ralph Cohen and Michael S. Roth (Charlottesville: University Press of Virginia, 1995), 370–81.

4. Schorske, *Vienna,* 19.

5. Ibid., 83.

6. Ibid., 62.

7. Ibid., 119.

8. Ibid., 145.

9. Hugo von Hofmannsthal, "Buch der Freunde," in *Aufzeichnungen,* ed. Herbert Steiner (Frankfurt am Main: S. Fischer, 1959), 60; Schorske, *Vienna,* 134, 172.

10. Schorske, *Vienna,* 183.

11. Ibid., 202.

12. ibid., 203.

13. As I discuss below, Dominick LaCapra has emphasized the ways in which Schorske's reading of Freud neglects critical dimensions that are a deep part of the "retreat from the political." For a reading of Freud that emphasizes the critical dimensions of psychoanalysis, see my *Psycho-Analysis as History: Negation and Freedom in Freud* (Ithaca: Cornell University Press, 1987). I have a different reading of some of the evidence Schorske uses in "Freud's Use and Abuse of the Past," chapter 11 in this collection. See also William J. McGrath, *Freud's Discovery of Psychoanalysis: The Politics of Hysteria* (Ithaca: Cornell University Press, 1986).

14. Schorske, *Vienna,* 206 n. 26.

15. Ibid., 266.

16. Ibid., 273.

17. Ibid., 271.

18. Ibid., 311.

19. Ibid., 318.

20. Ibid., 364.

21. Michael S. Roth, "Introduction," *History and . . . ,* 1–22.

22. Carl E. Schorske, "A Life of Learning," American Council of Learned Societies, *Occasional Papers,* 1 (New York, 1987), 13.

23. Schorske, *Vienna,* xvii.

24. Carl G. Hempel, "The Function of General Laws in History," *Journal of Philosophy* 39, 1 (1942): 35–48.

25. Louis O. Mink, "The Divergence of History and Sociology in the Recent Philosophy of History," in *Historical Understanding,* ed. Brian Fay, Eugene O. Golob, and Richard T. Vann (Ithaca: Cornell University Press, 1973, 1987), 169.

26. In this regard see F. R. Ankersmit, "The Dilemma of Contemporary Anglo-Saxon Philosophy of History," *History and Theory,* Beiheft 25: *Knowing and Telling History: The Anglo-Saxon Debate* (1986): 1–27.

27. See Michael S. Roth, *Knowing and History: Appropriations of Hegel in Twentieth-Century France* (Ithaca: Cornell University Press, 1988).

28. Ian Hacking, "Two Kinds of Historicism in Philosophy," in *History and . . . . ,* 296–318.

29. See Michael S. Roth, "Cultural Criticism and Political Theory: Hayden White's Rhetorics of History," chapter 7 in this collection. See also Wulf Kansteiner, "Hayden White's Critique of the Writing of History," *History and Theory* 32, no. 3 (1993): 273–95.

30. On changes within the American historical profession that are connected to these developments, see Novick, *That Noble Dream,* and my review essay, "Unsettling the Past: Objectivity, Irony, and History," chapter 1 in this collection.

31. It is perhaps worth noting here that Herbert Marcuse published *Eros and Civilization* in 1955 and that Norman O. Brown published *Life Against Death* in 1959. Marcuse and Brown, two of Schorske's closest intellectual friends, were using history (and psychoanalysis) to undermine political and cultural conditions they considered deplorably oppressive and to suggest an escape from this history.

32. Michael S. Roth, "The Ironist's Cage," chapter 8 in this collection, and Roth, "Foucault on Discourse and History: A Style of Delegitimation," chapter 4 in this collection.

33. Schorske, *Vienna,* 19.

34. Ibid., xxviii.

35. Ibid., xxv.

36. Ibid., xix.

37. See Michael P. Steinberg's comment on the necessity of recognizing fragmentation in "'Fin-de-Siècle Vienna' Ten Years Later: 'Viel Traum, Wenig Wirklichkeit,'" *Austrian History Yearbook* 22 (1991): 154.

38. See the introduction to the Wesleyan University Press reissue of *The Obstructed Path* (1968) and *The Sea Change* (1975) as *Between Commitment and Disillusion* (1987). In what follows I draw on my essay, "Narrative as Enclosure: The Contextual Histories of H. Stuart Hughes," chapter 2 in this collection.

39. See Carl E. Schorske, "Science as Vocation in Burkhardt's Basel," in *The University and the City: From Medieval Origins to the Present,* ed. Thomas Bender, (New York: Oxford University Press, 1988), 198–209; Lionel Gossman, "Cultural History and Crisis: Burckhardt's *Civilization of the Renaissance in Italy,*" in Roth, *Rediscovering History,* 404–27.

40. Schorske, *Vienna,* xxiii.

41. Dominick LaCapra, "Is Everyone a *Mentalité* Case? Transference and the Culture Concept" (orig. pub. in *History and Theory* 23, no. 3 [1984]: 296–311), in LaCapra, *History and Criticism* (Ithaca: Cornell University Press, 1985), 71–94.

42. Ibid., 82.

43. Schorse, *Vienna,* xxv.

44. For example, for Gay, the cosmopolitan scientificity of the medical world in which Freud worked makes any specific Viennese context not especially relevant to the founder of psychoanalysis. Gay also seems to suffer from the illusion that the lack of a particular, contingent context would make the theory more universal or scientific. See, for example, Peter Gay, *Freud, Jews, and Other Germans: Masters and Victims in Modernist Culture* (New York: Oxford University Press, 1978), 31–32.

45. This is a major component of the criticism in LaCapra's article cited above. La-Capra restated this criticism in a personal communication to me. I am grateful for his thoughtful and generous response to an earlier version of this essay.

46. Roth, "Narrative as Enclosure," 42–43.

47. LaCapra, "Is Everyone a *Mentalité* Case," 84.

48. Michel Foucault, *Discipline and Punish: The Birth of the Prison,* trans. Alan Sheridan (New York: Pantheon, 1977), 30–31.

49. Such a dialogue is, of course, what Dominick LaCapra has been calling for and often creating.

50. Carl E. Schorske, "History and the Study of Culture," in *History and . . . ,* 382–95.

PART 2

Uses and Abuses

• 4 •

Foucault on Discourse and History:
A Style of Delegitimation

At a time when the popular press has joined important figures in the academy in denouncing poststructuralist thinkers for avoiding morality and politics or repressing them for ignoble reasons, one can turn to Michel Foucault's writings for confirmation of the important contribution that poststructuralism has made to our ability to think seriously about our relationship to the past. His work also exemplifies how a rhetorical turn in philosophy and history does not necessarily preclude the development of an informed, critical stance on some of the crucial problems of modernity. Although this essay will be a critical examination of Foucault's use of an analysis of discourse to tell a history of the present, I should preface my remarks by saying that this criticism presupposes the great importance of Foucault's contribution to thinking about history and about politics. Foucault's historical analysis of discursive practices has done more than any other contemporary body of writing to wake those who think about the connection of past and present from their dogmatic slumbers. We must ask, however, where Foucault leaves us when we are thus awoken. Do we in fact have any more power to deal with the world around us than we did in our dreams?

Foucault's books tell the story of increasing repression and domination; even when we attempt to be free, he shows how the attempt leads to ever greater constraints. To enter into the work of Michel Foucault is to enter a world of critical pessimism. In this essay I will discuss how his genealogical analysis of discourse in fact creates a pessimism at the expense of criticism, and how his effort at delegitimation undermines the possibility of making history meaningful, which may be essential for any kind of political action or judgment.

I have argued elsewhere that Gilles Deleuze's interpretation of Nietzsche and Foucault's oeuvre as a whole should be understood as reactions against the Hegelian philosophy of history that was so influential in France from the 1930s through the postwar period. In this reaction there is not only a turn away from historical events and toward discourse, there is also a displacement of questions of meaning and direction in favor of an analysis of use or function.[1] Foucault's work illuminates both the powers and the limitations of rejecting the dialectical emplotment of history in favor of the construction of a genealogical history of the present. Foucault's writings are a sustained attempt to find a modern style in which a Nietzschean approach to the past can be coherently and persuasively maintained. And this Nietzschean approach is understood to be in large part charged by anti-Hegelianism:

> In order to liberate difference, we need a thought without contradiction, without dialectic, without negation: a thought which says yes to divergence; an affirmative thought the instrument of which is disjunction; a thought of the multiple—of dispersed and nomadic multiplicity that is not limited or confined by constraints of similarity; . . . We must think problematically rather than question and answer dialectically.[2]

Foucault's Nietzscheanism altered as it was confronted with different methodological possibilities and changing political choices. A genealogy of his thought might be developed that connected his work to his biography or that focused on his personal and political commitments to the antipsychiatry, prison reform, and gay rights movements,[3] but here I shall concentrate on how his anti-Hegelian and Nietzschean style of delegitimation develops in his major writings. What Deleuze said of Nietzsche he might also have said of Foucault: "Anti-Hegelianism traverses his work like a thread of aggressivity."[4]

Foucault, Nietzsche, and Interpretation Without End

Michel Foucault's writings on the past and his other political interventions displayed a sustained attempt to think and apply the lessons of Nietzsche within the contemporary theoretical conjuncture. An important part of this conjuncture had to do with a focus on language in a very broad sense, or on what Foucault preferred to call discourse. His Nietzsche, then, was not so much the theorist of the will to power but the thinker who examined at what price the subject can speak the truth, and "the relation between 'telling the truth' and forms of reflexivity, of self upon self."[5] And as he emphasized again at the end of his life, he came to this Nietzsche through Heidegger:

> Heidegger was always for me the essential philosopher. I began by reading Hegel then Marx and I started to read Heidegger in 1951 or 1952; and in 1953 or 1952, I no longer remember, I read Nietzsche. . . . All my philosophic becoming was determined by my reading of Heidegger. But I recognize that it is Nietzsche who took it over . . . I tried to read Nietzsche in the 50s, Nietzsche alone meant nothing to me! Whereas Nietzsche and Heidegger, that was *le choc philosophique!*[6]

If Heidegger remains an absent target of Foucault's writing, Nietzsche figures prominently in two important texts. By examining them in some detail, we should be able to assess to what extent it is helpful to think of Foucault's oeuvre as an example of a French Nietzscheanism, and how that oeuvre refigures the connection between history and knowing through an analysis of discourse.

In the Royaumont Colloquium of the summer of 1964 Foucault delivered a lecture on Nietzsche, Marx, and Freud. In this talk he examines what he elsewhere calls a new *epistēmē;* a new way of knowing and thinking about the world. An *epistēmē,* much like a paradigm in a Kuhnian sense, is a strategy of discourse through which we interact with objects and people around us, and with ourselves. The new discursive strategy that he examines in this essay is "interpretation." Of course interpretation existed well before the nineteenth century, but then it was aimed at the discovery of resemblances. In the nineteenth century, and in particular in the work of Marx, Nietzsche, and Freud, there arises again "the possibility of a hermeneutic."[7] This possibility is based on an awareness of the reflexivity of interpretation, and an increased attention to the meanings of the surface of signs (their interconnections) rather than a probe into their depths (their references).

It is particularly the reflexivity of interpretation—the idea that an interpretation can best be understood by turning interpretive strategies back on the interpretation itself—that leads Foucault to the second major characteristic of nineteenth-century hermeneutics: "Interpretation finally became an infinite task."[8] For these thinkers the task is infinite because no secure origin or goal acts as a standard for judging meanings.

Foucault notes that for Nietzsche there is no origin of meaning. As interpretation tries to get beneath signs to something more fundamental than them, it discovers only more interpretations. Meaning comes through the imposition of interpretations.[9] Signs, then, are not prior to interpretations; instead signs are always already the product of interpretations:

> Beginning in the 19th century, beginning from Freud, Marx and Nietzsche, it seems to me that the sign is going to become malevolent; I mean that there is in the sign an ambiguous and even suspect means of willing evil, and of *malveiller.* That is insofar as the sign is already an interpretation which does not present itself as such. Signs are interpretations which try to justify themselves, and not the inverse.[10]

In a world without beginnings, without a secure meaning to search out, the goal of interpretation becomes mysterious also. Interpretation for Nietzsche—as for Freud and Marx—is always incomplete, and a total hermeneutic is closer to *l'expérience de la folie* than it is to "absolute knowledge."[11] Dialectical thinking had erred in trying to attribute positive meaning and direction to the play of meaning.[12] In contrast to this appropriation of interpretation for something more secure, and in contrast to the semiologist's faith in the "absolute existence of signs"—and thus a possible systematization of their relationships—Nietzsche, Marx, and Freud leave us with a "hermeneutic which is enveloped on itself," an endless interpretation without foundation and without goal. For Foucault, this legacy defines the current discursive period and of course his own interpretation of it:

> The problem of the plurality of interpretations, of the war of interpretations, is, I believe, made strictly possible by the very definition of the interpretation, which goes on to infinity, without there being an absolute point beginning from which it is judged and is decided upon. Thus, the following: the fact that we are destined to be inter-

preted at the very moment where we interpret; all interpreters must know it. This plethora of interpretations is certainly a trait which profoundly characterizes Western culture now.[13]

Seven years after giving the lecture at Royaumont Foucault returned to Nietzsche in an essay that would define his historical approach to discursive practices for the rest of his life. In "Nietzsche, la généalogie, l'histoire," Foucault showed what was at stake in adopting a Nietzschean perspective, if not a method, on the past instead of either the traditional historiographical or the "metaphysical" modes of comprehending historical change.

Foucault begins his description of genealogy where his previous discussion of interpretation left off. Genealogy is an examination of the minutiae of history, not of great deeds. It rejects the "metahistorical deployment of ideal significance and of indefinite ideologies" and instead concentrates on the play of interpretations, on primal disparity and not bedrock essence.[14] In fact Foucault tries to steer genealogy between two dangerous points: Hegelian philosophy of history and conventional historiography.

The Hegelian philosophy of history—"metaphysics" in Foucault's essay—looks for an essence beneath historical events. Rather than seeking out the meaning that links all events and discourses in a coherent whole, the genealogist recognizes irremediable diversity and discontinuity. Genealogy thus depends on a notion of hermeneutics because it presupposes the primacy of interpretation over the sign; that is, the genealogist expects that the past will contain only more interpretations, and he or she does not seek out a basic truth or essence to serve as a standard of transhistorical judgment:

> If interpretation were the bringing slowly to light of meaning buried in the origin, then only metaphysics could interpret the becoming of humanity. But if interpretation is the violent or surreptitious appropriation of a system of rules (which in itself has no essential meaning), in order to impose a direction, to bend it to a new will, to force its participation in a different game, and to subject it to secondary rules, then the development of humanity is a series of interpretations.[15]

Whereas the metaphysical (Hegelian) historian searches for a *sens de l'histoire,* the Nietzschean genealogist makes use of a *sens historique.* The division between these two terms is the chasm that for Foucault separates traditional historiography or philosophy and his own work.

The search for a *sens de l'histoire* has been animated by a desire to give meaning and direction to the present by finding its development in the past. In a crucial sense this practice is always one of legitimation. To know the direction of history is to validate a certain contemporary practice, make it "realistic" or "reasonable" or "progressive." The point becomes clear when those in power justify the exercise of their power through an appeal to history, and Hegel himself gave the best example of this in the *Philosophy of Right*. When the State is viewed as the highest product of the final stage of history, the appearance of the divine on earth, criticism of it becomes quite literally a form of "non-sense."

But the legitimating function of a *sens de l'histoire* is relevant not only to those in power. The same function is operative for those who use history to criticize those in power, of whom Marx is the most obvious example. Marxist theory of history does not so much predict future historical change as justify a certain kind of political action aimed at bringing about these changes.[16] The effort to find a *sens de l'histoire* connects present to past in order to ground judgments and actions. History becomes that place to which one turns for continuity, stability, and the possibility of acting in a meaningful, that is, nonarbitrary way. Without nature or a god to guide us, a *sens de l'histoire* can legitimate an identity as well as a program for change.[17]

Foucault rejects legitimation through history as "metaphysical." The *sens historique* is counterhistorical when compared to the Hegelian approach to the past. Rather than providing stability or continuity, it disconnects the present and its pasts:

> The search for descent [*provenance*] is not the erecting of foundations, it disturbs what was previously considered immobile; it fragments what was thought unified; it shows the heterogeneity of what was imagined consistent with itself.[18]

Nietzschean genealogy sees the "becoming of humanity as a series of interpretations."[19] Instead of trying to weave together major events and worldviews into a master narrative of history, it focuses on the creation of discursive strategies for interacting with one's past and with others. Foucault uses genealogy to uncover the appearance of these strategies or interpretations and their eclipse. And the question "Interpretations of what?" is no longer admissible because of his view of language. Interpretations are primary; there is nothing beneath or behind an interpretation except another interpretation, and the same holds true for the work of the genealogist. The reflexive dimension remains crucial for Foucault. Genealogy cannot take itself for a science that regards the interpretations of the past from some suprahistorical point of view. Genealogy affirms itself as another in a series of interpretations, as a discourse among discourses soon to be revised. The *sens historique* is nonmetaphysical to the extent that it rejects all absolutes.[20]

In "Nietzsche, la généalogie, l'histoire," Foucault follows Nietzsche in calling history without absolutes "effective history.": At least since Ranke, historians have taken "metaphysicians" as easy targets for their empirical wrath, but Foucault is not linking genealogy with traditional historiography:

> "Effective" history differs from that of the historians in that it does not stand on any constant; nothing in man—not even his body—is stable enough for recognizing other men and being recognized by them. . . . It is necessary to destroy that which permits the consoling play of recognitions. To know, even in the historical order, does not signify to "re-find," and above all not to "re-find ourselves." History will be "effective" to the extent that it introduces discontinuity into our very being. Knowledge is not made for comprehension, it is made for cutting.[21]

Effective history will be a "countermemory" teaching us that we live without foundations, and that the events of our past do not contain the anticipation of meanings fully realized in the present or the future.[22] Effective history knows itself to be a partial interpretation in the service of particular interests in the present; its inquiry includes a genealogy of itself.[23]

If effective history knows itself to be an interpretation of still other interpretations that never lead to a stable identity or to comprehension, why should anyone do this kind of history? Foucault notes that its reflexive dimension makes genealogy a *carnival concerté*,[24] and that its first function is to parody those elements in the present that find their legitimation in a proud lineage. The second use of effective history is the "systematic disassociation of our identity.":[25] "The purpose of history, directed by genealogy, is not to discover the roots of our identity, but to commit itself, on the contrary, to its dissipation."[26] By dissolving the bases of our identity, effective history undermines the very foundation of our attempts to know ourselves. The genealogist not only asks about the difficulties of knowing a certain object—about the relationship between discourse and "the world"—but also undercuts the subject who would know. This is the third usage of effective history: to destroy the knowing subject by uncovering the hidden vicissitudes of the will to truth. And it is here that Foucault ends his essay, pointing out the way in which a genealogical, Nietzschean history can undermine the security of foundations, continuity, and identity, and place our will to know within the fabric of our desire to interpret.

Foucault's Histories of the Present

Although "Nietzsche, la généalogie, l'histoire" marks an important step in Foucault's account of his own work, it is no less a description of what he had already written than a program for what he intended to do. In *Madness and Civilization* and *The Birth of the Clinic,* Foucault's analysis of the discourse of medicine and psychiatry had already privileged the discontinuous and the destabilizing. It has been rightly pointed out that in the former he retained an essentialist notion of the "experience of madness" that remained pure and stable over time, but the work as a whole surely aims to undermine our faith in the categories of both mental illness and reason.[27] In *The Birth of the Clinic,* Foucault describes his project as both historical and critical insofar as it is concerned "with determining the conditions of possibility of medical experience in modern times."[28] But the entire point of determining these possibilities is to bring to mind the opportunities for change. In all his historical works Foucault situates himself at the beginning of a contemporary shift in the way we interact with the world (*epistēmē,* discourse formations, a prioris, paradigms). His histories are effective insofar as they contribute to hasten this shift by exposing the limits of the present structures of experience.[29]

The Order of Things can be situated in this nascent shift. The book was written when structuralism's critique of historicism and humanism was fashionable, and it contributed to this critique by providing an account of how the notion of "man" became the center of our thinking. The structuralist critique of humanism depended on an analysis of language in which the speaking subject had little or nothing to do with the meaning of what was said. We do not generate the meanings in discourse; we find ourselves always already within a discourse. If "man" or human history was not the origin of meaning, self-consciousness would no longer be the goal of knowing. Heidegger's critique of phenomenology and his notion of man as not the lord of beings but the shepherd of Being was crucial to Foucault's own critique of the human sciences. He not only contributed to the polemic against the "anthropologization" of knowledge, he also pointed to signs of the disappearance of "man" from our thinking and tried to show the transitory nature of "man" so as to hasten that disappearance.[30]

The Order of Things argues that a culture speaks and thinks through different *epistēmēs,* and that these *epistēmēs* limit the possibilities of perception, cognition, and expression. These limitations are unconscious because they are the very conditions of our discourse. Although Foucault says we are imprisoned within our own language and cannot describe our own *epistēmē,* his project is centered on the belief that a new beam of light is beginning to shine into our prison. As a perceiver of this new dawn, as an archaeologist who can place this light in relation to the past and present structures of experience, Foucault appears to have one foot in the modern world and one foot in whatever world will follow.[31]

The genealogist's act of interpretation is an act of will to foster change. The notion of *effective* history becomes more concrete when we see that the desired effect of interpretation is (at least in part) the disintegration of the structures of our discourse, by which Foucault means the dissolution of our contemporary conditions of experience and knowing. Foucault says nothing about the content of change because for him any future *epistēmē* is unknowable. It is perhaps the question why one would choose to foster change about which one knows nothing that leads him to examine in detail the mechanisms by which change takes place. How are different forms of power exercised in various movements for change, and in various resistances to these movements? This examination, although it does not directly answer the question "why one should," does provide a "thicker" interpretation, one that may make action in the present more open to discursive legitimation than it otherwise would be.

Foucault's work always had something to do with power, but with *Discipline and Punish* this concern emerged in the foreground. Whereas previously he had examined the possibilities of knowing and how these were maintained in language, with this book he began to examine the power/

knowledge constellation from the perspective of the exercise of power.[32] It is certainly true that the earlier investigations of the possibilities of knowing had much to do with power, especially insofar as the expression of these possibilities in discourse became important for institutions, disciplines, and conceptual change. In *Discipline and Punish* and his later works, Foucault's notion of discourse becomes thicker as it comes to emphasize the operations that depend on (and reinforce) ways of knowing. In a sentence that fits perfectly into his view of Nietzsche's *Genealogy of Morals,* Foucault stresses the connection of knowledge and power:

> We must admit that power produces knowledge . . . that power and knowledge directly imply one another; that there is no power relation without the correlative constitution of a field of knowledge, nor any knowledge that does not presuppose and constitute at the same time power relations.[33]

Discipline and Punish not only describes the birth of the prison, it explores the power/knowledge constellation that makes systematic normalization possible.

Foucault's understanding of power has been discussed in great detail elsewhere; here we need note only that he is attaching himself to an interpretation of Nietzsche that underlines the interconnection of the will-to-power and the will-to-truth. Most important, power is viewed not as something that inhibits truth but as something that produces truth. Thus power is not only repressive, it is creative. And the ability of a discursive strategy for the exercise of power to create truths, or a regime of truth, is the secret to the self-legitimation of the strategy.[34]

Foucault describes *Discipline and Punish* as a "history of the present," and here he means more than just "the history of a paradigm that is about to become outmoded." In this work the development of prisons—of penal "reform"—is linked to mechanisms of power which he clearly thinks need to be resisted now. Resistance to normalization means resistance to the network of power in which the prison has existed. Practical political work for prisoners and against a specific exercise of power has replaced more distant, if still vaguely apocalyptic, references to shifts in the structures of discourse:

> The meaning which bears and determines us has the form of a war rather than that of a language: relations of power, not relations of

meaning. History has no "meaning," though this is not to say it is absurd or incoherent. On the contrary it is intelligible and should be susceptible of analysis down to the smallest detail—but this in accordance with the intelligibility of struggles, of strategies and tactics.[35]

The contrast between relations of power and relations of meaning recalls that between *sens historique* and *sens de l'histoire*. The problem with the latter terms in each opposition is that they assume a generalizable or transcendent function that allows for judgment among particulars. In other words, considerations of meaning and considerations of the *sens de l'histoire* are totalizable. This conclusion is problematic for Foucault because genealogy assumes (and shows) the fragmentation and discontinuity of the past.[36] When Foucault criticizes the search for meaning in history, he is criticizing the notion that there is a uniform meaning or a uniform history, and he aims both at Hegelianism and at semiology:

> Neither the dialectic, as logic of contradictions, nor semiotics, as the structure of communication, can account for the intrinsic intelligibility of conflicts. "Dialectic" is a way of evading the always open and hazardous reality of conflict by reducing it to a Hegelian skeleton, and "semiology" is a way of avoiding its violent, bloody and lethal character by reducing it to the calm Platonic form of language and dialogue.[37]

Semiology is abandoned along with dialectics because both have a pretension to nonlocal knowledge. Foucault sees this pretension as an evasion of the *specific* connections of knowledge and power.[38]

That changes in the past have been fragmentary and discontinuous also shows us something about how our *sens historique* should foster change in the present. Analysis of history, if it is to be "effective" (that is genealogical), must not only examine how power and knowledge are related but also situate itself in the present in accordance with specific strategies and tactics of resistance, in accordance with another exercise of power. In the 1977 interview from which I have been quoting, Foucault makes clear that the emphasis on specific struggles, strategies, and tactics is a post-1968 phenomenon. One of the lessons of those *événements* is that the state is everywhere but that, in order to combat it without imitating its structure, one has to organize resistance at the micro or local level.[39] In this environment the role of the intellectual also changes. Whereas intellectuals had once spoken in the name of universal values and Truth, they now could speak "within specific sectors, at the precise points where their own conditions of life situate them."[40] The notion of discourse as being fragmentary and heterogeneous and of interpretation as being endless is connected to a view of the intellectual whose interventions have no pretension to totality. The valorization of the specific as opposed to the universal intellectual is connected to the dismissal of all attempts at universal history and to an antirepresentational politics that underlines the "indignity of speaking for others."[41]

The problem with this view of the intellectual—and of everyone who speaks—is that it effaces, or accepts the effacement of, public life. According to this view I cannot speak for you because I do not share the "conditions of life that situate you." The inability to share these conditions undermines one's ability to speak for—or to—anybody at all. Foucault has not only dissolved the possibilities for representation, he has also dissolved the possibilities of communication as a form of political participation. Such participation, certainly the heart of any democratic politics, requires that some conditions—Eric Weil called them traditions, or parts of the community that go without saying, Wittgenstein, forms of life—are shared. However, the emphasis Foucault puts on discontinuity, fragmentation, and division makes clear that our ability to share such conditions with others is, at best, very limited. Politics is thereby reduced to the pursuit of small, special interests (although since all interests are now "special," the word loses much of its force). There is no General Will to which the intellectual can attach him- or herself because there is no longer a public sphere that transcends our specific situations, struggles, and strategies; there is, in sum, no longer the possibility of community. Even more strongly, such a possibility has never existed; there has only been the exercise of a specific kind of power in whose interest the illusion of such a possibility functioned. At least this seems to be Foucault's view.[42]

Even in the 1977 interview, however, some doubts emerge. The view of the specificity of intellectuals can become a form of skepticism. We cannot speak for anybody because we can never know what anybody really thinks or wants. Such a skepticism might be theoretically amusing if joined to verbal and textual play, but in political terms it is surely impotent. The specific intellectual has renounced the universal, but what then can be the basis for his or her ability to join with other people, or to teach, learn from, or persuade other people, to work together for change? What, in other words, can serve as the forms of commonality essential for politics? Or does this skepticism entail an anemic view of politics as essentially the pursuit of private interest? Foucault's answer seems to be that our commonality is that we share in the regime of truth production. We are parts of a discourse, of a technology of producing truth; we are enmeshed in "the ensemble of rules according to which the true and the false are separated and specific effects of power attached to the true."[43] The critical intellectual's general task, then, is "that of ascertaining the possibility of constituting a new politics of truth." The point is not to change what people think but to change the way the "regime" produces truth.[44]

Here we return to the equivalent of the references to the vague shifts in our archive or *epistēmē* that animated Foucault's earlier works. The specific intellectual is supposed to work within his or her own situation for change. A university professor, for example, might argue for a democratization of the university or for more equality in hiring; at least these seem to be the kinds of things for which Foucault hoped the intellectual would argue. Of course there are no transcendent or even general criteria for evaluating arguments for change, and so an intellectual with opposed arguments would be just as specific. "Foucault," Paul Veyne tells us, "admits to being incapable of justifying his own preferences; he can appeal to neither a human nature, nor an equivalence to an object. Because knowledge is power, it is imposed and one imposes it."[45] Perhaps this is why Foucault was not satisfied with specificity as a positive political value. In any case the intellectual is also on a more general level insofar as he or she supports or undermines the regime of truth. There is no way to "emancipate truth from every system of power," just as there was no way to think without discourse or without *epistēmēs* or archives. The political task (for those who share Foucault's sympathies) is to "detach the power of truth from the forms of hegemony . . . within which it operates at the present time."[46]

Because we know that truth will always be attached to a system of power, we want to know not only that we are detaching the power of truth but to what new regime we are attaching it. This is the crucial political dilemma of the specific intellectual, but Foucault has nothing specific to say about it. This position recalls his earlier apocalyptic rhetoric, where nothing can be said of the next archive because we can think only within our own archive.[47] The epistemology seems to get in the way of the politics, although one might argue that the failure in political thinking is justified through an epistemology. In any case it seems that in shifting from large-scale talk about discursive possibilities to more specific local accounts of power, Foucault better positions himself to provide an account of the mechanisms of power and the possibilities for *specific* forms of desirable change. But this is not the case. Instead the gap separating the present and any goals for change remains supreme. It is a gap of theoretical silence, and it is the gap of politics.[48]

From Discourse to Style

Foucault's understanding of change starts from Nietzschean premises that were important to other French intellectuals in the 1960s and 1970s, but he does not display the faith in Being's progressive selectivity that comforted some of his contemporaries.[49] Foucault does embrace a Nietzsche who endorses the flux of things, who destroys the stable, continuous narrative that legitimates an identity and instead celebrates the blooming, buzzing confusion that might replace it. But he knows that there is no possibility of thinking or living in direct contact with this world of raw Power, Being, or Truth. These forces are always already interpreted, always already within the context of a regime. When Foucault talks of change, he is not talking of a liberation from the constraints of discourse; he is talking about the creation of a new discursive regime.

The problem is that there is no indication of what this regime will look like because of the epistemological point that one cannot describe future paradigms, only the present one and those of the past. To call attention to this epistemological point is not enough, however, because it also holds true for the much criticized Hegelian philosophy of history in any of its progressivist versions. One only has to think of the flight at dusk of Hegel's owl of Minerva or Kojève's notion that we have only dialectical knowledge of the human past. But neither Hegel nor Kojève left politics as simply a gap in theory.

They did not leave such a gap because with the Hegelian model all human change is mediated. Apprehending mediation within this model is equivalent to comprehending the meaning and direction of history. Thus for Kojève an understanding of the master/slave dialectic is the key for configuring history in such a way as to understand what kind of action is progressive.[50] For Foucault, as we have seen, history has no meaning and it certainly has no direction; that is, there is no possibility of mediation in Foucault, and this is perhaps the most important aspect of his Nietzschean approach to discourse and history *qua* reaction against Hegelianism. For Nietzsche, as for Foucault, there are events, but these are great irruptions into history. Change is not what we desire, work toward, and achieve only out of something that resists our purposeful labor, it is that which happens *between* archives; however, we can understand only that which occurs *within* an archive. Change is not something we intend, it is at best something we can one day (genealogically) map.[51] To borrow a phrase from Charles Taylor, Foucault leaves us with "strategies without projects."[52]

Foucault was sensitive to this criticism of his work. He did not merely mouth the evasion that the ideas of community and the possibility of nonarbitrary, nonprivate action had somehow been deconstructed with the deferral of metanarratives. Instead he pointed to his political action as that which indicated the direction in which he thought change should occur, and what he was willing to do to further such change.[53] His action was in principle nontotalizable, that is, one could not derive from it the foundation for a theory of progress or progressive action in general. The struggles he wrote about and supported were, in other words, "anarchistic."[54] Perhaps the key issues tying them together were: Who are we? How is it that a form of power "categorizes the individual, marks him by his own individuality, attaches him to his own identity, imposes a law of truth on him which he must recognize and which others have to recognize in him. It is a form of power which makes individuals subjects."[55] If Foucault's work did not indicate the direction of desired change, perhaps it could indicate how we have become subjects who desire to know this direction. Perhaps it could indicate how the connections have been formed between our ways of knowing and our ways of desiring. A critical understanding of these connections might help us to construct not a foundation but a framework for our action in the present. Foucault turned to the history of sexuality for this understanding because this history revealed how we are constituted as subjects.

The three volumes of the *Histoire de la sexualité* have more than one agenda, but the project clearly aims at an understanding of the history of how the subject has been constituted.[56] In other words, Foucault wants to show how various "technologies of the self" have created a specific notion of the individual in relation to his or her conduct, desires, and experience. These relations eventually situated sexuality in a moral domain, rather than in a "style of life."[57] The configuration placed sexuality within a network of power and truth which, in its Christian form, made desire not only something to be managed or molded but something to be condemned as inherently evil.

Foucault situates his late work in relation to other histories. He does not stress the difference between genealogy and history but instead notes that his essay is a philosophic exercise. At stake, he says, is "knowing to what extent the work of thinking one's own history can liberate thought from what it thinks silently, and to permit it to think otherwise."[58] He had already raised the idea of thinking in different ways in the introduction to volume 2: "There are moments in life where the question of knowing if one can think otherwise than one thinks and see otherwise than one sees is indispensable for continuing to look and to reflect."[59] How does a study of sexuality among the Greeks and Romans constitute a philosophic exercise? How should it help us to "think otherwise"?

The study of ancient sexuality can be seen as a part of a genealogy of morals; that is, Foucault finds that morality has little to do with following a rule, everything to do with how the self is understood. The difference between pagan and Christian morality is the difference in their strategies for forming an independent and free self.

> The evolution . . . from paganism to Christianity does not consist in a progressive interiorization of rule, of act and of responsibility; instead it produces a restructuration of forms of the relation to self and a transformation of practices and techniques on which this relation was based.[60]

Thus for Foucault, the study of ancient sexuality is a philosophic exercise because it shows how we first constitute ourselves as subjects who need rules by which to live. It helps us to think otherwise by calling attention to a way of life not determined or even conditioned by the attempt to follow a rule, one that instead can be described as the cultivation of a style.

> Among the Greeks, the same themes of restlessness . . . took form in a reflection which aims neither at a codification of acts, nor at a constitution of an erotic art, but in the establishment of a technique

of living. . . . The physical rule [*régime*] of pleasures and the economy it imposes are part of a whole art of the self.[61]

If Foucault's historical studies offered no criteria for evaluating change, they could explore possibilities in the past that might allow us to begin to think, and live, otherwise. They uncover neither models we are to imitate nor rules we are to try to follow, but innovations that might allow us to create other ways of being. These innovations provide not criteria for prediction—or even production—but material for aesthetic inspiration. The possibilities are not substitutes for lost foundations nor are they only the objects of nostalgia. Instead they are meant as contradictions to the historical givens that we take as natural or necessary.

We should note, however that the effort to "think otherwise" and to recover an ethics not tied to following a rule is in tension with the understanding of discourse found in Foucault's early works. Recall that he had stressed that an archive or *epistēmē* limited the possibilities of discourse and of thought, indeed that the archive or *epistēmē* established the conditions of possibility of discourse and thought.[62] What else could one do within an *epistēmē* but follow its rules? But as we have seen, Foucault situated his own work at the limits of our own possibilities of knowing and acting. In the final volumes on the history of sexuality, Foucault wants to expand these limits by imagining other forms of constraint, other regimes. But it should be clear that the project of "thinking otherwise" remains inherently problematical for the genealogist conscious of working within and not just on a history of the present.

If Foucault's work in the 1970s is clearly connected to Nietzsche's *Genealogy of Morals,* the last two volumes of the *History of Sexuality* are more closely tied to Nietzsche's *Birth of Tragedy.* There Nietzsche found in pre-Socratic Greece a time when life was justified as an aesthetic phenomenon, when the cruel bite of scientific Socratic irony had not yet corrupted an aesthetic balance between the Appolonian and the Dionysian. Foucault likewise finds in the Greeks a moment before the constitution of the subject as a moral problem. Here we can perhaps see how Foucault's reading of Nietzsche was mediated by Heidegger, the "essential philosopher."[63] Heidegger's search for a point before the fall is part of a long German fascination with the Greeks. Foucault does not adhere to this tradition completely; he does not search for a romantic origin that must be lamented, recaptured, or reiterated.[64] But he does find in the Greeks the notion of morality as a style that might allow us to escape the exigencies involved in establishing universal values through the creation of philosophical criteria legitimated by a notion of the subject.

> A moral experience essentially centered on the subject no longer appears to me to be satisfactory . . . The search for styles of existence as different as possible from one another appears to me one of the points on which contemporary research within particular groups can start. The search for a form of morality which would be acceptable to everyone—in the sense that everyone must submit to it— appears catastrophic to me.[65]

Foucault's failure to provide a criterion for judging change should be understood as a refusal. As Habermas pointed out, Foucault's critique of power depends on criteria from the "analytic of the true" (the Enlightenment tradition) that his criticism undermines.[66] In the terms we have been using, not only does Foucault offer his readers an alternative style, he provides them with a detailed criticism of their values and their limitations. Yet the criticism is attached only to a desire for change, not to an argument for legitimate change.

Deleuze's *Foucault* defends this style of criticism as a Nietzschean mode of the history of the present. He sees Foucault as having written a series of historical ontologies that examine the diverse conditions of power, truth, and the self. But these conditions are never apodictic, they are problematic:[67] "No solution is transferable from one epoch to another, but there can be encroachments where the penetration of problematic fields which form the 'data' of an old problem are reactivated in another."[68] However, Deleuze recognizes here the same problem that concerns Habermas: How is one to connect the various historical ontologies? How are concerns for change in the present to be connected to historical ontologies? "Finally," Deleuze writes, "it is practice which constitutes the only continuity from past to present, or inversely, the manner in which the present explicates the past."[69]

Once again the absence of a transhistorical criterion to connect the various epochs (clearly what Habermas thinks he can provide) with one another and with the present is filled by appeal to a practice. For Foucault's Greeks, who did not *feel* the absent criterion because they were not looking for it, "style" was the equivalent of "practice." For Deleuze's Nietzsche, the connection was made by a happy reading of the eternal return. The selectivity of the eternal return insured a form of progress that was not dependent on negativity; real (nonreactive) practice presumably gets selected. Present and past are linked by a cycle that forces out those (reactive) elements most deserving of criticism.[70]

At the end of his essay on Foucault, Deleuze rightly brings together the themes of his own interpretation of Nietzsche with his reading of his friends work. In regard to the future they can "indicate only germs [ébauches], in the embryological sense, not yet functional."[71] And in pages that will be either frightening or invigorating, depending on one's appreciation of science fiction, he speaks of both the difficulty of knowing the future and the importance of imagining a future in which new forces will be liberated. The liberation of these new forces includes what Foucault called the "death of man," and what Nietzsche named the "superman." In the final sentence of the work, which may recall Heidegger's remark that only a god can save us now, Deleuze adds: "As Foucault would say, the death of man is much less than the disappearance of existing men, and much more than the change of a concept; it is the advent of a new form, neither God nor man, of which one can hope that it will not be worse than its two predecessors."[72] By now of course we know that there can be no foundation for this hope. Foucault might have added that what is possible is a style of life in which it could be manifest, but we must recall that his focus on style of life, or on the construction of the subject, is apolitical—or at least a politics reduced to the private. Foucault's earlier work not only dismantled the notion of progress but also undermined the notion of social hope on which his own cultural criticisms fed.[73] In his later turn toward the subject Foucault finds perhaps a personal hope, an *ethos* that provides a possibility of individual freedom within any regime of discourse. The distance between individual freedom through the construction of a style of life and political freedom may, however, be as great as the distance between *epistēmēs*. In any case it is a distance, according to Foucault, about which we are reduced to silence.

The Nietzschean approach to history through an analysis of discourse insures that politics will occur in a realm that cannot be legitimated, because this realm either is that about which nothing can be said or is itself gestured to as the practical connection between ways of thinking and experiencing. The point here is not that an approach to (and emplotment of) historical events in a grand narrative legitimates, whereas the Nietzschean notion of interpretation critiques. Historicist connections between history and knowing can be an important way legitimating a critique or validating a form of delegitimation. Perhaps we can conclude that the discursive turn in French thought "represented" by Foucault is a radicalized strategy of delegitimation, because it makes no attempt to save itself from those things that are undermined. But this would be a strange use of the word *radical,* for the result of the practice can be a return, dizzying but a return nonetheless, to the status quo. In saying this I do not question the personal commitment of Foucault to a certain style of politics. However, his inability or refusal to justify that politics makes it a *personal* commitment, rather than a commitment that is in principle open to discussion, that is, a political one.

One may object that what counts as political here is foreign to the contemporary redefinition of the political for which Foucault deserves partial credit. His effort to think through how we have become subjects who desire certain forms of legitimation indicates that he took seriously the political problem of legitimation even as he tried to historicize it. His last books are an extraordinary attempt to escape these questions. Genuinely bothered by them, and unable to speak to them in a satisfactory way (even for himself), Foucault turned to genealogy for an understanding of their perhaps limited significance. Maybe our search for connections and criteria is as culture-specific as our sexual practices and our diets. To imagine and reflect on a culture that did not desire these connections and criteria might help us abandon our own search for them.

Despite his important political commitments, Foucault never elaborated a way of "thinking otherwise" that went beyond a style of delegitimation. This style (happily) does not provide us with a method of historical analysis or even with a "philosophy of discourse." Foucault's work does, however, leave us with provocations, suggestions, and questions that can stimulate our capacity to work through what is at stake in trying to think and live within discourse and without foundations.

Foucault's work, like much contemporary history and theory that focuses on discourse as the object of knowledge, leaves us with radical strategies of delegitimation without much attention to the reasons why we might want to use such strategies in relation to specific problems. These reasons cannot be reduced to epistemological issues, and thus the problem of political legitimation is not obviated by recent attempts to move beyond epistemology and foundationalism. New forms of legitimation might consist of narratives linking analyses of injustice with the needs of particular, historically contingent, communities. These forms of legitimation would also be expressions of political identification on the part of intellectuals; neither the forms nor the expressions would be foundational, but instead would be pragmatic. These pragmatic constructions would not depend on the necessity of discovering one's natural community or real comrades. Instead they would point toward the possibility of acknowledging commonality in the service of particular, contingent, but also vital political goals.

NOTES

1. See Michael S. Roth, *Knowing and History: Appropriations of Hegel in Twentieth-Century France* (Ithaca: Cornell University Press, 1988), passim. This essays draws extensively on the final chapter of the book.

2. Foucault, *"Theatrum Philosophicum,"* *Critique* 282 (1970): 899. Modified translation in *Language, Counter-Memory, Practice,* ed. Donald F. Bouchard (Ithaca: Cornell University Press, 1977), 185, 186.

3. A favorite trick of intellectual historians is to see the unity of a life tying together the parts of an oeuvre. Although this may sometimes be helpful, there is clearly no good reason for supposing the unity (even the intelligibility) of a life. Didier Eribon, *Michel Foucault,* trans. Betsy Wing (Cambridge, Mass.: Harvard University Press, 1991), James Miller, *The Passion of Michel Foucault* (New York: Simon and Schuster, 1992) and David Macey *The Lives of Michel Foucault* (London: Hutchinson, 1993). See also Michael S. Roth, "Reinscribing Michel Foucault," *Intellectual History Newsletter* 15 (1993), 57–61.

4. Deleuze, *Nietzsche et la philosophie* (Paris: Presses Universitaires de France, 1962), 9.

5. See the interview with Gérard Raulet (first published in 1983) collected in *Michel Foucault: Politics, Philosophy, Culture,* ed. Lawrence D. Kritzman (New York: Routledge, 1988), 30–33.

6. Foucault, "Le retour de la morale," *Les nouvelles* (28 juin–5 juillet 1984), 40.

7. Foucault, "Nietzsche, Marx et Freud," in *Nietzsche* (Paris: Les Editions de Minuit, 1967), 185. Hereafter NMF.

8. NMF, 187.

9. NMF, 190.

10. NMF, 191.

11. NMF, 188–89. In 1964 Foucault still held fast to the notion of a pure *expérience de la folie.* For a critical appraisal, see Jacques Derrida, "Cogito et histoire de la folie," in *L'Ecriture et la Différence* (Paris: Seuil, 1967), 51–97. Derrida's critique was originally made

in a lecture given in 1963. For a historical treatment of Foucault's early views on madness see Pierre Macherey, "Aux sources de l'*Histoire de la folie:* une rectification à ses limites," *Critique* 471–72 (août/septembre 1986): 753–74.

12. NMF, 191. See also Foucault's resistance to adding Hegel to the trilogy in the discussion following the article (194).

13. NMF, 195–96.

14. Foucault, "Nietzsche, généalogie et l'histoire," in *Hommage à Jean Hyppolite* (Paris: Press Universitaires de France, 1971), 146. Hereafter NGH.

15. NGH, 158. Modified English translation from *Language, Counter-Memory, Practice,* 151–52. Hereafter LCP.

16. See Michael S. Roth, "Review of Barry Cooper's *The End of History,*" *Political Theory* 13, no. 1 (1985): 148–52, and Roth, *Knowing and History,* chaps. 2, 5.

17. Thus Dewey can be rightly seen as legitimating hope and solidarity, even if he was a critic of his time. The contrast with Foucault is powerfully drawn by Richard Rorty in "Method, Social Science and Social Hope," in *Consequences of Pragmatism* (Minneapolis: University of Minnesota Press, 1982), 203–8.

18. NGH, 153; LCP, 147.

19. NGH, 158.

20. NGH, 159. The rejection of absolutes is clearly aimed at what Foucault calls the Platonic tradition (nature as absolute) and the Hegelian tradition (end, or *sens,* of history as absolute). It is also aimed at semiotics to the extent that it strives for a systematic (i.e., more than interpretive) understanding of past interpretations.

21. NGH, 160; LCP, 153, 154. For a critique of "continuous history," see Foucault, *The Archaeology of Knowledge,* trans. A. M. Sheridan Smith (New York: Harper and Row, 1972), 216.

22. NGH, 167; LCP, 162. Hayden White has talked about Foucault's project as a "disremembrance of things past," in "Foucault Decoded: Notes from the Underground," *History and Theory* 12 (1973): 23–54; reprinted in *Tropics of Discourse: Essays in Cultural Criticism* (Baltimore: The Johns Hopkins University Press, 1978), 233.

23. LCP, 163.

24. NGH, 168.

25. NGH, 169; LCP, 162.

26. NGH, 168.

27. See Derrida's critique of Foucault cited above, and Foucault's response, *Histoire de la folie* (Paris: Editions Gallimard, 1972), 583–603. See also the critical commentary on the "nondebate" by Alain Renault and Luc Ferry in *La Pensée 68* (Paris: Editions Gallimard, 1985), 120–29, and the historical essay by Macherey cited above. Georges Canguilhem has underlined the centrality of *Histoire de la folie* in Foucault's oeuvre as a whole, "Sur l'*Histoire de la folie* en tant qu'événement," *Le Débat* 41 (1986): 37–40.

28. Foucault, *The Birth of the Clinic: An Archaeology of Medical Perception,* trans. A. M. Sheridan Smith (New York: Vintage, 1973), xix.

29. I am drawing here on the first part of my "Foucault's 'History of the Present,'" *History and Theory* 20, no. 1 (1981): 32–46. See also the 1984 interview in which Foucault

says about his work on the history of prisons, "I wanted to make it [the penitentiary situation] intelligible, and, therefore, criticizable" (Kritzman, *Foucault: Politics, Philosophy, Culture,* 101).

30. Foucault, *The Order of Things: An Archaeology of the Human Sciences* (New York: Vintage, 1970), 384.

31. Ibid., 207. See Roth, "Foucault's 'History of the Present,'" 39.

32. Since I am interested here in Foucault as a Nietzschean thinker, I have stressed the role genealogy has played throughout his work, rather than dividing his work into archaeological and genealogical phases. For a subtle, nuanced discussion using this division, see Paul Rabinow and Hubert L. Dreyfus, *Michel Foucault: Beyond Structuralism and Hermeneutics,* 2d ed. (Chicago: University of Chicago Press, 1983), especially 104–25. Rabinow and Dreyfus see a clear shift in Foucault's interests away from discourse after May 1968.

33. Foucault, *Surveiller et punir: Naissance de la prison* (Paris: Editions Gallimard, 1975); translated by Alan Sheridan as *Discipline and Punish: The Birth of the Prison* (New York: Pantheon, 1977), 27.

34. On Foucault's truth/power connection see, for example, Rabinow and Dreyfus, *Michel Foucault,* 126–42, and Larry Shiner, "Reading Foucault: Anti-Method and the Genealogy of Power-Knowledge," *History and Theory* 21 (1982): 382–98.

35. Foucault, "Truth and Power," in *Power/Knowledge: Selected Interviews and Other Writings,* ed. C. Gordon (New York: Pantheon, 1980), 114.

36. In a 1978 interview Foucault claimed that he aimed to dissolve discontinuities in favor of showing the intelligibility of practices. Here he is simply backing (rightly) away from the paradox of establishing discontinuity as a principle in a philosophy of history. Foucault's work aims to make history's fragmentation and heterogeneity intelligible without appeals to foundations or goals. If one rejects looking for a *sens de l'histoire,* one cannot find this *sens* in discontinuity. See Kritzman, *Foucault: Politics, Philosophy, Culture,* 100.

37. Ibid., 114–15.

38. See Remo Bodel, "Foucault: pouvoir, politique et maîtrise de soi," *Critique* 471–72 (1986): 908.

39. Note Deleuze's remark that "we have no need to totalize that which is invariably totalized on the side of power" ("Intellectuals and Power," in LCP, 212). In an interview conducted not long before his death, Foucault commented on how the ties between the events of 1968 and Marxism broke the latter's grip on political thinking in France; see *The Foucault Reader,* ed. Paul Rabinow (New York: Pantheon, 1984), 385–86.

40. Foucault, "Truth and Power," 126.

41. Deleuze says that Foucault's fundamental lesson was the "indignity of speaking for others," and "the theoretical fact [?] that only those directly concerned can speak in a practical way on their own behalf" ("Intellectuals and Powers," 209). See in this regard Mark Poster, *Foucault, Marxism and History: Mode of Production vs. Mode of Information,* (New York: Blackwell, 1984) 153–57.

42. At the end of his life Foucault spoke about the rights of persons being "immanent in the discussion." It is important to note, though, that Foucault was talking about discus-

sion at least partly in contradistinction to politics rather than linking discussion and participation. See *The Foucault Reader,* 381–82.

43. Foucault, "Truth and Power," 132.

44. Ibid., 133.

45. Veyne admires greatly his friend's "warrior ethic," which includes an understanding that the enemy has good reasons for fighting too. "Le dernier Foucault et sa morale," *Critique* 471–72 (1986): 937–38.

46. Foucault, "Truth and Power," 133.

47. See my description of this condition in "The Ironist's Cage," chapter 8 in this collection.

48. Ian Hacking points to this same "gap" but does not view it as a weakness in Foucault's work. Hacking claims that Foucault, like Kant, disconnected freedom (and politics) from knowledge, precisely because there are no truths to know about the good life. It is not clear, though, that the fact that there are no truths to know about the good life requires that we undermine our capacity to discuss our projects to construct a better life; that is, that we undermine our capacity for political participation. See "Self-improvement," in *Foucault: A Critical Reader,* ed. David C. Hoy (Oxford: Blackwell, 1986), 235–40. I called attention to Foucault's Kantlike position in "Foucault's 'History of the Present,'" 38.

49. See the critique of Deleuze's reading of Nietzsche in Roth, *Knowing and History,* 194–201.

50. See Ibid., 94–124, and Roth, "A Problem of Recognition: Alexandre Kojève and the End of History," *History and Theory* 24 (1985): 293–306.

51. See Deleuze, "Écrivain non: Un nouveau cartographie," *Critique* 343 (1975): 1207–27, and Deleuze *Foucault,* 31–51.

52. Charles Taylor, "Foucault on Freedom and Truth," *Political Theory* 12, no. 2 (1984): 168.

53. Foucault, private communication, 1981. Rabinow and Dreyfus seem to accept this defense; see "Habermas et Foucault: Qu'est-ce-que l'âge d'homme," *Critique* 471–72 (1986): 857–72; English version, "What Is Maturity? Habermas and Foucault on 'What Is Enlightenment?'" in Hoy, *Foucault: A Critical Reader,* 109–22. The defense is repeated in the interviews in *The Foucault Reader,* where Foucault goes so far as to say that he "never tried to analyze anything whatsoever from the point of view of politics" (385).

54. Foucault, "The Subject and Power," in Rabinow and Dreyfus, *Michel Foucault,* 211. Even if he refused to thematize his various political gestures, his appeal to them is an appeal to what he thought was "progressive" at any particular moment. Foucault has been taken to task for his inability to provide a ground for positive action or for his own critique. See, for example, Michael Walzer, "The Politics of Michel Foucault," in Hoy, *Foucault: A Critical Reader,* 51–68; Nancy Frazer, "Michel Foucault: A 'Young Conservative'?" *Ethics* 96 (1985): 165–84; Habermas, *The Philosophical Discourse of Modernity: Twelve Lectures* (Cambridge, Mass., 1987), chaps. 9, 10. David Hoy puts these criticisms into an intellectual context in his introduction to *Foucault: A Critical Reader* (1–25). Foucault "responds" to some of those criticisms in the interviews in the *Foucault Reader* by saying he belongs to no political group.

55. Rabinow and Dreyfus, *Michel Foucault,* 212.

56. This part of the agenda only becomes clear in volumes 2 and 3. Volume 1 is more concerned with showing how the idea of "repression" is inadequate for making sense of sexuality, in part because power is creative and not just repressive. See, for example, the interview with Foucault, "On the Genealogy of Ethics: An overview of Work in Progress," in Rabinow and Dreyfus, *Michel Foucault,* 229–52.

57. Hayden White has written provocatively on the importance of rhetoric and style in Foucault's work before that work had an explicit concern with style ("Michel Foucault," in *Structuralism and Since* ed. John Sturrock [Oxford: Oxford University Press, 1979], 81–115).

58. Foucault, *Histoire de la sexualité,* vol. 2: *L'usage des plaisirs* (Paris: Editions Gallimard, 1984), 15.

59. Ibid., 14.

60. Ibid., 75.

61. Ibid., 155–56. See also, for example, 30, 106, 107, 111, 133, 224, 248, 275–78; vol. 2: 49, 58, 85, 116, 117, 272–73.

62. Yet another way in which Foucault's project might be seen as a strange historical complement to Kant's. See Roth, "Foucault's 'History of the Present,'" 38–39.

63. Deleuze points out that Foucault's "Heraclitism" is more profound than Heidegger's, because he goes on to say—with a discretion that gives a content to his notion of irresponsibility—"phenomenology is too pacific, it has glorified too many things" (*Foucault* [Paris: Les Editions de Minuit, 1986], 120).

64. As Deleuze nicely puts its, for Foucault there is no Greek miracle, as there is for Heidegger (*Foucault,* 121).

65. Foucault, "Le retour de la morale," 41.

66. Habermas, "Une flèche dans le coeur du temps présent," *Critique* 471–72 (1986): 799. See also the article by Rabinow and Dreyfus in the same issue, "Habermas et Foucault: Qu'est-ce-que l'âge d'homme," 857–72. English versions of both these articles are in Hoy's collection. The Habermas page reference in the English edition is 107–8. Foucault, with Habermas in mind, talks of a "consensus model" as a critical principle but not a "regulatory principle," in *The Foucault Reader,* 379.

67. Deleuze, *Foucault,* 122.

68. Ibid.

69. Ibid.

70. See Deleuze, *Nietzsche et la philosophie,* and *Nietzsche* (Paris: Presses Universitaires de France, 1967), and Roth, *Knowing and History,* 194–201.

71. Deleuze, *Foucault,* 139.

72. Ibid., 141.

73. See Rorty, "Method, Social Science and Social Hope," 206–8. Habermas's criticism of Foucault, cited above, is also relevant here, although social hope need not be founded on criteria acceptable to the Enlightenment tradition.

Natural Right and the End of History:
Leo Strauss and Alexandre Kojève

I wish you a speedy and complete recovery, and I hope it will be given to us to see each other alone or else in good company. The possible localities of such a meeting, if any, are in your opinion, if it has not changed, restricted to a certain part of the surface of the earth. I am more open minded in this respect.

—Leo Strauss

Yes, you are right, we must surely have thought about the same things. And I am sure we fully agree that in this situation, philosophy—if not "consoling"—is nevertheless as reliable and satisfying as ever.

—Alexandre Kojève

Over the last decade there has been a lively debate in the human sciences about the nature of modernity. Can it be that we have passed from a modern to a postmodern age, and if we have made this transition, how can we evaluate the history that has led to it? Or is it the case that the transition is marked exactly by our inability to make such evaluations? Habermas, Lyotard, Jameson, and Rorty, these are some of the names that cram footnotes in the contemporary debates about our place in our history or about our placement of history. The revised and expanded edition of *On Tyranny* recalls two older positions on the nature of modernity: those of Leo Strauss and Alexandre Kojève.[1] In their debate about tyranny (originally published in 1954), and in their correspondence (published in 1991), we see articulated the radical alternative positions in regard to the modern, and in regard to the possibilities and obligations of philosophy in modernity.

The philosophical legacies of Leo Strauss and Alexandre Kojève at first glance indicate little common ground for discussion. Strauss's interpretations of ancients and moderns hung together in a radical conservatism which he professed in a university, while Kojève brought his amalgam of Hegel,

Marx, and Heidegger to his work as a progressive bureaucrat in the French Finance Ministry. Yet one has known for some time of their connection through students who made the journey from the University of Chicago to Paris, and from some scattered published comments. The expanded edition of *On Tyranny* allows us to reconstruct some of the most important points in their dialogue on the connections between philosophy, politics, and history. By doing so we should be able to understand the development of their work, and its significance for a contemporary understanding of modernity and the relation of politics and philosophy in our time.

In this chapter I shall discuss the early stages of this dialogue: Kojève's response to Strauss's *Political Philosophy of Hobbes,* which took the form of notes on the connection between Hobbes and Hegel, and Strauss's response to Kojève's *Introduction à la lecture de Hegel.* These texts form the background to their exchange on Xenephon's *Hiero.* This exchange on the role of philosophy in history will be the subject of the third section of this chapter. The reconstruction of some key aspects of their conversation through the early 1950s allows us to see how their pursuit of the quarrel between Ancients and Moderns is a crucial contribution to our understanding of the possibilities of making meaning from and of finding truth beyond our own historical situation.

Hegel and Hobbes

In *The Political Philosophy of Hobbes* Strauss referred to Alexandre Kojevnikoff, with whom he "intented to undertake a detailed investigation of the connection between Hegel and Hobbes."[2] Strauss made the comment in a footnote to a passage dealing with the link between the fear of violent death and self-consciousness. Hegel, the "authoritative judge" in "questions which bear on the philosophy of self-consciousness," was cited in support of Hobbes's fundamental idea that the origin of virtue was in fear.[3] Kojève—who Strauss would later say understood the Hegel-Hobbes connection better than anyone else alive[4]—seemed to agree with Strauss about Hegel's support for Hobbes's understanding of virtue and self-consciousness, and thus in turn added weight to Strauss's own critical view of Hobbes's essential modernity.

Kojève wrote to Strauss after reading the Hobbes book, which he praised highly. Indeed, although he claimed not to know Hobbes well, Kojève thought that Strauss's interpretation was so strong that "it could not be otherwise."[5] In response to an earlier request from Strauss, Kojève went on to make a comparison between Hobbes and Hegel. In this comparison we can see in embryo some of the important points of their later debate. Kojève took as a given Strauss's interpretation of Hobbes, especially of the English philosopher's anticlassical modern position on the political. Kojève went on to use Hegel to develop his own ideas about philosophy and modernity, ideas sharply opposed to those on which Strauss focused in his later work. Kojève's response to the Hobbes book drew on the reading of Hegel that he was developing in the mid-1930s in Paris at the École Pratique des Hautes Études.[6]

Kojève argued that the "major difference" between Hobbes and Hegel was that only the latter dialectically synthesized ancient and modern philosophy by integrating a *summum bonum* grasped through reflection into the modern approach to history. The ancients had conceptualized the necessity for some general standard of judgment but had not paid enough attention to historical particularities. The moderns, on the other hand, paid so much attention to them that they lost the capacity to think coherently about transhistorical judgment. As the dialectical synthesis of these two positions, Hegel took the messiness of historical change into account without losing an anchor for judgments about historical change. Indeed he showed how the transhistorical standard would emerge out of historical particularity. Thus, according to Kojève, the "ideal State" of Plato was realized (achieved and grasped in thought) through history and at the end of history; it was the "realization of the kingdom of heaven." As Kojève wrote, "Although [the state's] final cause is also philosophical *knowledge,* this knowledge is a knowledge *of* action, *through* action."[7] The modern doubt about the "transcendent eternal order by which man's reason was assumed to be guided," was replaced in Hegel's work, Kojève argued, by the certain knowledge of the meaning and direction of human action over time. Thus, for Kojève's Hegel, the attention to history did not lead to relativism but to a knowing that understood the connection of knowledge to time.

Although both Hegel and Hobbes underlined the importance of fear at the origins of self-consciousness, Kojève thought the "concrete difference" between the two philosophers was that Hobbes "overlooked the value of work, and thus underrated the value of struggle." Fear of death leads only to religion and unhappiness; human vanity leads to work and struggle (for recognition). For Kojève's Hegel, work and struggle produced the ideal state in which there was mutual recognition and satisfaction, and a philosophy (Hegel's) that fully comprehended this state and the history leading up to it. The ideal state—universal and homogeneous—was the "end of history," and when Kojève wrote this letter to Strauss, he thought we were in the final moments of its complete realization.

The reader of Kojève will see in this response to Strauss's Hobbes book the crux of his interpretation of Hegel. Kojève used the master/slave dialectic as a schema to understand the stages of work and struggle in history. In this schema the human is defined by the presence of the desire for recognition—a desire that could be satisfied only with the conservation of its object—and the will to risk one's life in order to satisfy this desire. The realm of the human and of history is defined specifically in contradistinction to the realm of the animal and nature. The desire for recognition is the motor of history, and Kojève used the master/slave dialectic as an allegory of human development: There was bloody battle followed by the rule of the masters over the working slaves. The masters, however, could not satisfy their human desire because they were recognized by *mere* slaves. Eventually the slaves deposed the masters through revolution but they remained in servitude in relation to their work. This is the bourgeois condition. Real freedom would come only through the universal recognition of all and each as citizens. Thus the "final synthesis" of this dialectic is when "the *fight* of a *worker* leads to the *work* of the *fighter.*"[8] The freedom of universal recognition was, for Kojève, full satisfaction. It was also the end of history, since once the desire for recognition was satisfied there would be no force to create historical (human) change. There would be merely the activity of beings seeking to satisfy animal (nonhuman) desires. In other words, rather than engaging in action to achieve freedom and recognition, after the end of history "people" would find ways to acquire, let's say, video machines. The end of history, for Kojève, was the "definitive reality" that served as a transhistorical standard for judging all action. This end was not, as for Kantian thinkers, a horizon that retreated as one approached it but a realizable goal for political action in the contemporary world.[9]

Most critics of Kojève have taken one of two approaches to the interpretation of Hegel that culminates in the "end of history." The first is to argue that Hegel never said *that,* and to criticize Kojève for willfully distorting the ideas of a more reasonable philosopher.[10] The second is to claim that the idea of the end of history is not necessary to save historicism from relativism, or that, if we do need this concept to make judgments about historical change, we certainly have not experienced the ending of history.[11] Unlike Strauss's response, neither of these lines of criticism engaged Kojève on his own terms.[12] It should be emphasized, however, that Kojève was well aware of the personal or even violent nature of his reading of Hegel.[13] The Kojèvian response to those who claim that we cannot have knowledge of historical change but that we can still speak reasonably about it would echo Hegel's comment about the Christian consolation for suffering in this world: without doubt, an ingenious solution. This solution might be satisfactory to *intellectuals* (a term of derision for Kojève and Strauss) who wanted to go on speaking at any price, but it would not do for the philosopher.

The End of History: Realm of Freedom or Definitive Mediocrity?

Strauss's criticism of Kojève's reading of Hegel and of his understanding of modern philosophy had nothing to do with these other approaches. In his letter of August 22, 1948, we can see many of the themes of Strauss's later work, especially *Natural Right and History,* themes that both illuminate and show the stakes involved in Kojève's understanding of the connection between philosophy and history, and the gap that separated both from nature.

The critique can be divided into two categories: the first is based on the view that without a teleological philosophy of nature history can be given no order, nor can we know if it is "one and unique," a single process; the second criticizes the fundamental value Kojève attaches to the universal satisfaction of the desire for recognition and asserts that it is the quality and not the universality of recognition that counts. It is not the idea of the "end of history" as such that Strauss attacks: rather he tries to show that this concept does not do the job that Kojève assigns to it; that is, it will not allow the philosopher to determine reasonably the value of specific historical actions.[14]

Strauss points to the philosophy of nature implicit in Kojève's reading of Hegel. The primary distinction between "the human" and "the natural" quite clearly presupposes a conception of nature, but more important, this (unargued for) conception allows Kojève's Hegel to organize the field of historical events. In other words, the theory of a desire that begins history and the satisfaction that closes it are a form of the philosophy of nature, even though Kojève conceives this theory specifically against even the possibility of speaking philosophically of nature. If not for the naturalist base, Strauss argued, there would be no reason to assume that history does not repeat itself indefinitely or that there are not many different histories, with no underlying unity:

> Indeed, it is evident that the philosophy of nature is indispensable. How can the uniqueness of the historical process . . . be accounted for? Only a teleological concept of nature can help out here. If nature is not structured or ordered with a view to history, then one is led to a contingency even more radical than Kant's transcendental contingency.[15]

If a hidden concept of Nature gives direction to the master/slave dialectic, then Kojève's Hegel has not effected a synthesis of ancient and modern thought but has merely suggested a classical solution to the problem of contingency without arguing for it.

We see in Strauss's criticism a theme that has a crucial role in his philosophy as a whole: historicism that divorces itself from a philosophy of nature results in either incoherence or relativism. Kojève hopes to meet Strauss's objection without giving up his theory of history by using the "end of history" as a standard of judgment. Both agreed on the necessity of having such a standard. As Strauss wrote in *Natural Right and History*:

> to the extent to which the historical process is accidental, it cannot supply man with a standard, and that, if that process has a hidden purpose, its purposefulness cannot be recognized except if there are transhistorical standards. The historical process cannot be recognized as progressive without previous knowledge of the end or purpose of the process.[16]

Although both Strauss and Kojève agreed on the need for some stable criterion of judgment, they were radically opposed in regard to what that criterion might be. The "knowledge of the end or purpose" of the historical process can be known, Kojève tells us, because the process is essentially complete. This knowledge is itself a product of the historical process and not something transhistorical by virtue of its participation in Eternity. Kojève has to (and does) accept the complaint that he is advocating the worship of success (although he wants to substitute "honor" for "worship"), since he endorses Schiller's dictum that *die Weltgeschichte ist das Weltgericht*.

Strauss does not confine himself to criticizing Kojève's criterion of judgment because it is the product of historical development. He also questions the value of the "end of history" as Kojève conceives it. The essential feature of this final state is that in it the fundamental human desire is satisfied because there is universal recognition. Strauss points out an ambiguity here: Is Kojève claiming that humanity is in fact satisfied in this Endstate or that it should be satisfied therein? Kojève has to affirm the former since he has no criterion for establishing the "should" other than the satisfaction itself; that is, in the Endstate, "is" and "ought" must coincide, and it is one of the principal tasks of the philosopher to describe how they do so.

According to Strauss, in describing the final coincidence of "is" and "ought" in an Endstate of universal recognition, the essential facet of the human is left out. "In the Endstate great deeds are impossible," he points out, and the best among persons will never accept definitive mediocrity, even if the state created the conditions in which all were equal. Strauss summarizes his disagreement with Kojève as follows:

> In any case, if not all human beings become wise, then it follows for almost all human beings the end state is identical with the loss of their humanity, and they can therefore not be rationally satisfied with it. The basic difficulty also shows itself in this, that on the one hand the End-State is referred to as the State of warriors-workers, and on the other hand it is said that at this stage there are no wars and as little work as possible (indeed, in the strict sense of the term, there is no more work at all, since nature is definitively conquered).[17]

According to Strauss, only if the fundamental (or the highest) human desire is for wisdom will an Endstate—ruled by the wise—satisfy what is best in humanity. Thus even if history is going in the direction that Kojève claims for it, the satisfaction that it brings to people might not coincide with making them wise, unless we are willing to equate wisdom with idleness. Furthermore, by failing to make wisdom a component of the end of history, Kojève has not provided an idea of universal satisfaction, since philosophers will be satisfied by nothing less than wisdom.[18] The mastery of nature is the triumph of technology, but this victory does not show that people have discovered the highest goal in the service of which to employ their technē. Indeed the "progress" that Hegelianism applauds may threaten the possibility of this discovery by destroying the conditions in which philosophy can exist. In a word, philosophers would never trade the search for wisdom for the accomplishment of equality.

Politics, Philosophy, and Legitimation

The debate between Strauss and Kojève about the role of history in philosophy is also a debate about the role of philosophy in history; that is, about the value of philosophy for historical change and political action. This is the theme of their debate in *On Tyranny*. Their dialogue raises the essential questions about the desire and responsibility of the philosopher vis-à-vis the political/historical realm. It also underscores the problem with Kojève's claim that this realm had already been completed in the definitive triumph of us slaves, and with Strauss's appeal to a group whose self-confidence in knowing the essential questions would be the only legitimation it need deign to seek.

Hegel identifies the history of philosophy with the philosophy of history because of his view that persons necessarily become (self) conscious of the changes created in them by their actions in the world. Self-consciousness, although stimulated by philosophy, tends naturally to grow. It is important to note that in this regard Kojève separated his own position from Hegel's; that is, Kojève thought that philosophy, far from being an extension of human nature, had always to struggle against a natural human tendency to remain the same. If self-consciousness grows in history— and in turn promotes historical development—it is because of the philosophers' "incessant efforts."[19] Thus Kojève admits the possibility that people will be satisfied with the "security of their well-being" in an efficient state without worrying at all about the realization of universal recognition; or, the possibility that some will prefer the perfection of an "absolute silence" to the wisdom of a complete and coherent discourse.[20] These two historical possibilities can be described as "antiphilosophical," and if either is realized, the end of history would look quite different from the way that Kojève's Hegel conceives it.

Kojève sees the philosopher's task in politico-pedagogic terms. Philosophy is dependent on politics and can also serve to guide it. The dependency derives from the fact that philosophers have to begin the process of reflection from the given historical reality created, in large part, by politics. Furthermore, if they are not to live in isolation, philosophers must coexist peacefully with the polity, at least to the extent that it would permit them to philosophize. Philosophers can serve as guides for politics on the basis of what Kojève sees as their three advantages over other members of the polity—expertise in dialectic or discussion, liberation from prejudices that permits a greater appreciation of historical reality, and the ability to see the whole rather than to simplify through abstraction.[21]

The question then arises as to whether philosophers will *want* to be political persons, and it is in their response to this question that the point of disagreement between Strauss and Kojève becomes most clear. For the latter, philosophers, like all persons, desire recognition. They attain it, however, not through bloody battle but through dialectic or discussion. It is through discussion that wisdom (or progress toward it) becomes manifest and is admired by those who can understand what is being said. It is as pedagogues that philosophers can most easily come into conflict with the state, which itself is pedagogic to the extent that its authority is not exclusively based on violence. Thus Kojève concluded:

> Consequently, to want to influence the government to accept or establish a philosophic pedagogy, is to want to influence the government in general; it is to want to determine or co-determine its policy as such. But philosophy cannot renounce pedagogy. Indeed, the "success" of the philosophic pedagogy is the only "objective" criterion of the truth of the doctrine of the Philosophy (at least of its anthropological part) . . .
>
> If one does not want to be content only with the subjective criteria of "evidence" or "revelation" (which do not do away with the problem of madness), it is then impossible to be a Philosopher without wanting to be at the same time a philosophic pedagogue.[22]

Philosophers must assume responsibility for their pedagogy, and that responsibility is, in large part, political. The retreat from this responsibility is, for Kojève, the mark of intellectuals who do not accept the risk that comes with philosophizing, and whose political responsibility has to be forced on them by others.[23] Thus philosophers, in contrast to intellectuals, want to be political persons—teachers responsible for their teaching—to the extent that they want to be philosophers.

Strauss's view of the philosopher vis-à-vis politics is diametrically opposed to Kojève's. If the latter belongs to the Hegelian tradition in which the highest form of philosophy is the state philosophy, the former belongs to the tradition which underlines that the philosopher must be forced to return to the cave in order to rule. Not that Strauss thinks philosophers are without the advantages that Kojève attributes to them; both agree on the capacity of philosophers to guide the polity. For Strauss, however, philosophers who want to rule, who desire recognition, cease for that reason to be philosophers.[24] It is not that philosophic inquiry needs to be conducted in solitude but that the demands of the political are always in conflict with the requirements of the philosophical. If philosophers are more adept at discussion, political persons have to know when to stop talking and get back to work; if the former are liberated from prejudices and thereby have a view of the whole, the latter share in the prejudices (opinions) of the community and know their own place. Perhaps *the* lesson of political philosophy, for Strauss, is that the conflict between politics and philosophy is irremediable; to forget this conflict is to invite disaster in both domains.

Strauss does not offer his own teaching as a prophylactic against the possibility of an apocalyptic marriage of philosophy and politics but as a protest against the acceptance of their union as eternal. For him modern thought is founded upon this marriage, and its implications form the fundamental assumptions of contemporary life. The "idea of progress" is born of this unholy union: the idea that by combining theory and practice we are solving the most important problems. Modern thought is concerned with the triumph over Necessity (Nature or Fortuna) as the crucial step toward their solution. Strauss points out, though, that the modern tradition has almost nothing to say about the world people will live in after this step is taken. The realm of freedom provides satisfaction and protection but it offers no clues for happiness or excellence. In a passage in Strauss's *Thoughts on Machiavelli*—underlined in Kojève's own copy of the book—the author summarizes his view of modern philosophy:

> The new philosophy lives from the outset in the hope which approaches or equals certainty, of future conquest or conquest of the future—in the anticipation of an epoch in which the truth will reign, if not in the minds of all men, at any rate in the institutions which mold them. Propaganda can guarantee the coincidence of philosophy and political power. Philosophy is to fulfill the function of both philosophy and religion. . . . The domination of necessity remains the indispensable condition of every great achievement and

in particular his [Machiavelli's] own: the transition from the realm of necessity into the realm of freedom will be the inglorious death of the very possibility of human excellence.[25]

If philosophers participate in the struggle against nature at the expense of the contemplation of the natural, they forget the basis of philosophy; in accepting the realm of freedom as the realm of the comfortable, they deny the possibilities of excellence. If the goal of all human effort is the triumph over nature, victory removes the very ground of the human.

Strauss thus rejects Kojève's political criterion for a "successful" philosophy. Although he agrees that a standard of judgment is necessary, he denies that history or modern self-consciousness can meet this necessity. For him the solution would not be to evade the demand for a standard through the claim of being postmodern. This ironic evasion of the demand for a transhistorical standard would be for Strauss simply a disguise for abandoning philosophy. For him there is another alternative to the modern: "The classical solution supplies a stable standard by which to judge of any actual order. The modern solution eventually destroys the very idea of a standard that is independent of actual situations."[26] For Strauss the independent transhistorical standard must be based on the supposition that there is an "eternal and immutable order within which history takes place, and which remains entirely unaffected by History."[27]

Kojève's review of On Tyranny asks how this supposition can be legitimated, how the philosopher's "subjective certainty" of a natural order can be differentiated from the paranoid's certainty that everyone is out to get him or her. Given Strauss's insistence on the self-sufficiency of the life of the philosopher[28]—the philosopher's indifference to the admiration (even the welfare) of other people—and on the natural limits on the number of persons capable of being philosophers, the possibilities of "intersubjective certainty" are practically nonexistent. The shared beliefs within a sect (or school) of philosophers—to say nothing of political scientists—are clearly not an adequate form of legitimation, even if the friendship and loyalty among the sect's members does alleviate some of the existential dilemmas resulting from this inadequacy.[29]

Strauss's reply to Kojève's subjective certainty criticism was that the philosopher did not pretend to have "objective certainty," only the "genuine awareness of the problems, i.e., of the fundamental and comprehensive problems."[30] Kojève's challenge was only side-stepped here, however, as criteria for determining what is "genuine," "fundamental," and "comprehensive" still need to be established. Strauss's final point in this regard seems to have been merely the renewed assertion that the philosopher's "self-admiration or self-satisfaction does not have to be confirmed by the admiration of others in order to be reasonable."[31] Indeed he compared this self-admiration with the "good conscience" that did not "require any confirmation from others."[32]

In response to Strauss's "Restatement," Kojève asked whether Torquemada or Dzerzhinski had "bad consciences."[33] The appeal to an "eternal and unchangeable order" provides a "stable standard" only as long as people agree about the significance of this order. Since the order does not effectively command agreement, insofar as there is disagreement, the appeal does not provide a solution to Strauss's "problem of relativism" and seems only to substitute obscurantism for nihilism. To use a metaphor that Strauss had borrowed from Schopenhauer via Weber: the philosophy of nature is not a cab that one can stop at one's convenience. How can moral certainty or self-satisfaction avoid the problem of legitimation? Strauss's failure to adequately respond to this question gives further weight to Kojève's view that a discursive appeal to a "natural order" is ineffective, since even if there is such an order, he does not see how we can speak reasonably about it. One can choose silence—one can even call this choice an openness to being—but otherwise one either "chatters" in a modern way or one is an Hegelian.[34]

The Hegelian regarded the approaching universal and homogeneous state as good because it was final: reason must coincide with the world; reason *is* the coincidence of discourse and the world. Whether one approved of the world was not relevant here. Not flinching from Strauss's description of the Endstate as the state of Nietzsche's "last man," Kojève went on to describe its philosophers as administrators who educated the posthistorical "Automatons."[35] He was no longer here celebrating the joys of the universal and homogeneous state or the "realm of freedom"; instead he was describing a process he saw being actualized in history. And he saw no way out. We may note that Kojève wrote the letter just cited on the stationery of the Secrétariat d'Etat aux Affaires Economiques.

Throughout his writings Kojève rejects the possibility of using a suprahistorical criterion for judging historical development; that is, he chooses what he calls philosophic knowing through a re-collection of history and rejects what he calls theological knowing through a suprahistorical Absolute.[36] We can note that Strauss's critique of the modern tradition raises problems that Kojève confronted in his first articles on the Russian mystic Vladimir Soloviev.[37] Translated into the language of Soloviev, Strauss is asking if the end of history has really come to coincide with the suprahistorical Absolute that is the ultimate criterion of judgment. Indeed with this question Strauss is expressing his profound doubts about whether humanity can ever create its own salvation through history. He emphasizes that Kojève's choice obliges him to recognize the end of history as "salvation," even if this result fails to reach humanity's highest aspirations. Kojève accepts the obligation since he holds fast to the view that salvation can only come to us from ourselves. Even in his later work, when his view of the quality of the supposed "salvation" approaches Strauss's, he does not try to find an escape from its source; that is, by the end of the 1940s when the end of history seemed less like a goal that one wanted to achieve than a world that one had to learn to live within, Kojève shifted from a concern with historical recognition through struggle and work to a concern with reconciliation—via philosophy—with the "posthistorical world" of ex-slaves. It is not at all clear that Strauss's critique of Kojève's conception of the "end of history" was instrumental in changing the function of that conception in the latter's philosophy as a whole. It is clear, though, that the function did change by the mid-1950s, as Kojève reappraised the positive potential of his historic present. During the seminar on Hegel and in the *Esquisse d'une Phénoménologie du Droit,* the "end of history" is discussed as both necessary and good. Since Kojève did not think that the Endstate had been fully realized, he was self-consciously making propaganda to persuade others to work for it. Although never losing his conviction that the world was becoming "universalized and homogenized," he described it in his late works in critically ironic rather than utopian or prophetic terms:

> If man becomes an animal again, then his arts, his loves and his play must also become purely "natural" again. It is therefore necessary to admit that after the end of history men would construct their edifices and works of art as birds build their nests and spiders spin their webs, would perform their musical concerts in the manner of frogs and cicadas, would play like young animals, and would indulge in love like adult beasts.[38]

This was, he said, the era we now lived in. An era in which "the Russians and Chinese are only Americans who are still poor," and in which the only question was whether the snobbism of Japanization would prevent the total "return to animality" found in "the American way of life." Thus the realm of freedom turned out to be the final example of the cunning of reason.

The dialogue between Strauss and Kojève does not end in reconciliation, which is to be expected since both are philosophers willing to accept the apparently unhappy implications of their respective positions. If the value that the former put on philosophic friendship did not meet the latter's demand for effective legitimation, it certainly did not blind Strauss to the risk that a sect of philosophers would develop who thought they knew the *really* fundamental problems and questions better than other philosophers or political scientists. This was a risk that Strauss was apparently willing to run, and he saw it as much less dangerous—intellectually, and certainly politically—than the risks that Kojève's position entailed. In response to Kojève's claim that through Hegelianism we see the completion of history, Strauss asks whether this goal has in fact been worth the effort. Kojève's only reply can be that the End is the result of the effort, and so we have to recognize it as "worth it" or withdraw (preferably in silence) from historical reality. In constructing his version of Hegelianism, he makes such a withdrawal philosophically impossible, for to go "beyond history" for him means learning to live with the results of it. As Hegel writes in the preface to the *Philosophy of Right:* "There is less chill in the peace which knowledge brings." In this regard, however, Strauss's comment on Burke in *Natural Right and History* is directly applicable to Kojève's Hegel. Burke, Strauss said:

> comes close to suggesting that to oppose a thoroughly evil current in human affairs is perverse if that current is sufficiently powerful; he is oblivious of the nobility of last-ditch resistance. He does not consider that, in a way which no man can foresee, resistance in a forlorn position to the enemies of mankind, "going down with guns blazing and flags flying," may contribute greatly toward keeping awake the recollection of the immense loss sustained by mankind, may inspire and strengthen the desire and the hope for its recovery, and may become a beacon for those who humbly carry on the works of humanity in a seemingly endless valley of darkness and destruction.[39]

Kojève underlined the first sentence of this passage in his copy of the book with a note: "cf Hegel."

The dialogue between Strauss and Kojève thus underlines the power of and the dangers in their respective positions. It reminds us that confidence in one's virtuous (or creative) works in the "valley of darkness"—whether in the name of a classical or a postmodern detachment from the historical—may indeed be simply a form of blindness, and it underlines the "immense loss" in making the ideology of progress into the one and unique development of History as Reason. In so doing the confrontation of their positions may contribute to opening a clearing in which philosophy can challenge the so-called reason of history without giving up in advance its cause (or its games) for lost, and accepting in return only the "good conscience" (or sophisticated cynicism) of the comfortable sect of antimoderns.

After commenting on their declining physical health, in June 1949 Strauss wrote the following to Kojève:

> What is of course depressing is the fact that the older one grows, the more clearly one sees how little one understands: the darkness gets increasingly dense. It is perhaps a questionable compensation that one sees through the lack of clarity in the ideas of chatterers and cheats more easily and quickly than in earlier years. The happiness of contemplation is really only available from time to time, so says the philosopher.[40]

Despite their differences (or was it because of them?) Kojève and Strauss found the happiness of contemplation in their exchanges. Despite the fragility of philosophy's place in the contemporary world (or was it because of this fragility?) they sustained their dialogue about modernity and the relation of politics and philosophy to it.

NOTES

1. Leo Strauss, *On Tyranny,* rev. and expanded ed., including the Strauss-Kojève correspondence, ed. Victor Gourevitch and Michael S. Roth (New York: The Free Press, 1991). In this chapter I have drawn on the introduction to this edition of *On Tyranny,* which I coauthored with Victor Gourevitch.

2. Strauss, *The Political Philosophy of Hobbes* (Oxford: Clarendon Press, 1936), 58 n.

3. Ibid., 57.

4. *On Tyranny,* 192.

5. Ibid., 231.

6. For a detailed account of that reading see Michael S. Roth, *Knowing and History: Appropriations of Hegel in Twentieth-Century France* (Ithaca: Cornell University Press, 1988), chap. 5.

7. *On Tyranny,* 232.

8. Ibid.

9. Kojève's most overtly political essay in this regard is "Hegel, Marx et Christianisme," *Critique* 3–4 (1946): 308–12, 339–66. At the close of this essay he noted that all interpretations of Hegel were programs for work and struggle and that they had the significance of political propaganda.

10. Examples of this approach can be found in Patrick Riley, "Introduction to the Reading of Alexandre Kojève," *Political Theory* 9, no. 1 (1981): 5–48; and Dennis J. Goldford, "Kojève's Reading of Hegel," *International Philosophic Quarterly* 22, no. 4 (1982): 275–94, and Shadia B. Drury, *Alexandre Kojève and the Roots of Postmodern Politics* (New York: St. Martin's Press, 1994), chapters 1–6. The most important contemporary example in this regard was the critique of Tran Duc Thao, "La phénoménologie de l'esprit et son contenu réel," *Les Temps Modernes* 36 (1948): 493–519.

11. See, for example, Michel Darbon, "Hegelianisme, marxisme, existentialisme," *Les Etudes* 4, nos. 3–4 (1949): 346–70. Mikel Dufrenne thought that God saved us from relativist historicism, while Jean Desanti settled for Marx (as revealed by the party): "Actualité de Hegel," *Esprit* 17, no. 9 (1948) 396–408; and "Hegel, est-il le père de l'existentialisme," *Nouvelle Critique* 56 (1954): 91–109.

12. Barry Cooper accepts Kojève's notion of the Endstate and uses it in a very interesting way to "make sense of our modernity" (as did the more popular use of Kojève by Francis Fukuyama discussed in chapter 9). See Barry Cooper, *The End of History: An Essay on Modern Hegelianism* (Toronto: University of Toronto Press, 1984).

13. In a letter (October 7, 1948) responding to Tran Duc Thao's review in *Les Temps Modernes,* Kojève described his interpretation of Hegel as an "oeuvre de propagande destinée à frapper les esprits." We can also note in this regard Kojève's marginalia to an article by Aime Patri, "Dialectique du Maître et de l'Esclave," *Le contrat social* 5, no. 4 (1961): 231–35. Patri wrote, "under the pseudonym of Hegel, the author (Kojève) exposed a personal way of thinking"—Kojève added: "bien vu!" In the preface to his history of philosophy and Hegelian wisdom, Kojève wrote: "Finally, the question of knowing if Hegel "truly said" what I have him say would seem to be puerile."

14. *On Tyranny,* 236–38.

15. Ibid., p. 237.

16. Strauss, *Natural Right and History* (Chicago: University of Chicago Press, 1953), 274.

17. Ibid., 238.

18. We can note that for Strauss the dissatisfaction of philosophers was crucial, for they were among the best of people.

19. Kojève, *Introduction,* 2d ed. (Paris: Gallimard, 1967), 398.

20. Ibid., p. 278.

21. *On Tyranny,* 148–50.

22. Kojève, "L'action politique des philosophes," *Critique* 41/42 (1950): 145; *On Tyranny,* 163.

23. Ibid., 166–67.

24. Ibid., 203.

25. Strauss, *Thoughts on Machiavelli* (Chicago: University of Chicago Press, 1958), 298. Kojève underlined the last sentence of this passage and noted in the margin: "cf. Kojève."

26. *On Tyranny,* 210–11.

27. Ibid., 212.

28. See the excellent discussion of this point in Victor Gourevitch, "Philosophy and Politics," *Review of Metaphysics* 22, nos. 1–2 (1968): 80–84. My view of the Strauss-Kojève exchange owes much to this article and even more to extensive conversations with its author.

29. *On Tyranny,* 196.

30. Ibid.

31. Ibid., 204.

32. Ibid. Strauss placed "good conscience" within quotation marks.

33. Ibid., 255.

34. Ibid., 256.

35. Ibid., 255. By attaining wisdom the philosophers become "gods."

36. The distinction between theological and historical knowing runs through all Kojève's work, and he regarded the "choice" between the two modes as fundamental and prephilosophical. See, for examples, his review of Alfred Delp's *Tragische Existenz: Zur Philosophie Martin Heideggers,* in *Recherches Philosphiques* 5 (1936–1939): 415–19; *Introduction à la lecture de Hegel,* 293; "Hegel, Marx et le Christianisme," 347, 363f. *On Tyranny,* 153–61. See also Strauss, "Jerusalem and Athens: Some Introductory Reflections," *Commentary* 43 (1967): 45–57; "On the Mutual Influence of Theology and Philosophy," *The Independent Journal of Philosophy* 3 (1979): 111–18. On Kojève's copy of the typescript of Strauss's lecture, "What is Political Philosophy?" Kojève wrote "Strauss = Theology" alongside his friend's discussion of political theology.

37. See Roth, *Knowing and History,* 83–93.

38. *Introduction a la lecture de Hegel,* 436 n. See also the discussion of this passage below, 153–54.

39. *Natural Right and History,* 318.

40. *On Tyranny,* 242. The last sentence, which Strauss wrote in Greek, Latin, and English, refers to Aristotle, *Metaphysics,* Book XII, ch. 7, 1072b, 25.

• 6 •

Thin Description: Richard Rorty's
Use of History

Richard Rorty is one of the most insightful, provocative, and consistently readable philosophers writing today. His major work to date, *Philosophy and the Mirror of Nature,* has had an enormous impact on the self-understanding of Anglo-American philosophers, as it has provided a useful way for thinking about the history of philosophy for those both in and outside the profession. Since the publication of that book Rorty has written numerous essays on a wide variety of topics across diverse fields.[1] While remaining a participant in important discussions in Anglo-American philosophy, he has also entered into wide-ranging debates with important figures in French and German cultural criticism. He seems to be no less at home when appropriating the work of Davidson and Sellars than he is when criticizing Habermas and Foucault or praising the (limited) significance of Derrida's recent writings. In the last ten years, at least, Rorty has developed not only a clear voice within the philosophical community but he seems to be developing into a philosopher who is also a public intellectual much like one of his heroes, John Dewey.

Philosophy and the Mirror of Nature established Rorty as a radical critic of mainstream philosophy, especially the evolution of epistemology since Kant. As Ian Hacking has noted, "No matter how loosely we construe membership in an analytic and primarily anglophone tradition, Rorty was the first member to apply the technique of historicist undoing to that tradition."[2] In other words, Rorty showed how the problems of philosophy had been constructed in particular historical circumstances—in response to specific conditions—and that in our own circumstances these problems were no longer worth pursuing. More specifically, he described how the tradition of philosophy as a tribunal of reason had gone bankrupt, and how it might be replaced by philosophy finding a place as part of the conversation of our culture. If there were no general principles of cognition or belief to be applied to specific propositions or actions, then philosophers were no longer referees in their cultures' debates but rather participants in their discourses.

Philosophy and the Mirror of Nature met with a predictable response from those professors of philosophy who had not noticed that epistemology was dead, who were unaware that the legitimacy of their arbitration (on such issues as, Is this theory scientific? Is this kind of behavior moral in all circumstances?) had been undermined. The cogency of Rorty's presentation was sometimes challenged or he was accused of "not being careful" in his redescription of the tradition of Western philosophy. Did Rorty get Plato right in the same book that discussed Descartes, Kant, Heidegger, and Dewey? How, after all, could he? The guardians of the tradition had no trouble finding disputes about specific interpretations. But there were also many, with less invested in this tradition, who complained about the idea of "philosophy as conversation," which seemed like a slim benefit to have gleaned from destroying the dominant strains in the canon of philosophy.[3]

For all his professional iconoclasm Rorty was a firm believer in the progress of Western history and the strength of political liberalism. He might be willing to undermine the legitimacy of cultural foundations or natural ends, but he did so thinking we were already doing pretty well without them, thank you. Thus on the one hand Rorty offended traditionalists by emphasizing the historical specificity of what some had thought to be eternal problems or questions, while on the other hand he enraged radicals by defending contemporary Western values and institutions after having redescribed them as foundationless. The revolutionary in philosophy was a political liberal and so was not easily placed among those radicals most vocal in the world of "theory."[4]

Contingency, Irony, and Solidarity answers the question: How can you aim to undermine the foundations and the telos of the West while also wanting to defend its core liberal values? Another version of this question is: How can you have Heidegger and Dewey in your pantheon of heroes, Nietzsche and Habermas? The quick answer is that you can have both desires only when you realize that these values do not need the traditional buttressing, and you can have both sets of heroes when you realize that each was heroic in a distinct way. In this book Rorty wants to have it both ways, though not at the same time. He wants to keep distinct questions about politics or institutions from questions about pleasures. In other words he distinguishes between the private and public without giving one priority over the other. Of course this distinction is not natural: the world does not present us with essentially private and public aspects. But Rorty redescribes modernity in such a way as to encourage liberalism as a public doctrine and ironism as a private pleasure that is compatible with that doctrine.

Much of the support for this public-private split comes from a particular picture of Western history. It is historicism that freed us from the need to appeal to foundations, and it is a kind of historicism that Rorty hopes will provide us with the possibilities of solidarity even as it leaves room for the irony-riddled search for personal autonomy. Rorty's versions of Western history are very general, and he makes no claims to originality in this regard. But I think we can see that his use of history is crucial for his establishment of the pervasiveness of contingency, the context and the content of irony, and the hope for and extension of solidarity.

Contingency, Irony, and Solidarity is divided into three parts, each containing three chapters.[5] The first, "Contingency," moves from a discussion of the historically particular aspects of language, of selfhood, and ultimately of a liberal community. The second part, "Ironism and Theory," contains a chapter on the connection of ironic theory with liberal hope, another devoted to readings of Proust, Nietzsche, and Heidegger, with a concluding chapter on Derrida. Part 3, "Cruelty and Solidarity," explores the connections between the private and public as seen by Nabokov and Orwell. The former's worries about the public effects of the pursuit of private joys and the latter's worries about what happens to intellectuals in a world without a private realm are brought to light in separate chapters. The book concludes with a brief chapter on solidarity, on why it is possible to have a community that can tolerate private pursuits, and pursuers of the private who can tolerate community.

Rorty sees philosophy since Hegel as caught in a kind of trap. Having given up on the commitment to an idea of a common human nature in favor of an historical account of how we got to where we are, philosophers have still been divided between those for whom self-creation is the dominant desire and those for whom the desire for a more just and free human community dominates. This division mirrors the one that Rorty has seen between contemporary German and French thinkers.[6] French postmodern thinkers seemed primarily concerned with standing apart, with achieving a brilliance that separated them from the rest. Their German counterparts, on the other hand, were concerned with finding a path back to community, with fitting in, or at least with fitting together. For Rorty both groups are in the post-Hegelian historicist tradition. They have given up on finding the eternal or on constructing the unchangeable. The "new standoff" that takes place on this common ground is between those who are primarily concerned (or should be) with the private and those who are primarily concerned (or should be) with the public. *Contingency, Irony, and Solidarity* suggests a way beyond this impasse. By dropping the demand for a single theory, by giving up the dream of a way to overcome the private/public split, Rorty means to propel historicism beyond its current standoff.

One may notice the riff on the Hegelian style here. We are encouraged to do so even in the tripartite structure of the book, or in the way the American finds a path beyond the German/French battles. Rorty—in good Hegelian fashion—wants to move us beyond the dilemmas of Hegelian historicism without having recourse to a foundationalism of any kind. However, the synthesis that he proposes is an ironic one; that is, he wants to break through the entanglements of public and private theories by cutting them apart, not by bringing them together in a higher form. In other words, his historicism aims at undermining the desire for synthesis—for a unified theory that would negate the public/private distinction—thus preserving the virtues of the private and the public by removing the universalizing tendencies of each.

A reflexive difficulty is immediately evident here. A theory, *X*, that described how the current impasse of private and public could be overcome would still be a kind of synthesis even if it argued for the preservation of the distinction between the two domains. In other words, in order to thematize the rightfulness of the distinction, *X* would be constructed at a level beyond this distinction.[7] Rorty escapes this reflexive difficulty by not offering a theory about the private and public. Instead he presents several narratives relevant to each domain and points out the dangers or silliness that result from collapsing one into the other. The historicist and nominalist culture to which he hopes to be contributing would happily settle for such narratives to connect with its past and with its utopian futures (xvi).[8] This culture would be a liberal one, one in which as Rorty says borrowing from Judith Shklar, "cruelty is the worst thing we can do" (xv).

The historicizing narrative of the book provides a story of our liberation from ways of thinking that made us subservient to a god or nature. The Enlightenment and the Age of Revolutions helped us see that Truth was not something we discovered but rather something we made. Kant and Hegel, as it were, went half-way: showing how much of what we regarded as true was the product of our efforts but reserving another domain (the noumenal, Spirit) as that where Real Truth was to be found. "What was needed," Rorty emphasizes "was a repudiation of the very idea of any-thing—mind or matter, self or world—having an intrinsic nature to be expressed or represented" (4). What was needed, in other words, was Donald Davidson.

Rorty reads Davidson as spelling out the implications of Wittgenstein's treatment of vocabularies as tools (13). Davidson is the first philosopher to break completely with the idea that language is a medium of either repre-sentation or expression (10). This break allows us to dispense completely with the subject-object picture of knowledge. We can also view different vocabularies not in terms of whether one more adequately represents or expresses than another but in terms of how they help us cope with differ-ent situations at different times. And we should not expect these vocabu-laries to fit together into a coherent whole any more than we would expect all the tools in our kit to work together.[9]

The Davidsonian view of the contingency of language provides Rorty with a way of thinking about the development of European culture. If lan-guage is not a medium, if it has no essential task of representing or expres-sing something greater than it (for example, Spirit, Reality, Being), then we can say that language has no intrinsic purpose. We are thus led to an evolu-tionary view of language: new forms are developed not to fulfill some des-tiny but "as a result of a great number of sheer contingencies" (16). Think of new forms in language as metaphors, as relatively unfamiliar noises or marks. Some die out quickly; others are fit enough to survive, but also to become ordinary expressions. Perhaps one could give a causal account of this process, but it occurs without any prearranged purpose. When strong poets, philosophers, or scientists come along they can impose new ways of talking. Their metaphors are found to work. But we can bet that pretty soon some new strong poets will come along, changing yet again our vocabularies and hence our actions and identities (20).

Rorty here brings Davidson's view of language together with Nietzsche on history:

> A culture in which Nietzschean metaphors were literalized would be one which took for granted that philosophical problems are as temporary as poetic problems, that there are no problems which bind the generations together into a single natural kind called "humanity." A sense of human history as the history of successive metaphors would let us see the poet, in the generic sense of the maker of new words, as the shaper of new languages, as the vanguard of the species. (20)

Rorty borrows the schema for the rise of modernity from Hans Blumenberg and extends it as a call to "no longer worship *anything* . . . where we treat *everything*—our language, our conscience, our community—as a product of time and chance" (22).[10] Understanding the contingency of language leads to an understanding of the contingency of history. But how do we make this history our own?

A history without a telos can be acknowledged and adopted by a self without an essence. This brings Rorty to Freud. Freud's great contribution to our understanding was to "turn us away from the universal and to the concrete" (34). This means that Freud taught us that there were no general standards against which to measure the development of the self. Rather its development is the product of an amazing variety of impressions brought together to "set the tone of a life" (37). Some of these constellations will be accepted as productive and even progressive, whereas others will be judged as marginal or even neurotic. The acceptance or judgment will depend on the contingent collection of values dominant at a given time. There is no essentially human pattern to which individual lives conform.

Thus in Rorty's account Freud is a thinker who broke away from any attempt to unite the public and private. Sure, these came together from time to time in a happy coincidence of purposes: specific facets of Leonardo's relationship with his mother conditioned his attempts at satisfactions, the results of which others would find interesting. We call people geniuses whose idiosyncrasies happen to catch on. "To sum up," Rorty says, "poetic, artistic, philosophical, scientific or political progress results from the accidental coincidence of a private obsession with a public need" (37). And obsessions can be pursued at great risk despite the fact that they are based on sheerly contingent personal experience.

Our willingness to cling to our identities or pursue our obsessions despite the contingency of their evolution is important for Rorty because he wants to argue that societies, too, can fight for their values even while knowing they are historically contingent and not given by nature or God. However it may be for societies (we shall return to this later), it seems doubtful that obsessives pursue their objects while conscious of their contingent place in their lives. We can see this place as contingent, but it is the belief in the necessity of the activity that makes it an obsession. In his writing on the self, though, Rorty is not concerned with motivation but only with the acknowledgment found in Freud (and also in Nietzsche and Harold Bloom) that there are no general rules of self-construction, no substance of one's personality to be actualized, only more or less happy constellations of fortuitous impressions and actions (41). Freud provides powerful accounts of how these impressions and actions can be redescribed into, if not whiggish narratives, commonly unhappy constellations: meaningful memories with which we can live.[11]

The last chapter of section 1, "The Contingency of Community," sketches Rorty's view of a liberal utopia. The discussions of language and of the self were meant to move us away from the search for foundations and perhaps stimulate a taste for the benefits of "redescription." The culture of liberalism would be a culture of redescription, a culture that understood itself as the product of the contingencies of history without valuing itself any less for so being. People living in such a culture would know that the vocabularies they use are not the only ones and are not closer to reality, to God, or to nature than the others that may be available. For Rorty's liberal community the recognition of contingency is freedom (46).

Of course the question that arises here is whether a foundationless community would also be rudderless. Would not a liberal community that saw its own values as contingent be unwilling to defend them against competitors or invaders who wanted to impose other values? This is the so-called relativist predicament, and Rorty uses his discussions of language and the self to show its irrelevance. Those who worry about this predicament still leave a space from which a neutral perspective can rank vocabulries or selves. The dilemma of relativism is thought to arise when this space is empty and the objective rankings go unmade.[12] But Rorty's first two chapters showed how we might do without this space—not think of it as empty but recognize that it has never existed. For him "there is no such thing as the 'relativist predicament,' just as for someone who thinks that there is no God there will be no such thing as blasphemy. For there will be no higher standpoint to which we are responsible and against whose precepts we might offend" (50).

When you give up on the idea of a higher standpoint, you find another way of arriving at propositions that are ranked as true. A liberal community does this by committing itself to the free and open exchange of ideas. Truth will be whatever is produced by such exchanges (52). According to the historical sketch provided in *Contingency,* the Enlightenment fostered this idea through its commitment to the so-called scientific method, but it obscured the idea in its rhetoric about the scientist getting in touch with Reality. Although this rhetoric has probably been useful, it now needs to be replaced in the following way:

> We need a redescription of liberalism as the hope that culture as a whole can be "poeticized" rather than the Enlightenment hope that it can be "rationalized" or "scientized." That is, we need to substitute the hope that chances for fulfillment of idiosyncratic fantasies will be equalized for the hope that everyone will replace "passion" or fantasy with "reason." (53)

The result of this charter would be the valorization of the poet's ability to alter our vocabularies and our sense of who we are and what we are doing, rather than of the warrior's ability to conquer people less valuable than we, or the priest's or scientist's abilities to get us in touch with something bigger and better than ourselves.

Rorty's picture of a liberal utopia is really the center of the book, his attempt to show what postmetaphysical people living together might look like. He wants to imagine a culture that would not feel the absence of an epistemologically clean standpoint from which to legitimate their deepest values, a culture that would replace such a standpoint with a narrative about how we happened to arrive at these values, and about how dearly held these values really are. A culture cured of metaphysics would be one for which the question, "How do you really know that this story is the right one," would make no sense, but also one that would welcome alternative accounts of who it had become. People in such a culture would identify as deeply with the story they see as their own as people identify with their own account of their lives, even as they realize that this life has been shot through with contingency. It is still theirs. "Citizens of my liberal utopia," Rorty writes, "would be liberal ironists . . . people who combined commitment with a sense of the contingency of their own commitment" (61).

One of the crucial features of a liberal culture that identifies with contingency is its separation of the private and public realms. Remember that a liberal is someone for whom cruelty is the worst thing. Why? For Rorty this question is unanswerable and must be deflected. There are no *reasons* to be given for why one should hate cruelty; no *criteria* to be offered that enable us to determine when cruelty is taking place. Instead we can historicize. We can see that in the development of the West there has been an evolution of our moral consciousness such that the range of actions that count as cruel and the range of people against whom it is forbidden to be cruel has grown. The breadth of our "we intentions" has been extended in the rise of modernity, although attempts to *found* universal obligations (instead of recognizing that somebody is enough like us to deserve our protection from cruelty) have met with failure. Rorty's historicism amounts to telling a story of the history of the West that aims at stimulating a solidarity about the achievements of tolerance and the acceptance of contingency.

But the story Rorty tells is very thin.[13] In fact he just gives us a paragraph here and there to remind us of the stories that are available elsewhere. He seems more interested in saying that narratives should replace arguments than he is in what specific kinds of belief might come from the narrative form of his historicism. His readings of Nabokov and Orwell in the last section of the book show how fictional narratives contribute to his understanding of morality, pleasure, and irony, but they provide little in the way of a story of "how we got to where we are." Such a story Rorty does want to claim, however, should replace arguments aimed at justifying why we do what we do. Thus history, particularly cultural history, is given a great importance after the death of epistemology. The redescriptions found in historical narratives, and not logical or empirical discoveries, provide us with the contexts for either our contemporary pride or contempt. These contexts can shape our beliefs and actions.

Rorty seems to mean by argument the kind of final, unanswerable proofs sought by the logical positivists who were so important for his own intellectual development. However, there are certainly reasoned explanations that emerge out of narratives (but not only there) that can be helpful in defining cruelty and our stance toward it. After all, arguments in a general sense are useful in helping us recognize cruelty (by helping us see, for example, that given our other beliefs her pain should count for us as much as his), and even in setting up criteria (historically contingent though they may be) that enable us to reduce the systematic cruelties of our organizations. Rorty's call to replace argument by narrative works only insofar as one thinks that arguments aim at finality and closure whereas narratives allow for contingency and irony. Such thinking, however, neglects the roles arguments might play in open-ended conversation as much as it neglects the totalizing ambitions of many narrative forms.

After confronting what we can call the Anglo-American objection to the epistemological nonchalance of his liberal utopia, Rorty considers two objections to his historicism. The first, from Michel Foucault, can be formulated as the ironic question: Do you really *believe* this self-congratulatory story about the "development" of the West? The second, from Jürgen Habermas, can be formulated as a worried plea: Are you really going to offer no more legitimation to the development of the West in modernity than this mere *story?* Rorty summarizes the situation as follows: "Michel Foucault is an ironist who is unwilling to be a liberal, whereas Jürgen Habermas is a liberal who is unwilling to be an ironist" (61).

One can locate Foucault's irony at many levels, but perhaps it is most clearly visible in his account of—or discounting of—historical progress; that is, he is ironic about one of the few things that escapes Rorty's irony. Take, for example, Foucault's view of the history of madness: where one might see the evolution of more rational and humane views of the insane developing with the decriminalization of insanity and the secularization of the ways in which we think about it, Foucault points out how modern conceptualizations of mental illness function to legitimate normality at the expense of the integrity of the experience of madness. Similarly, he showed how the substitution of incarceration for the torture of criminals did not express an increasingly humane society but one that had integrated discipline and control throughout its political and social apparatuses. His final project on the history of sexuality poked through the rhetoric of liberation and raised questions about how talk about sex had acquired its own imperatives that had little to do with increasing freedom.

Foucault's books have an ironic form because they show us that even when we attempt to be free the attempt can be shown to lead to ever greater constraints. His genealogical investigations show how a culture proud of its progress toward freedom and tolerance is really a world of increasing domination and repression. His writings lead us into a world of critical pessimism or, as I now prefer to put it, into the ironist's cage.[14]

Thus, although Foucault sees that modern societies have abolished obvious forms of cruelty and domination, they have created subtle yet sharp networks of constraint that are more pervasive and more difficult to resist than anything imagined by earlier tyrants. Ironically, even good intentions have led to more oppression. As a result of his genealogical investigations, Foucault resists any attempt to propose solutions to the dilemmas he uncovers: "My position is that it is not up to us to propose. As soon as one 'proposes'—one proposes a vocabulary, an ideology, which can only have effects of domination."[15] Foucault is right to say that with a proposition is implied a vocabulary (an "ideology" is just a "bad vocabulary") but that only means that a community of some kind is projected. And Foucault seems to think that such a projection is always a form of domination.[16] Rorty believes Foucault thinks this way because of his commitment to self-creation, or the desire to be fully autonomous. The French writer's commitment to this desire, which others have described as a valorization of transgression, leads him to be ironic about any efforts to promote community or solidarity. His ironic historicism forces Foucault to reject even the self-consciously contingent vocabulary of liberalism as only yet another inhibition on (and so target for) transgression.

Rorty does not criticize Foucault's irony or effort at autonomy; he just thinks it is misplaced—that is, it is a mistake to try to create public institutions that would guarantee or even promote self-creation. These would lead to disasters (sometimes the kinds of disasters that Foucault is so good at exposing) or further objects of ironic derision. The liberal realizes that public institutions should only try to reduce cruelty and pain. However, in the liberal culture Rorty imagines there would be plenty of room for those people (like Foucault and Rorty) who get pleasure from self-creation or transgression. Thus Rorty wants to place Foucault's irony and transgressive spirit in the private realm. Of course this may seem like an effort to domesticate Foucault. It is. Rorty is clear (and, I think, persuasive) about not allowing the intellectual or artist who thinks that self-creation is all to imagine a society built on the model of this individual pleasure. Don't slip "into a political attitude which will lead you to think that there is some social goal more important than avoiding cruelty" (65).

It is not at all clear, however, that Foucault can be best redescribed as someone who slipped away from thinking that avoiding cruelty was our most important social goal. He certainly cannot be fitted into a category of thinkers who value self-creation above all else. After all, Foucault is concerned with the creation of local forms of solidarity based on resistance to certain forms of power. This is not to minimize his differences with Rorty. The French thinker would certainly reject the pragmatist's self-congratulatory tale about the development of postmetaphysical liberalism, and he could do so on pragmatic grounds. Such a tale can create blindness toward certain forms of cruelty that are systematically produced in contemporary liberal societies. These forms of cruelty may go unnoticed by those who created and listen approvingly to the liberal tale. Although Rorty is concerned with this problem of attention in regard to Nabokov's novels, a Foucauldian response to Rorty's pragmatic historicism would be to point out how it enables the perpetuation of particular forms of cruelty.[17]

Even if Rorty does not want social policies that would promote creativity and autonomy (he can go as far as to say he wants policies that guarantee free and open communication), he does see the "strong poet" as the hero of a liberal culture. That means that the culture values creating new ways of coping with the world and the self instead of discovering truths out there. This is where Habermas's objections become most relevant. He thinks that Rorty mistakenly aestheticizes the pragmatist picture of modern culture by collapsing the distinctions between philosophy and literature.[18] Although they may not have any substantial political disagreements, Habermas wants to "reconstruct a form of rationalism" whereas Rorty wants to replace rationalism with a poeticized view of culture, a view that values not problem solving, but redescription (67–68).

Habermas sees his work as a continuation of the Enlightenment, as another facet of the "incomplete project of modernity." Although the path of what he calls "subject-centered reasons" was a poor one, the desire to reach a universally legitimate form of reason was and is fundamental to the health of our would-be democratic societies. The idea of "undistorted communication" is supposed to provide a better path to this goal than earlier self-understandings of the Enlightenment (67). For Habermas this idea ensures that if different groups enter an ideal speech situation with the same problem, they would come up with the same conclusion. Preserving the universal character of reason would enable us to escape relativist dilemmas by providing us with a basis for our social criticism (and for reason generally) as well as a goal for our lives in common.

Rorty is willing to give up on this basis and goal because he thinks that criticism of certain parts of a society can be tied to other parts of it that one is not criticizing at the moment,[19] while there need be no goal for our lives in common other than that of avoiding cruelty. As for a general legitimation of Reason as opposed to Unreason, the poetic pragmatist is clear: "reasonable" is just a compliment we give to a belief we like. Furthermore, he wants to stress the "radical diversity of private purposes" and the "radically poetic character of individual lives" (67). These aspects of our lives, ones stressed by Nietzsche, Heidegger, and Derrida, for example, would be erased in any updated universalism. Rorty agrees with Habermas that these aspects (and the thinkers just mentioned) are irrelevant to our political, our public lives. But since Rorty, unlike Habermas, does not privilege the political he still finds these aspects and these thinkers worth considering, caring for, and playing with.

As Rorty wants to replace the scientist with the poet as the hero of modern culture, he wants to replace efforts at religious or philosophical justification with an historical account of how we got to where we are (68). The account would help us see why the Enlightenment thinkers tried to buttress their approach to the world and the self with a foundationalism that could compete with the religious approaches. It would also enable us to see why such buttressing was no longer necessary for the maintenance of our rejection of cruelty, for our desires to preserve a domain of private pleasure and for our efforts to increase the bounds of solidarity.

The only kind of "private pleasure" that interests Rorty in this book is "ironism." Ironism is a pleasure available to liberal intellectuals: to intellectuals who live with radical contingency and so recognize that everything can be otherwise. Ironists are people who know that what they know can (and probably will) be redescribed in another vocabulary, and that there is no useful way of trying to see which vocabulary is more authentic or more realistic. The ironist aspires to be somebody who gets in on some rede-scription, who manages to change some parts of the vocabularies being used. The ironist wants to be a strong poet.

We can see that Rorty's picture of the ironist closely resembles Lyotard's picture of the postmodern artist. For Lyotard the modern artist was still hung up on trying to represent the conditions of representation. He or she was still tied to the idea of something "out there" that could be brought into the picture. The postmodern artist and writer, on the other hand, "are working without rules in order to formulate the rules of what *will have been done*."[20] Rorty borrows from Harold Bloom in order to define the ironic condition and anxiety of influence in these intellectuals. They must use an inherited vocabulary in order to create a new one. They feel the impulse to throw off the past because they *feel themselves to be a part* of the past. Ironists do not inspire themselves by aiming at a vocabulary that will be final or closer to something bigger than themselves or their community. They recognize the contingency and the transitoriness of even their most successful creations.

Who are these ironist intellectuals? Rorty offers illuminating readings of Proust, Nietzsche, Heidegger, and Derrida that clarify the conditions and limits of ironism. Nietzsche and Heidegger admired the strong poets as much as anybody ever has. In fact we might even say that they admired them too much, hoping that if a poet was *really* strong that he or she would tap into the ur-vocabulary or deepest essence of things. Of course each wanted to be that poet. In other words, Nietzsche and Heidegger wanted to overcome the authority of the tradition of metaphysics; but how could they do so without claiming some authority of their own? The development of ideas like the "will-to-power" and the "call of Being" were attempts to limit the possibilities of ironic redescription or the Hegelian tradition of philosophical one-upmanship. Nietzsche and Heidegger wanted to be such strong poets so they would not simply end up being somebody else's Oedipal father.

Proust and Derrida fit the description of ironist intellectuals more neatly because they are satisfied with mere redescription. They succeed in the task Coleridge described as "creating the taste by which they will be judged," but they do not then try to find a way to finalize or even legitimate that taste (97). Proust is a hero for Rorty because he creates his self through a redescription of the contingencies of his life and the lives of those around him without pretending to have "found himself" or to have exhausted the possibilities of redescription. Indeed Proust's understanding of involuntary memory makes the whole process of remembrance and of writing the novel a product of contingency. His dedication to the project is not undermined by his understanding of the accidental series of causes leading up to it.

Derrida seems to have learned not only from writers such as Proust but from the failures of philosophers like Nietzsche and Heidegger; that is, he learned that the attempt to be more than a redescriber is an empty grab at nostalgia for foundations. Rorty rejects readings of Derrida as having provided a method of deconstruction that allows us to know something special and deep about language, desire, or time by systematically undermining particular texts. Instead he embraces the extreme playfulness of some of Derrida's more recent work that "drops theory" and gives free rein to the associations that thinking about his theoretical predecessors produce: "There is no moral to these fantasies, nor any public (pedagogical or political) use to be made of them; but, for Derrida's readers, they may nevertheless be exemplary—suggestions of the sort of thing one might do, a sort of thing rarely done before" (125). Like Proust, Derrida does something rarely done before with language without pretending that he has done something that cannot be redone. He drops the pretension (common to Nietzsche and Heidegger) of having escaped from the contingency that rules the lives of the rest of us and accepts that contingency as the condition of his own life and art.

Even if Rorty is right about Derrida and Proust, it is not clear what role "accepting contingency" should have in his judgments about their achievements. He certainly does not want to say that they recognize that life is *really* contingent and that their achievements are based on a sort of realist intuition. I suppose that he admires their work in part because they are able to maintain their commitments to their projects without the metaphysical consolation on which Heidegger and Nietzsche depended. These German thinkers were the real obsessives, pursuing a project not because it happened to be his own, but because each believed that his project was the only real project to be pursuing. To call this belief "metaphysical consolation" is just to say we don't like it, not to show that it undermined their accomplishments.

In Rorty's story Nietzsche and Heidegger are simply more primitive than the contingency-accepting ironists Proust and Derrida; that is, his historicism describes a path of secularization that now has the broader meaning of a process in which we give up dependence on beings "out there," and see ourselves as the subjects (not the masters) of our own fate. At certain times belief in something out there—"nature," "God," "Reality"—has enabled us to create extraordinarily useful tools and institutions. Liberalism itself was given a shot in the arm by an effort to make the doctrine conform to nature or reality. Even so, according to Rorty we are now able to kick away the ladders that have been so important to us (194). Doing so will help us have a more tolerant liberalism, a liberalism that recognizes more forms of pain as significant and hence worth combating, as it leaves more room for irony and other private pleasures. Proust and Derrida have kicked away their ladders. They are up-to-date, the highest praise an historicist can give.

It may be the ease with which he celebrates the foundationless present, his lack of angst and his refusal to be dramatic about conflict, that many of Rorty's readers find so irksome. His commitment to liberal solidarity and his criticisms of some popular academic forms of "radical critique" often seem like a happy embrace of the status quo. Does the narrative describing our ascent to the present result only in our assenting to it?

The final section of *Contingency, Irony, and Solidarity* examines conflicts and connections that can emerge between the public and private realms. How can the pursuit of aesthetic bliss and ironist self-creation be a threat to the liberal program of avoiding cruelty? How does the liberal program deepen our understanding of ironism and the role of the intellectual in contemporary society? It is important for Rorty's general project to deny that there are any "philosophical answers" to these questions; that is, no answers will win agreement because they are formally more rational than their competitors. There are responses to be made to these questions, however, and in the modern period many of these can be found in the novel. Rorty turns to the narratives of Nabokov and Orwell for meditations on the connections and tensions between ironism and politics, between the private and the public.

How might art and torture be connected? Here is a question that allows for a comparison of the apparently private-oriented Nabokov with the apparently public-oriented Orwell. Rorty's readings are partial, contingent.

He reads Nabokov here to examine how the pursuit of the private pleasure of aestheticism can lead to an inattention to cruelty. And he reads Orwell as not just denouncing a possible totalitarian future but of probing the role that an ironist intellectual might have when there is no longer any social hope.

Both writers help us "sort out our relations to this world" through their creations of characters who expand our notions of human possibilities. Nabokov's contribution is the "monster of incuriosity": the genius whose pursuit of his very real talent closes his eyes to suffering despite an effort (for the sake of his genius) to remain attentive. Humbert and Kinbote remain "incurious about the people whose lives provide their material," and in creating them Nabokov acknowledges that "there is no synthesis of ecstasy and kindness" (160). Rorty finds a moral in Nabokov's aestheticism: "to notice what one is doing, and in particular to notice what people are saying. For it might turn out, it very often does turn out, that people are trying to tell you that they are suffering" (164).[21] Orwell's contribution was the intellectual monster. In *1984* O'Brien has the cerebral talents and tastes that attract him to (and make him attractive to) Winston. These are the traits of the ironist, but in *1984* there is no room for the radical doubt that makes ironism, in Rorty's sense, possible. There is no room for this doubt because there is no possible future: there is only the future guaranteed by the party. Without doubt and the social hope that can come with it, O'Brien turns his intellectual talents to other ends: "to feel the pleasure of twisting and breaking the special, hidden, tender parts of a mind with the same gifts of his own" (187). The result of this torture is the destruction of Winston's ability to reconstitute the narrative of his life; in Elaine Scarry's sense (important for Rorty), he cannot remake his world.[22]

In his discussion of Orwell Rorty returns to his historicism, emphasizing both how contingency is important to it and pointing to its increasingly dark shades in the twentieth century. The novelist helps him see that "it just happened" that liberal democracies have developed that condemn torture, and that they are not the necessary actualization of some immanent human essence. But that means that "it may just happen" that these democracies are not only contingent but ephemeral; that they will disappear and be replaced by regimes that seek out ever more subtle forms of cruelty as they close off the possibilities of social hope. Furthermore, the history of these societies in the world of the twentieth century has been a kind of torture for the liberal ideal of avoiding cruelty and reducing social pain. I

mean that the events of this time may have destroyed our ability to reconstitute a narrative of our history that leads to a political future of "human
dignity, freedom and peace."[23] For Rorty Orwell described this torture,
and events have "confirmed" his description (182). Can liberal historicism
redescribe this recent past in such a way as to reconstitute a vision of our
future that will inspire dedication and solidarity despite its contingency?[24]

The ironic redescription championed in much of the book certainly
does not lend itself to the kind of inspirational heroic historicism that liberalism may need in the contemporary world. But that does not mean that
ironism is incompatible with the kind of solidarity that such a historicism
would encourage:

> The ironist—the person who has doubts about his own final vocabu-
> lary, his own moral identity, and perhaps his own sanity—desperately
> needs to *talk* to other people, needs this with the same urgency as
> people need to make love. He needs to do so because only conversa-
> tion enables him to handle these doubts, to keep himself together, to
> keep his web of beliefs and desires coherent enough to enable him to
> act.   (186).

In a world where doubt is still permitted, and in a liberal culture in which it
would be encouraged, conversation, not cruelty, can be the source of satisfaction for the ironist. Conversation can lead to a kind of solidarity, one that
is based not on some discovery of a common essence but on an acknowledgment of connections and shared beliefs that tie people together. It is crucial
for Rorty that the realization of the contingency of these connections and
beliefs need not undermine our willingness to preserve them, even at great
risk. He notes that this is the fundamental premise of the book (189).

Rorty is successful in showing that there are probably no good philosophical arguments (in his narrow understanding of "argument") for abandoning this premise. There is no necessary incompatibility between contingency and commitment, between irony and solidarity. But one would
expect an historicist to want to show more than that; to want to provide
narratives of solidarity or historical accounts of how commitments are
maintained in the face of great adversity.[25] Although an acknowledgment
of contingency may not undermine the beliefs of ironists, perhaps it does
(or has) undermine(d) the beliefs of other people. Perhaps they are more
like the obsessives than they are like Proust and Derrida and Rorty. And

what if most people do need the "illusion" of foundationalism to maintain their networks of liberal solidarity? How can the poetic pragmatist condemn this illusion or even call it by that name?

The chapter on solidarity is the shortest in the book, although it is here that perhaps the most detail is needed. What kind of detail would this be? I suppose one could call it narrative detail or at least historicist density. We do not need arguments explaining why we *should* feel solidarity; Rorty is the first to agree that it is more than a little absurd to think that these feelings are created out of syllogistic reasoning. But we certainly can use narratives (historical and otherwise) that explore what happens to people who count for us when solidarity breaks down in the face of evil and what can happen (or what has happened) when solidarity and hope in the future combine to reduce cruelty. These narratives will often have to do with questions of pain and our reaction to it; that is, they will belong to Rorty's public domain. But they will often also have to do with "the purpose of life" or the "adequacy of our current vocabulary," and hence belong to his private domain. Indeed the problem of separating public and private in regard to these narratives will probably be as hopelessly difficult as separating content and form. There may be occasions in which we wish to talk about these aspects separately, but keeping the separation clean and rigorous seems about as likely as finding more-than-contingent criteria for deciding whether politics is more important than art.

Rorty quotes a story from William James that will work as an example of a narrative that produces the public/private fuzziness I have in mind. James describes himself as walking in the forest and coming upon a cabin in a clearing. He detests the despoliation of the landscape, the horrid pigpens and muddy gardens. But he thinks again after talking with the mountaineer who lives there:

> I had been losing the whole inward significance of the situation. Because to me the clearings spoke of naught but denudation, I thought that to those whose sturdy arms and obedient axes had made them they could tell no other story. But when *they* looked on the hideous stumps, what they thought of was personal victory. . . . In short, the clearing which to me was a mere ugly picture on the retina, was to them a symbol redolent with moral memories and sang a very paean of duty, struggle and success.

I had been as blind to the peculiar ideality of their conditions as they certainly would also have been to the ideality of mine, had they a peep at my strange indoor academic way of life at Cambridge.[26]

(38)

In this description of his "overcoming a certain blindness," James provides Rorty with a perfect example of redescription, of the contingency of vocabularies, and of the tolerance that can emerge from an acceptance of the latter and a celebration of the former.[27] But for Rorty all of this goes on in the domain of the private, and this demarcation must itself be redescribed. Surely there are social consequences (consequences that have an impact on who feels pain) to whether one remains blind in James's sense. One certainly cannot legislate the overcoming (the "coming-to-attention," the "consciousness raising") for specific individuals, but politics cannot be reduced to legislation.[28] To mention just one public aspect in this regard, the educational policy of a polity is crucially political, and certainly all education in (at least) the humanities today would have an impact on whether people were encouraged to expand their vision in the way James describes. What would be the result of this expansion? James responds in this way: "It absolutely forbids us to be forward in pronouncing on the meaninglessness of forms of existence other than our own; and it commands us to tolerate, respect and indulge those whom we see harmlessly interested and happy in their own ways, however unintelligible these may be to us. Hands off.[29] How could decisions about education that would effect overcoming a certain blindness be redescribed as private without just encouraging a new blindness to one of the crucial facets of liberalism? Surely the overcoming and the social tolerance that James describes has everything to do with avoiding cruelty and reducing pain.[30]

Education and social tolerance is not the only area where Rorty's private/public distinction becomes exceptionally fuzzy. At times it works very well, because it enables him to cut through a lot of "theorizing" that is supposedly political. However, no attention at all is given to some of the antiliberal ways in which this distinction has been used. This issue does not emerge in his discussions of Foucault and Habermas, but it would have if more gender-conscious cultural criticism were addressed. In this case it would have become clear, for example, that one of the important problems with the public/private distinction in liberal culture is that for many people, especially women, it is *not believable*.[31] In other words, under the guise of this distinction other things have been going on; or, in Rorty's terms, cruelty was unnoticed because it was declared private. It is clear, however, that a systematic blindness to the cruelty inflicted on a group of people is a public matter and needs to be described that way to be combated.[32]

This issue should recall some of Foucault's concerns, which cannot be reduced to either an effort at self-description or a delight in transgression; that is, he was concerned with overcoming our blindness to certain forms of cruelty, and he saw the disguise (i.e., a redescription about which we are suspicious) of "the private" as often facilitating this blindness. Many of his redescriptions were aimed at reducing this cruelty. It is in this regard that his work has been important for feminists, whose own suspicions about the public/private distinction are not taken into account in Rorty's book. The ways in which gender intersects with solidarity in the development of the liberal use of the public/private distinction should have a prominent place in a historicist redescription of liberal culture. The objections to the public/private distinction that Rorty does consider are either divorced from any community under the guise of theoretical suspicion or are attached to a community via some refurbished universalism. Feminist objections to the public/private distinction present another mix, since they clearly promote a form of solidarity even as they usually reject universalism. If the slogan "the personal is the political" is extraordinarily problematic as a prescription of the way things should be, it is a powerful redescription of how the category of the personal has done much cruel political work against women. "The personal is the political" can also make a claim to (re)appropriate certain kinds of experience as valuable, as worthy of value. Recognizing the contingency of the public/private distinction means recognizing that it can work and has worked against important aspects of the culture of liberalism that Rorty is trying to promote, even if it might still be used (in conditions of equality) in the service of this culture.

Pointing out the contingency of the public/private distinction so important for *Contingency, Irony, and Solidarity* opens up important parts of its presentation to historicist redescription. Doing so confirms more than it undermines, of course, the central claims of the book which, after all, are put forward as elements of a conversation. The book depends on even as it calls for historicist narratives that will provide liberal culture with a sense of itself—with a strong but contingent meaning and direction. Although he has not presented these narratives here in any detail, Rorty has provided an important stimulus to the kinds of redescription in which they would be engaged. The stimulus comes, in part, from the crucial moral, political, and aesthetic functions that he gives to these redescriptions, despite an ironic acknowledgment of their contingency.

In *Contingency, Irony, and Solidarity* Rorty has written a brief but powerful work that forcefully expands on the critical task of *Philosophy and the Mirror of Nature,* enriching the idea of philosophy as conversation by engaging some of the most important questions raised about his views. His ironic historicism has set new standards for how philosophy can speak of language, self, and society without speaking only to philosophers.

NOTES

1. This essay is a discussion of *Contingency, Irony and Solidarity,* published by Cambridge University Press in 1989. References to this work will be given parenthetically in the text. A two volume collection of Rorty's philosophical papers: *Objectivity, Relativism and Truth,* and *Essays on Heidegger and Others* was published by Cambridge University Press in 1991.

2. Ian Hacking, "Two Kinds of New Historicism for Philosophers," in *History and . . . . : Histories Within the Human Sciences,* ed. Ralph Cohen and Michael S. Roth (Charlottesville: University Press of Virginia, 1995), 298.

3. Cornel West's sympathetic view of Rorty's critique of philosophy emphasizes his antiprofessionalism: "[Rorty's] plausible yet objectionable uses of Wittgenstein, Heidegger, and Dewey and his creative misreadings of Quine, Goodman, and Sellars yield the most adversarial position in American academic philosophy since the fervent antiprofessionalism of William James." ("Afterword," in *Post-Analytic Philosophy,* ed. John Rajchman and Cornel West [New York: Columbia University Press, 1985], 266). See also Rorty, "Philosophy in America Today" and "Cavell and Skepticism," in *Consequences of Pragmatism* (Minneapolis: University of Minnesota Press, 1982), 211–30, 176–90.

4. The essay in which one can see this combination most clearly is "Post-Modern Bourgeois Liberalism," *Journal of Philosophy* 80, (1983): 583–89.

5. The book is based on Rorty's Northcliffe and Clark Lectures of 1986 and 1987. Some of these had already been published in the *London Review of Books.*

6. Richard Rorty, "Cosmopolitanism Without Emancipation: A Reponse to Jean-François Lyotard," in *Objectivity, Relativism, and Truth* (Cambridge: Cambridge University Press, 1991), 211–22. See also "Habermas and Lyotard on Postmodernity," in *Habermas and Modernity,* ed. Richard Bernstein (Boston: MIT Press 1985), 161–76.

7. Rorty discusses this kind of self-referential paradox in "The Priority of Democracy to Philosophy," in *The Virginia Statute for Religious Freedom: Its Evolution and Consequences in American History,* ed. Merrill D. Peterson and Robert C. Vaughan. (Cambridge: Cambridge University Press 1988), 270–72. See also Alexander Nehamas, "Can We Ever Change the

Subject?: Richard Rorty on Science, Literature, Culture, and the Future of Philosophy," *Boundary* 2, no. 10 (1982): 395–413.

8. Rorty does not regard the creation of such a culture as a utopian dream, seeing this process as analogous to secularization. "A postmetaphysical culture seems to me no more impossible than a postreligious one, and equally desirable" (xvi).

9. See also Richard Rorty, "Pragmatism, Davidson, and Truth," in *Truth and Interpretation: Perspectives on the Philosophy of Donald Davidson,* ed. Ernest LePore (Oxford: Blackwell, 1986), 333–55.

10. See Hans Blumenberg's *The Legitimacy of the Modern Age,* trans. Robert M. Wallace (Cambridge, Mass.: MIT Press, 1983).

11. See Michael S. Roth, *Psycho-Analysis as History: Negation and Freedom in Freud* (Ithaca: Cornell University Press, 1987), passim.

12. Rorty's presentation here is close to Heidegger's understanding of Nietzsche on the death of God. See "The Word of Nietzsche: 'God is Dead,'" in *The Question Concerning Technology and Other Essays,* trans. William Lovitt (New York: Garland, 1977), 53–114.

13. Alexander Nehamas has discussed Rorty's "focus on the logical rather than on the institutional and ideological features of the metaphor of the mirror of Nature: "Can We Ever Change the Subject," 408. See also West, "Rorty's historicist sense remains too broad, too thin—devoid of the realities of power; his ethnocentric posthumanism is too vague, too nonchalant—and unmindful of the decline of liberalism" ("Afterword," 268; and see 270) and West, *The American Evasion of Philosophy: A Genealogy of Pragmatism* (Madison: University of Wisconsin Press, 1989), 194–210.

14. See chapter 8 in this collection.

15. Michel Foucault, *Politics, Philosophy, Culture: Interviews and Other Writings, 1977–1984,* ed. Lawrence D. Kritzman (New York: Routledge 1988), 197.

16. Rorty: "It is as if thinkers like Foucault and Lyotard were so afraid of being caught up in one more metanarrative about the fortunes of 'the subject' that they cannot bring themselves to say 'we' long enough to identify with the culture of the generation to which they belong" ("Habermas and Lyotard on Post-Modernity," 172).

17. I should add that Rorty would welcome this "pointing out." He has already said that the power of Foucault's work comes from the ways in which it shows us forms of cruelty about which we otherwise would not know. The issue on which the Foucauldian response to Rorty might focus would be whether the latter's historicist narrative helped us to avoid being cruel or merely to avoid acknowledging cruelty.

18. Habermas, *The Philosophical Discourse of Modernity: Twelve Lectures,* trans. Frederick Lawrence (Cambridge, Mass.: MIT Press 1987), 209ff.

19. In this regard he is close to Blumenberg (*The Legitimacy of the Modern Age,* 184). See "Habermas and Lyotard on Post-Modernity," 167.

20. Jean-François Lyotard, *The Post-Modern Condition: A Report on Knowledge,* trans. Geoff Bennington and Brian Massumi (Minneapolis: University of Minnesota Press, 1984), 81.

21. Rorty underlines this moral despite his earlier polemical assertion that there is no such thing as the voice of the oppressed (94). Is not the voice of the oppressed what people use to tell you they are suffering?

22. Elaine Scarry, *The Body in Pain: The Making and Unmaking of the World* (Oxford: Oxford University Press, 1985), passim.

23. Rorty here is in part writing in reaction to Raymond Williams, *Orwell* (London: Flamingo 1984).

24. Rorty has argued that the Left has evaded this historicist task under the mask of theoretical sophistication. See his "Thugs and Theorists: A Reply to Bernstein," *Political Theory* 15, (1987): 564–80.

25. Rorty says that "surely" Danes and Italians who saved Jews in World War II usually did so not because they were fellow human beings but because they were fellow members of the same union or profession, or fellow bocce players. Now it *may* be true that, if asked, these people would have used more parochial terms than *fellow human beings* to describe their connection to the Jews in question. But there is nothing sure about it. Historical accounts of local constructions of solidarity, narratives that show how the contingencies in these constructions fell together, help us understand how contingent and meaningful communities come together (and fall apart).

26. William James, "On a Certain Blindness in Human Beings," in *Talks to Teachers on Psychology*, ed. Frederick Burkhardt and Fredson Bowers (Cambridge, Mass.: Harvard University Press, 1983), 134.

27. One can only say "can emerge" because other versions of redescription (the first James used, for example) can result in humiliation.

28. As James says, "But how can one attain to the feeling of the vital significance of an experience, if one have it not to begin with? There is no recipe which one can follow" ("On a Certain Blindness,"144).

29. Ibid., 149.

30. Rorty certainly endorses James's "Hands off" but does not think that any issues arise for political philosophy after this declaration is made. Thus he has nothing to say about how social tolerance can be encouraged or inhibited by the policies of a political regime. On Rorty's view of education and liberalism see his article on Allan Bloom, "That Old-Time Philosophy," *The New Republic* 198, no. 7 (1988): 28–33.

31. For a feminist critique of Rorty's public/private distinction see Nancy Fraser, "Solidarity or Singularity: Richard Rorty Between Romanticism and Technocracy," in *Unruly Practices: Power, Discourse, and Gender in Contemporary Social Theory* (Minneapolis: University of Minnesota Press, 1989), 93–100. One of Fraser's major concerns is the absence of the possibility of oppositional solidarity in Rorty's view of politics. I do not see that this absence is entailed by the public/private distinction he makes, but it certainly is created by the kind of historicist narrative on which he depends.

32. This is not to say that Rorty uses the public/private distinction in the old sexist ways. He does not. The reduction of cruelty and pain is, according to him, a public matter, no matter where this cruelty takes place. However, Rorty does not pay attention to the historical construction of the public/private distinction as a weapon against women, and also against lesbians, gays, and racial and ethnic minorities. Had he done so, the question of how his version of the distinction could be seen as useful by these groups might have been addressed in a helpful way.

Cultural Criticism and Political Theory: Hayden White's Rhetorics of History

Political theory has had a symbiotic relation to the theory of history at least since Hegel. Indeed, when one begins to think rigorously about politics, one must sooner or later begin to integrate the historical field into any conception of what counts as political or with what kinds of politics are possible or desirable. Even the most abstract models of the political must show how historical events can be made sense of, determined, or inspired. Thus a political theory contains or implies a conception or a vision of history just as theories of history contain or imply a conception or a vision of the political. Political theorists have been sensitive to this interconnection, especially if they have been a part of recent debates about Marxism and historicism or about ways in which structuralism and poststructuralism have affected the possibilities of diachronic understanding.

Hayden White does not have a "theory of history" in the sense usually of interest to political theorists; that is, he does not provide a way of putting historical events together into a meaningful whole nor does he provide a reasoned explanation of why this cannot be done. Instead White is a theorist of *history* in its other meaning: the written record of past events. Thus White's subject is not, for example, whether there has been progress and freedom or increasing domination and normalization in the modern period but, rather, how the liberal mode of understanding the past and the Foucauldian mode emplot past events into coherent stories, or meaningful narratives. White probes the status of these stories, *qua* stories and *qua* histories, and he shows how they compare as linguistic or rhetorical constructions. Finally White offers a rhetorics of historical writing that should change the way we think about the possibilities of any theory of historical events.[1]

In the late 1960s philosophy of history in America had only recently emerged from what we can call a Hempelian paradigm;[2] that is, philosophers were concerned with whether historiography could be a science, and if so, how it could develop causal laws about historical change. In the late 1960s there was more interest in understanding what historians did when they wrote about the past and less effort to tell them what they must do to behave like scientists. Philosophers began to look again at the "autonomy of historical understanding" and thus at the form in which this understanding was expressed.[3] One can rightly say that analytic philosophy of history began to take a linguistic or even a narrativist turn, as philosophers concentrated on the textual products of historical work.[4]

White came to reflect on the status of history, not from the side of the philosopher who is interested in various kinds of knowledge but as a historian of the founding modern theorist of history, Vico, and as a practitioner who saw his colleagues resisting theoretical questions by appealing to their special place as mediators between art and science. In the earliest essay reprinted in these books, "The Burden of History," White shows how the historian's conception of both art and science was based on antiquated nineteenth-century notions. Historians had isolated themselves from the intellectual community by ignoring more recent developments in science and art that emphasized the constructivist qualities of both enterprises. In this passionate and polemical piece, White calls for historians to be not only more concerned with the connections between the pasts they study and the present from which they study them but to "plunder" the experimental developments in the arts and sciences for metaphors that will change the content of their concerns and the forms in which they are expressed. As White emphasized,

> the "*burden of the historian*" in our time is to reestablish the dignity of historical studies on a basis that will make them consonant with the aims and purposes of the intellectual community at large, that is, transform historical studies in such a way as to allow the historian to participate positively in the liberation of the present from the *burden of history.*[5]

All of White's work since this essay clearly has aimed at liberating historical writing and understanding from its nineteenth-century burdens, although, as we shall see, it has not always been clear how *this* liberation would help free our present from the weight of our past.

Metahistory is an attempt to get historians out from under their nineteenth-century burdens through a detailed explication of the works of some of the great nineteenth-century historical writers.[6] White examines four types of "realism" exemplified in the works of Michelet, Ranke, Tocqueville, and Burckhardt and then three philosophical repudiations of realism in Marx, Nietzsche, and Croce. Here, it seemed, was intellectual history on the grand scale. The evolution of historical thinking has long been a preferred topic among historians and, in going back to the nineteenth century, White was pointing to what he himself called their golden age. White took the philosophers of history more seriously than most of his colleagues would have, but on the whole his subject was recognizably within this reflexive branch of intellectual history.

But White's book has a basic ahistorical core with which historians have great difficulty coming to terms, but which also gives the book genuinely theoretical import. White reads his nineteenth-century authors through the lens of contemporary literary theory, specifically theories of rhetoric and genre.[7] For White the four types of realism can be understood as four styles of emplotting historical events into stories. The genres were romance in Michelet, comedy in Ranke, tragedy in Tocqueville, and satire in Burckhardt. And the philosophers of history privileged particular tropes, or figures of speech: Marx emphasized metonymy and synecdoche to organize the historical field, whereas Nietzsche relied on metaphor and Croce on irony. None of these authors used a single genre or trope exclusively, but each of them represented the past through a preferred rhetorical function.

In White's reading of Marx, for example, he shows how the writer had two different strategies for representing the past. First, his political economy was mechanistic and law-bound. Metonymy—taking the part for the whole—ruled here, as economic relationships were seen to determine the whole of our historical interactions. The genre of this strategy of representation was tragedy, insofar as all economic development increased basic conflicts; wealth coming at the cost of increasing misery for more and more people.

The second strategy of representation had, however, a quite different form. In describing changes in the superstructure, Marx relied on synecdoche—an essential attribute standing for the object—as properly human relations would ultimately come to exist in society at the end of (pre)history. The content of this form is the genre of comedy; a story in which contradictions are dissolved and harmony reigns. Thus White shows how Marx's poetic or rhetorical emplotment of the historical field leads to a story in which *specific* historical events have a tragic sense, but in which this sense is incorporated into a larger comic paradigm. Within this paradigm Marx is able to affirm the potential meaningfulness of history given the possibilities for radical action to bring the story to its proper ending.

A summary of the conclusions of White's reading of Marx or the other authors cannot do justice to the rich detail of his textual explications. My point here is to discuss the theoretical strategy of his representation of the nineteenth-century historians and philosophers. White is not concerned in *Metahistory* with whether a history or a philosophy of history is more realistic than another. He is not concerned with their scientific character. Instead he examines how what Barthes called the "reality effect" is created by all historical writing. Different ways of creating this effect generate different plots and also different kinds of ideologies.[8] The metahistorical element in all historical writing is the "precritical," "deep structural content" of the writing. This content can always be understood through some combination of the four tropes, which exhaust the possibilities for representing the past in language. Thus the critic of historical writing armed with the theory of the tropes can understand not so much the "autonomy of historical understanding" but the kinship of writing about history with writing in general and the possibilities available to this form of expression for making particular stories out of the past for particular purposes.

Note that White never claims that the historical writer set out to write under the sign of metaphor or that comic emplotment was Marx's conscious organizing principle as he wrote. Instead White's analysis of the formal properties of the text is dependent neither on some notion of the author's intention nor on an appeal to a context, nor even on conventions one knows about independently of the text. Thus White's attempt to articulate how a text achieves its effects is very far from, let's say, Quentin Skinner's effort to get at what a text *really does.* Likewise, his rhetorical analysis has little in common with J.G.A. Pocock's effort to uncover the language (or paradigm) available to a political theorist. Pocock looks for the discursive form that a content took in a particular context; White looks for the content of particular narrative forms.[9]

What, then, had White done in *Metahistory* to help historians escape their nineteenth-century burdens? By using a formalist strategy to focus on the construction of types of realism, White displaced epistemological questions and questions about objectivity in favor of an inquiry into literary or poetic structure. Historians did not find story types in the past; they formed the past into story types. The interesting questions for White were not about the correspondence of a story with its "reality"; there was no reality *that could be considered* apart from some meaningful emplotment of it. Instead he was interested in how writers *created* criteria for what would count as realistic to give their own stories authority. White's readings were meant to undermine this authority in order to expose the moral, political, and aesthetic choices that motivated the adoption of any particular form of the rhetoric of realism. Claims of objectivity and of realism were always attempts to mask these fundamental choices, attempts that a tropological critic could help us see through.

In his subsequent essays, many of which are collected in *Tropics of Discourse* and *The Content of the Form,* White continued to examine historical writing as a rhetorical structure. By eliding the question of correspondence, and in thinking about reference as a linguistic function, he was clearly moving history and literature more closely together. "The differences between a history and a fictional account of reality," White wrote, "are matters of degree rather than of kind."[10] White was in no way undermining the status of history here, since he recognized the power of literature to teach us about reality.[11] If history was once again to have wide cultural significance, it could no longer deny the literary imagination as its "own greatest source of strength and renewal." And if historians were to be self-conscious about what they did, they needed the theories of representation provided by those working in rhetoric and linguistics.[12]

But theories of representation are also representations, and one wants to know why the tropes, for example, are given such importance as a "deep" content. White sees his four tropes everywhere, not just in contemporary literary theory or in the nineteenth century. Not only does he depend on Burke and Frye for models, he returns to Vico's notion that our forms of consciousness are "given by language itself."[13] Freud, Jakobson, Levi-Strauss, and Piaget all provide theories compatible with tropology, and Foucault is shown to have a tropological system of explanation, whether he knows it or not.[14] Like his structuralist cousins across the Atlantic, White seemed to think he had the key to unraveling the meaning of all language taken, if not as myth, then as figurative discourse.

But in the final essay reprinted in *Tropics,* "The Absurdist Moment in Literary Criticism," White shows how structuralism passes into poststructuralism, as the theories of language are themselves shown to be merely signs of language. And the same can be said for the theory of tropes. Literary theory turns on itself to ensure that there are no privileged places from which to constitute meaning. Furthermore, there are no privileged sciences for understanding how others constitute meaning. The structuralists whom White "profited from" in writing *Metahistory* were becoming deconstructionists who showed that his profit had no value.

Rather than celebrate the playfulness of deconstruction that results from this shift, White sees the hypostatization of theories of discourse as a sign of our sterile and mutilated cultural condition. It is sterile and mutilated because deconstructionists not only see how meaning is imposed on reality but they see all meaning as an arbitrary imposition to be unraveled by the critic who then unravels his or her own enterprise. Derrida, then, emerges not as a critic of structuralism but as a victim of its point of view. White's own use of tropes was meant to move us "beyond irony" by showing us the moral, political, and aesthetic choices that remained open to us.[15] Once we understood that it was we who construct our narratives out of the past, the appeal to history should become not a constraint on freedom but one of the ways in which we could choose to give meaning to our lives. But if we were "always already" embedded in an arbitrary figure of speech, where was the place from which we made our choices?

White's most recent collection of essays, *The Content of the Form,* attempts to answer this question. One of the most important places where these choices are found is in narrative, and the essays contained in this book examine the powers and functions of narrative in representing the real. In turning to narrative, White clearly thinks he is getting to the core cultural significance of historical writing and of realism in general. "To raise the question of the nature of narrative," he writes, "is to invite reflection on the very nature of culture, and possibly, even on the nature of humanity itself."[16]

A narrative is a rhetorical strategy through which we mold our experience into a meaningful whole that can be communicated to others. White is especially interested in discourses that "narrativize" or pretend that it is experience that "speaks itself as a story."[17] Through this technique the story achieves what we call *realism,* since the telling appears to be homologous with the way things happened. When we think of our history as narrativized we think of it as having an intrinsic meaning and thereby an intrinsic moral and political sense. Narrativized histories, for example, see the past as being *really* the development of class struggle or *really* the evolution of liberty. Marxist or liberal stories of our past, then, appear not as stories at all but as transparent accounts of the way things really were and are. As well-ordered narrative accounts, they "give reality the odor of the ideal."[18]

Crucial for White's approach to historical writing is the idea that we endow the past with meaning because "in itself" it has none.[19] The historical writer must form the past into a narrative because the past is formless, or at least it does not have the rhetorical forms that alone make it meaningful in communication. White does not provide metaphysical arguments about the nature of the past prior to its textualization but instead notes that our history comes to us always mediated by texts and thus always formed by tropes (usually) in a narrative. His own work explicates how the mediation achieves its effects.

One of the most global of such effects is the expulsion of the possibility of history's meaninglessness. Indeed in "The Politics of Historical Interpretation: Discipline and Desublimation" (1982) White shows how, in the creation of history as a discipline, it was precisely this possibility that was foreclosed. Those utopians who viewed history as a sublime, formless spectacle were excluded from the modern notion of being genuinely historical. "True" historical consciousness—the Left and the Right could agree—was realistic and objective and at least tried to *find* the meaning in the past. But this creation of a realistic paradigm itself had a political component. The kind of politics that one can develop in relation to history will be quite different if one starts from the conviction that we must give a meaning to history rather than find a meaning and direction in it.

Perhaps now we can see more clearly what White means by the "content of the form." The meaning of a piece of historical writing should not be confused with either its referent or the intention behind it. Instead the writer's discourse achieves certain effects because of the way in which it is put together. The particular components of its narrative form reveal much about its moral, political, and aesthetic content. By getting at this component, White shows the content of any putatively realistic form.

Political theorists will rightly see in this style of reading a variation on the tradition of "ideology critique." But White, following Althusser and Jameson, does not think of ideology as a distortion of reality but rather "as a certain practice of representation whose function is to create a specific kind of reading or viewing subject capable of inserting himself into the social system that is his historically given potential field of public activity."[20] Thus a historical narrative—whether of a radical or a conservative kind—projects a reader who develops "realistic" attitudes about oppression, freedom, and the possibilities for change. These attitudes are of course meaningful, but they are also, White wants us to see, imaginary and open to change.

Here, however, the politically minded reader wants to point out that if all texts "project attitudes" as realistic, all texts are ideological. There is then no reason for engaging in ideology critique. The political point of showing the ideological character of an expression—that it masks a reality one would want to change—seems to vanish in a kind of relativism in which all texts mask, since that is what rhetorical structures must do. White seems to be party to a rhetorical relativism that would be part of the postmodern playfulness that he had earlier described as the symptom of a mutilated and sterile culture.

But the relativist charge is simply not appropriate to White. In all his work he is trying to show not that all texts are created equal because they are all rhetorical, nor the vacuous notion that there is nothing outside the text, but rather that the criteria for distinguishing among texts cannot be found in an appeal to history. White's work has effectively demolished the notion that history can be a neutral testing ground for the validity of certain texts by exposing the ways in which historical writings create criteria of realism that themselves cannot be judged *according to history.* We may have other grounds for distinguishing texts, and ultimately for establishing a vision of history; but an appeal to the past as meaningful before our appeal to it is unmasked by White as being always an ideological attempt at dissimulating our constructive will under the guise of an objective realism.

Metahistory and White's essays show how historical writings create referents or sign systems that the reader is supposed to regard as necessary, or objective, or as natural. This is the ideological move. By exposing the ways in which texts make this move, White does not of course hope to lead us to a more genuinely realistic connection with our history. Instead he means to make us aware of the enormous possibilities that are opened once the authority of realism is broken down. Breaking down this authority is not, it must be underlined, a new ground for politics, and White never pretends that it is. However, his work is a sort of clearing operation that suspends the burden of history *qua* burden of realism; realism that had made nineteenth-century social practice into its "criterion of plausibility." This clearing allows us to think again about the enormous range of choices there are in establishing our connection to our past and thus in developing a stance in the present.

White's critical analysis of historical realism should not, however, be confused with a rejection of narrative. How could one "reject" the, perhaps, universal effort to endow our pasts with meaning? In his readings of Ricoeur's pious approach to narrative, and Jameson's Marxist one, White evinces his respect for the view that life may make sense only insofar as we can tell it in the form of a story.[21] Jameson and Ricoeur resist the ironic response that the meanings they discuss are "only stories," despite their understanding of how narratives are put together. White too has wanted to go "beyond irony" in his rhetorical analysis by insisting that such analyses give us "the knowledge necessary for a free choice among different strategies of figuration."[22]

Here we reach the limits of White's ongoing project; so far, he has had very little to say about how such choices are made. This choosing seems to be beyond rhetoric, although we would never know about it but for its rhetorical expressions. As a critic of those expressions, White's own rhetoric leads us to the questions of why we turn to history in the first place. What do we want from the past, and what shall we do with our history once we understand that it can no longer function as a court of appeal? White leads us to these questions, but he also carefully avoids them. Perhaps he cannot do otherwise given the position he has created for himself as a critic of history writing.

In this regard a fruitful dialogue might develop between White's poststructuralist understanding of how our historical sense is put together and how some political theorists' understand the process of politics without foundations. This dialogue is long overdue, since contemporary theory must rethink not only the political status of new modes of knowing but also the possibilities and dilemmas that unfold when these modes are confronted with the burdens of history. Such a conversation would be one of the best ways in which to foster a cross-fertilization among literary, political, and historical theory that would help us rethink our connections with the past.

If the relationship between political theory and historical theory is to remain productive, then we must learn to think about the forms through which we make meaning out of our past and how those forms are related to the ways in which we now live and desire to change. Rather than measuring realism and distortion, White's thinking about history forces us to reconsider our criteria for evaluating the stories we tell and, in so doing, opens up to political questioning our connection to the past as we imagine "it really was" and hence to the future as we might imagine it could be.

NOTES

1. This chapter discusses the following books by Hayden White: *Metahistory: The Historical Imagination in Nineteenth-Century Europe* (Baltimore: Johns Hopkins University Press, 1973); *Tropics of Discourse: Essays in Cultural Criticism* (Baltimore: Johns Hopkins University Press, 1978); *The Content of the Form: Narrative Discourse and Historical Representation* (Baltimore: Johns Hopkins University Press, 1987).

White follows Paolo Valesio in using "rhetorics" to indicate the theoretical study of discourse by analogy with "poetics" to indicate the theoretical study of poetry. See White, "'Figuring the Nature of the Times Deceased': Literary Theory and Historical Writing," in *The Future of Literary Theory*, ed. Ralph Cohen (New York: Routledge, 1989), n. 15; and Valesio, *Novantiqua: Rhetorics as a Contemporary Theory* (Bloomington: Indiana University Press, 1980), chap. 1.

2. Louis O. Mink wrote that "it could be said without exaggeration that until about 1965 the critical philosophy of history *was* the controversy over the covering-law model." See Mink, "The Divergence of History and Sociology in the Recent Philosophy of History," in *Historical Understanding*, ed. Fay, Golob, and Vann (Ithaca: Cornell University Press, 1973/1987). Cited in Richard T. Vann, "Louis Mink's Linguistic Turn," *History and Theory* 26, no. 1 (1987): 2. Carl G. Hempel's, "The Function of General Laws in History," *Journal of Philosophy* 39 no. 1 (1942): 35–48.

3. See Mink, "The Autonomy of Historical Understanding" (1965), reprinted in *Historical Understanding*. Other philosophers developing this perspective were Dray, Gallie, and Danto.

4. On this development, see F. R. Ankersmit, "The Dilemma of Contemporary Anglo-Saxon Philosophy of History," *History and Theory*, Beiheft 25: *Knowing and Telling History: The Anglo-Saxon Debate* (1986), 1–27.

5. White, "The Burden of History" (1966), *Tropics*, 41.

6. Very helpful accounts of White's analysis in *Metahistory* can be found in the issue of *History and Theory*, Beiheft 19 (1980) devoted to six critiques of the book. See also Frederic

Jameson, "Figural Relativism or the Poetics of Historiography," *Diacritics* 6 (Spring 1976), 2–9.

7. His important influences in this regard seem to have been Vico, Nietzsche, Kenneth Burke, and "modern, especially semiotic linguistics." See White, "'Figuring the Nature of the Times Deceased,'" n. 18.

8. But the connections between emplotment, argument, and ideological implication are described only as affinities. In White's formalist readings not very much attention is paid to authorial intention.

9. See J.G.A. Pocock's very helpful "Introduction: The State of the Art," in *Virtue, Commerce and History: Essays on Political Thought and History, Chiefly in the Eighteenth Century* (Cambridge: Cambridge University Press, 1985), 1–34.

10. White, "Interpretation in History" (1972–1973), *Tropics,* n. 78.

11. White, "Historical Text as Literary Artifact" (1974), *Tropics,* 99.

12. Ibid.

13. White, "Interpretation in History," *Tropics,* n. 80.

14. Freud and Piaget are made to complement each other's and Jakobson's understandings of tropes in the introduction to *Tropics.* Levi-Strauss is discussed briefly in "Interpretation in History," reprinted in the same volume.

15. *Metahistory,* vii, 434. See Jameson's critical comments in "Figural Relativism," 9.

16. "The Value of Narrativity in the Representation of Reality" (1980), *Content,* 1.

17. Ibid., 2.

18. Ibid., 21.

19. This idea is subject to some controversy. See White's (1984) own magisterial account in "The Question of Narrative in Contemporary Historical Theory," in *Content;* and Ankersmit, "The Dilemma." For contrasting views see the extraordinary second volume of Paul Ricoeur's *Time and Narrative* (Chicago: University of Chicago Press, 1983); and David Carr, "Narrative and the Real World: An Argument for Continuity," *History and Theory* 25, no. 2 (1986): 117–31.

20. "Droysen's *Historik:* Historical Writing as a Bourgeois Science" (1980), *Content,* 86.

21. "Getting Out of History: Jameson's Redemption of Narrative" (1982), *The Content of the Form,* 167; and "The Rule of Narrativity: Symbolic Discourse and the Experiences of Time in Ricoeur's Thought" (1985), *The Content of the Form,* 181.

22. White, "'Figuring the Nature of the Times Deceased': Literary Theory and Historical Writing," 24. See also *Metahistory,* 434.

• 8 •

The Ironist's Cage

Not long ago, an issue of trendy *Spy* magazine explored the ways that contemporary culture had become a culture of irony. From car advertisements that contain only obvious falsehoods to fashions that play off negative judgments about earlier styles, irony is all around us. People and institutions with power are often as ironic about themselves as their critics are about them. However, irony has long been and continues to be an effective form for various stripes of cultural criticism; from Marx in his treatment of utopian socialism to Allan Bloom in his treatment of liberal education, the ironist undermines our ability to take his or her object seriously. We are disengaged from the object. Ironist critics who are also interested in social change, however, must preserve a clearing in which their readers can reconnect to a project of political action. When this clearing can no longer be maintained, the ironic form comes to have an extraordinary privilege.

This privileging of irony is often the result of the inability to sustain belief in the possibilities of significant political change. This is certainly the case for one of the most influential figures in twentieth-century French thought, Alexandre Kojève. As the function of revolution changes in his philosophy of history—that is, as the possibility of meaningful revolution disappears from his historicism by the mid-1950s—he becomes increasingly ironic in his criticism of contemporary life. In this regard his later work is emblematic of much of contemporary cultural criticism in France and elsewhere. Discovering scant possibilities of significant political change, post-Kojèveian critics of contemporary culture and society have found themselves in what I call the "ironist's cage."

The intellectual history of twentieth-century France was deeply marked by a confrontation with Hegel, a philosopher whose delayed impact on French culture might be seen as an example of what Freud called *Nachtraglichkeit,* or deferment.[1] Alexandre Kojève, a Russian emigré who did his advanced work in philosophy in Germany, developed a wildly original and deeply influential interpretation of Hegel in a seminar at the École Pratique des Hautes Études from 1934 to 1939. In attendance at the seminar at various times were Maurice Merleau-Ponty, Jacques Lucan, André Breton, Gaston Fessard, George Bataille, and Eric Weil.[2] For Kojève's Hegel, History was the revelation of Truth, and this truth was revealed primarily through the various turns taken by the master-slave dialectic. Why was this version of Hegelianism so powerful? Kojève's Hegel was a dramatic pragmatist. He tied truth and successful action together, and he saw progress accomplished through bloody battles for recognition. The master-slave dialectic was the motor of history, and the desire for mutual and equal recognition was its fuel. Kojève claimed that by reading Hegel through lenses ground against the texts of Marx and Heidegger, he was able to make sense of the totality of history and of the structure of human desire. History and desire became understandable when their ends and their goals became clear. Kojève claimed to provide this clarity, and if that was not enough, he couched his interpretation as a form of political propaganda which would further the revolution that would confirm the interpretation itself. As he wrote in 1946,

> we can say that, for the moment, every interpretation of Hegel, if it is more than small talk, is only a program of struggle and work . . . and that means that a work of Hegel interpretation has the significance of a work of political propaganda. . . . it is possible that the future of the world, and therefore the meaning and direction of the present and the significance of the past, depend, in the final analysis, on the way in which we interpret Hegelian texts today.[3]

Kojève situated the reading of Hegel which he developed in his seminars in the 1930s just before a revolution that would be a final confirmation of the interpretation itself. I have shown elsewhere that this faith in the meaning and direction of history—a faith I call heroic Hegelianism— waned by the 1950s. In this decade Hegelian historicism was displaced by a conceptually well-tooled structuralism that no longer claimed to find meaning and direction in history and that no longer needed confirmation by a future turn of events. Some Hegelian thinkers (Jean Hyppolite most prominently among them) abandoned historicism during this period, but Kojève stuck with his version of history as the revelation of truth. He did, however, change the place of revolution in his philosophy of history, and it is this shift that is most relevant to the irony of his later writings.[4]

By the early 1950s Kojève saw his work not as a form of propaganda aimed at stimulating a revolutionary self-consciousness but as a commentary on a history that had already run its course. In shifting the place of revolution in his understanding of history, Kojève changed the form of his philosophy: he abandoned engaged dramatic pragmatism in favor of detached ironism. I examine the shift in Kojève's conceptualization of revolution not only out of an interest in his writings for their own sake but because his posthistorical ironic philosophy of history has become a dominant mode of what today is called postmodern cultural criticism.

I

Let us begin by examining the importance of revolution in Kojève's reading of Hegel. It would not be too much to say that revolution is built into the very structure of his understanding of history, since that understanding is constructed on the frame of the master-slave dialectic. In this frame humans are defined by their desire for recognition—a desire that can be satisfied only with the conservation of its object—and by their will to risk their lives in order to satisfy this desire. The confrontation with an other leads to bloody battle followed by the rule of masters over their working slaves. The masters, however, can never satisfy their quintessentially human desire because they are recognized by *mere* slaves. The slaves, on the other hand, through their work and through the changes seen in the natural world as the result of their efforts, can begin to attain some satisfaction: They can see themselves in their creations. This form of satisfaction is progressive or historical insofar as the work that produces it can be built on.

But it is not work alone that creates historical progress. For Kojève's Hegel, there must be bloody battles, wars, and revolutions, in which people risk their lives not just for animal satisfactions but for recognition. According to Kojève, these moments reveal the properly human and hence the properly historical. Eventually the slaves take over, but they remain in servitude in relation to their work. In other words, they become bourgeois. Real freedom comes only through universal recognition of all and each as citizens. This freedom would define the Endstate, the end of history, after which all previous developments would become comprehensible.

The transition from aristocratic Christian society to bourgeois society is accomplished in the French Revolution. Hegel is its philosopher. The transition from bourgeois liberal society to a socialist Endstate is the revolution that Kojève sees on the horizon in the 1930s and 1940s. It would probably not be too much to say that he saw himself as its philosopher. For Kojève's Hegel, the Old Regime died of internal causes, the symptoms of the disease being what we call the Enlightenment. The Revolution itself, however, provided a crucial historical lesson. The Reign of Terror revealed the dynamic of Absolute Freedom in which people were able to grasp the essential lesson that freedom was the power to negate and that absolute freedom led to death. Only after this confrontation with death could one realize that mutual and equal recognition for all was the only way out of the master-slave dialectic.

According to Kojève, the French Revolution destroyed the belief that our desires could be satisfied only in the hereafter. The Enlightenment provided the philosophical antecedents of the Revolution by undermining the legitimacy of Throne and Alter. In this dialectical schema, the self-consciousness promoted by the Enlightenment was a necessary condition of the Revolution. Not until Christianity and the tradition of Platonic other-worldliness were understood could they be negated. Thus revolution and philosophy were tied closely together by Kojève. To have progressed from one stage of history to the next, it was necessary to have self-consciousness of the earlier epoch; or, as Kojève put it, "it was necessary that at each dialectical turn there was a *Philosopher* ready to take consciousness of the newly constituted reality."[5] Without the stimulus to self-consciousness provided by philosophy, humans tend naturally toward stasis, to withdraw into what they are already sure of, and to reject even the possibility of the new. The self-consciousness provided through philosophy, Kojève emphasized, has been a necessary condition of historical progress, just as historical progress has nourished self-consciousness.

This connection between self-consciousness and philosophy shines a new light on Kojève's claim that the history of the world depends on how one reads Hegel. Hegel provided the philosophical complement to the Revolution by destroying the idea that truth had an extratemporal basis or legitimacy. History was the only reservoir from which one could draw meaning and direction, and self-consciousness enabled one to tap into this source. If History was the court of world judgment, there was no one to whom those who lost the bloody struggles for recognition could appeal. In the mid-1930s the importance of historical action probably seemed clear enough to a Russian emigré who had come to France from Germany. During and immediately after the struggle against Nazism and fascism, the whole of the past and future seemed to Kojève to hinge on this presumably final state in the master-slave dialectic.

Given Kojève's radical, even violent interpretation of the *Phenomenology*, it might be useful here to recall the more common criticisms of Hegel as a philosopher whose work tended toward a positivist legitimation of the status quo. Marx's own criticisms of Hegel's so-called idealism placed the philosopher in the camp of conservatism. Lenin's kind words about Hegel's *Logic* may have helped somewhat, but it was really the discovery of the philosopher's early texts in the beginning of the twentieth century that made the common criticisms seem inadequate and stimulated a revival of interest in Hegelian thinking about history. These texts drew attention away from the philosopher of the Logic and the System, and made people aware of the thinker who struggled to reconcile personal alienation, religious longing, and political hope. Surrealists, Marxists, and budding existentialists saw in Hegel's early writings elements that could help them work through some of their own attempts to link, respectively, the instincts with radical action, the personal with the political, and historicity with history.[6]

Even before he arrived in France, Kojève was concerned with making sense of the progress of human institutions and action without recourse to an atemporal criterion of judgment such as an unchanging idea of "nature" or God. He recognized the need for some transhistorical standard and argued that Hegel had identified this criterion as the end of history. This end was not—as it was for Kant—a horizon that retreated as one approached it but, rather, a realizable goal of human action. In other words, in the 1930s Kojève thought that Hegel's philosophy promoted the self-consciousness appropriate to the final stage of history, a stage that would be characterized by mutual and equal recognition and thus satisfaction of the fundamental human desire. It was not difficult during this period to find the enemies of equality, and so the battle lines for the final struggle for recognition were clear. Philosophy and revolution were to be linked in what would be the culmination of world history.

Perhaps in response to some criticisms of his views by Leo Strauss, however, and certainly in response to the increasingly congealed political situation of the early 1950s, Kojève abandoned his heroic Hegelianism.[7] He continued to believe that the culmination of world history would define the truth of all previous events, and he continued to write of Hegelian philosophy as providing the knowledge of this truth. Instead of situating this philosophy at the onset of the culmination, however, in his later work Kojève claimed that the end of history had already occurred. And if history had already ended, as Kojève wrote in the 1967 edition of his *Introduction à la lecture de Hegel,* this would mean the end of the human:

> If Man becomes an animal again, then his arts, his loves and his play must also become purely "natural" again. . . . Men would construct their edifices and works of art as birds build their nests and spiders spin their webs, would perform their musical concerts in the manner of frogs and cicadas, would play like young animals, and would indulge in love like adult beasts. But one cannot then say that all this "makes Man *happy.*" One would have to say that post-historical animals of the species *Homo sapiens* (which will live amidst abundance and complete security) will be *satisfied* [*content*] with their artistic, erotic and playful behavior, inasmuch as, by definition, they will be contented with it.[8]

Kojève went on to say that this era is the one we live in. The end of history has already arrived, and it appears as form without content, rituals without faith, and the absence of action, properly so-called. The final stage of world history and the end of philosophy that coincides with it make possible universal satisfaction, as they signal the death of all properly human Desire.

Thus revolution in Kojève's later work no longer brings about the triumphant ascension of humanity but, instead, signals for those who see that we live on the other side of it a final decadence in which humans are distinguished from other animals only by their snobbism. Kojève's early combination of Marx, Hegel, and Heidegger in the service of claiming the future of the world is thus incorporated into a Weberian perspective on the routinization of life: The closure of the end of history is an iron cage in which human animals can engage in a variety of activities without struggle because their essential desires have been satisfied. In this iron cage, the struggle for recognition is replaced by conspicuous and endless consumption; historical change is replaced by animalistic repetition.

I have argued elsewhere that the major question that arises in regard to Kojève's work by the 1950s is why it exists at all. What is the point of writing philosophy after the end of history? The philosopher himself tells us that he wrote to promote self-consciousness about our posthistorical condition. But within the Kojèvian framework, self-consciousness is tied to historical progress. Yet the self-consciousness that Kojève was promoting was the knowledge that further historical progress was impossible. I have argued that his effort to open the path of self-consciousness to an understanding of our contemporary (Hegelian) situation itself counts against the claim that this situation can lead nowhere. The effort to close the circle of Hegelian wisdom and to communicate that closure to others allows for an opening as wide, or as narrow, as the self-consciousness to which this effort is addressed. Thus the commitment to the possibilities of self-consciousness reveals a commitment to the possibilities of light that might yet emerge at the end of the posthistorical tunnel.[9]

Once it became clear that revolution was no longer immanent, the only political rhetoric possible for Kojève's Hegelianism was the rhetoric of irony. This Hegelian had nothing outside of history to which he could appeal to anchor his criticism of contemporary life, and he refused to project into the future a goal that we were supposedly working toward. Instead Kojève pointed out how nothing of historical significance had happened since Hegel's day, except perhaps in our becoming more and more like animals as we had less and less to do with history.

The irony of Kojève's late work results from his valorization of self-consciousness without the possibility of progress. In this regard, understanding the development of his work can help us to grasp a crucial facet of French thought and critical theory generally since World War II; that is, the ironic form of much contemporary cultural criticism stems from either its rejection of self-consciousness as a plausible goal for intellectual work or its refusal to connect self-consciousness with a vision of historical progress.

2

One of the master ironists of recent French thought was Michel Foucault. His irony can be located at many levels, but perhaps it is most clearly visible in his account of—and discounting of—historical progress. Take, for example, his history of madness. Where others saw increasingly rational and humane views of the insane developing with the decriminalization of insanity and the secularization of the ways in which we think about it, Foucault described how modern conceptualizations of mental illness functioned to legitimate normality at the expense of the integrity of the experience of madness. Similarly, he showed that the substitution of incarceration for the torture of criminals did not express an increasingly humane society but one that had integrated discipline and control throughout its political and social apparatuses. His final project on the history of sexuality poked through the rhetoric of liberation and raised questions about how talk about sex had acquired its own imperatives that had little to do with increasing freedom.

Foucault's studies are ironic because they show us that even the attempt to be free can lead to ever greater constraints. His genealogical investigations unmask a culture proud of its progress toward freedom and tolerance as really a world of increasing domination and repression. His writings lead him into a world of critical pessimism or, as I would now prefer to put it, into the ironist's cage.

When Max Weber described how the Protestant desire for material objects had passed from being a "light coat" to being an iron cage, he blamed the process on fate. Secularization had left us, he said, with specialists without spirit and sensualists without heart, a description not unlike the Kojèveian picture of the end of history. But whereas Kojève's account of the culmination of history in the snobbism of the Japanese or the emptiness of Russo-American materialism was sketched with ironic lines, Weber's picture was painted with somber, tragic hues. Weber's foreboding wonder about the possibilities of breaking out of his version of the end of history—routinization—through charismatic leadership, finds an echo in Heidegger's famous line that only a god could save us now. Heidegger's description of the history of Western metaphysics as a slippery slope on which we fell away from a memory of Being hooks in well with the Weberian description of the iron cage. For Heidegger, our use of technology was a tragic attempt to make the world a home for ourselves. It was tragic because every effort to free ourselves from forms of natural or cultural pain resulted in our falling farther and farther away from the possibilities of living out the "destiny of a genuine humanity." For Heidegger, even Nietzsche's ironic appreciation of this falling was yet another example of the tragic inability of Western thought to think itself out of its iron cage. Thus Heidegger made room for himself: We needed this sage of the Black Forest to hear the call of Being and hence open a clearing as an escape from the history that imprisoned us.

How did the iron cage of Weber and of Heidegger become the ironist's cage of Kojève, Foucault, and, as I suggest, many others? The first step was to break away from a crucial aspect of the Hegelian style, namely, the effort at philosophical one-upmanship. Hegel did not criticize the tradition by showing that his predecessors in philosophy and other domains of cultural production languished in error; instead he described how their work foreshadowed—with various degrees of primitiveness—the truth, by which he meant his own philosophy. In his later work, Kojève accepted Hegel while abandoning this feature of the Hegelian style. Kojève saw Hegel (and not himself) as the last philosopher: It was not possible to include *The Phenomenology of Spirit* in a yet more universal picture. In the tradition of one-upmanship, the philosopher shows us the light while telling a story about how his predecessors lived in the dark. Thus for Hegel, Kant had yet to discover the truth about the connection of history and philosophy, and for Heidegger, Nietzsche had yet to realize that simply reversing metaphysical propositions did not free one from the prison of metaphysics. In this tradition the newest philosopher exposes the limitations—the bars on the cage—of his or her predecessors. We are urged out of the cage by someone who can see in. However, in the ironic trashing of this tradition, all that a philosopher can offer is a description of the *inside* of the cage. For Kojève, Hegel's universal truth does not enable us to step into the light of a Heideggerian Being; it only shows us the details of our own situation, our own imprisonment behind the bars of a closed, because completed, history. Rather than providing a melodrama of the heavy burdens of our captivity as seen from the outside, ironist critics present a landscape of the possibilities absent for them as well as for us.

Foucault's work leads him into the ironist's cage, then, not only because of the ways in which he undermines the idea of progress but because of his insistence that all forms of knowing are bound by the discursive constraints of what he variously called an *epistēmē,* an *archive,* or what we might call a paradigm. This insistence locks him behind the bars of irony because of a combination of two factors: his recognition that his own approach is bound by the discursive constraints of the present *and* his desire to contribute through his work to destroying these constraints. The combination of these factors can also account for the vaguely apocalyptic tone taken in many of Foucault's works. The tone is apocalyptic because to destroy the discursive constraints would be to destroy the world as we can know it and, perhaps, to liberate all sorts of possibilities hidden in the present. The tone is vague because Foucault is in the discursive cage with the rest of us. From our side of the constraints nothing can be said about the world beyond the bars. Before he attempted to respond to criticisms by Nancy Fraser and Jürgen Habermas focusing on his failure to identify criteria for change, I described Foucault as "straddling the San Andreas fault of experience," emphasizing his hope to shake things up despite his inability to say anything about why one would have confidence in the quaking.[10] We can now think of Foucault, like Kojève after he had abandoned faith in a meaningful revolution to come, as hammering within and upon the ironist's cage.

The caged Foucault was most readily seen when he attempted to make connections between his genealogical writings and his political commitments. In a dialogue published in 1977 Marie Odile-Faye asked the genealogist if at some point we might pass beyond the stage of criticism to propose something. Foucault responded as follows: "My position is that it is not up to us to propose. As soon as one 'proposes'—one proposes a vocabulary, an ideology, which can only have effects of domination."[11] Knowing only the cage of constraint, the ironist can provide maps of the bars around us, but anything more than that might prove to be just another kind of confinement. We might ask: Why bother even preparing the maps? Why bother (recall the question to Kojève) writing philosophy after the end of history? Foucault does not have the courage of Kojève's late lack of conviction, and so his irony breaks down in a naive expression of faith: "It is simply in the struggle itself and through it that positive conditions emerge."[12] Foucault is hoping, I suppose, that we won't notice the glib optimism or the completely unclear use of the word *positive*.

Similarly, Richard Rorty recently called attention to the importance of irony in Derrida's writing, which becomes hyperbolical in his later work as he gives up any pretense of contributing to a systematic project and settles for a proliferation of allusion and a reconfiguration of memories. It is a mistake, Rorty persuasively argues, to think of Derrida as refuting some other philosophers or schools of thought or as creating a new method that can be taught to graduate students.[13] Derrida, at least in his more recent work, is ironic in regard to the possibilities of method, and his irony is expressed in the proliferation of the connections he makes among theorists, artists, novelists, and poets. These connections may work for readers in showing them shades of meaning previously obscure, but they are not to be built on—except, perhaps, ironically. If Heidegger reached beyond *poesis* for the unhappy destiny of attempting to become its theorist, Derrida simply allows the creative use of language to take over. For him theory can only exist in ironic tension with—and even as an example of—*poesis.*

But Derrida does not, of course, always write in the mode of irony, and I would like briefly to look at a recent passage on Heidegger, which, I think, illuminates his own response to the ironist's cage. The passage is from *De l'esprit: Heidegger et la question,* published in 1987. This text appears at an important conjuncture in the evolution of deconstruction and must be read not only in relation to other texts on Heidegger but in relation to Derrida's writings about Paul de Man. More generally, these texts appear at a moment of intense reflection on the political status of deconstruction. Questions about this status have always been raised, to be sure, but with the increasingly contested American appropriation of deconstruction, along with the controversies surrounding Paul de Man and, more important, Heidegger, these questions have taken on a new urgency. In *De l'esprit,* Derrida is considering how a value-laden notion of evolution informs parts of Heidegger's work:

> This humanist teleology, I do not intend to criticize it. It is more urgent, no doubt, to recall that, in spite of all the denigrations [dénégations] or all the avoidances that one would like, it remained (. . . and this has not changed completely today) the price to pay in the ethico-political denunciation of biologism, racism, naturalism, etc. If I analyze this "logic," the aporias or the limits . . . in which we see this humanist teleology encumbered it is more to exhibit than formalize the terrifying mechanisms of this program, all the double constraints which structure it.[14]

Derrida goes on to say that he knows not whether these constraints can be escaped nor whether the humanist teleological program can be transformed. He does insist that this program cannot simply be avoided but must be recognized in its subtle and cunning forms.

What does this passage on humanist teleology have to do with the iron-ist's cage? I read Derrida here as saying that despite the fact that we can see through the theoretical and practical weaknesses of humanist teleology (by which I suppose he principally means Marxist historicism), we must also recognize that ethical or political criticism of great historical dangers de-pends on this humanism. Rather than taking this recognition as an invitation to skepticism about the ethical or political realm—a skepticism that would guard its theoretical sophistication by paying the price of impotence and complicity—Derrida seems to see the role of deconstruction as being a witness to the dangers inherent in the use of humanism to combat specific historical threats. Here he avoids both the blind optimism that Foucault fell back on in saying that in struggle, good things happen and the hyper-bolic skepticism that would make deconstruction irrelevant to politics. The ironist can do no more than point out that if humanism is used to combat racism, the use itself becomes a danger for those who believe, let's say, in equality. If no position is privileged by being outside of our historical/linguistic cage, however, for Derrida this does not mean that all positions should be treated equally. Someone will still ask, of course, how the philosopher can establish the relative merits of positions without any privileged point of reference. A response, I suggest, cannot be given that will satisfy the exigencies of the interlocutor; only an ironic account of the question's own dream of escape from the cage can be offered.[15] In Der-rida's and Foucault's cultural criticism, the impossibility of escape is no longer a fact to be lamented or even a loss to be mourned; it is, rather, the condition of our discourse and our action. They have provided a sophisti-cated acknowledgment of the dangers in the conditions for speech and action, but while doing so, they pay much less attention to how we speak and act with one another despite (and through) our various forms of con-finement.

3

If Kojève, Foucault, and Derrida are all working within the ironist's cage, there is an important difference between the Hegelian and the post-structuralist use of irony. For the Hegelian, irony is meant to wake us from our dogmatic slumbers and to provoke self-consciousness. And self-consciousness is tied to action, which can be given meaning and direction. Neither Foucault nor Derrida gives a parallel function to self-consciousness.

Indeed, perhaps because of what has come to be called the "critique of the subject" and the "critique of totality," self-consciousness is not an important category for either writer. The result is that Foucault was incapable of connecting his commitment to certain forms of political struggle with his genealogical investigations, and Derrida's deconstruction has the curious result of being an appeal to prudence. In other words, Derrida is able to show how slippery and sometimes how dangerous any form of action or discourse can be. The form of the showing has tended to be outrageous or at least transgressive: Yet what can the lesson of this practice be if not "Be careful out there," or rather "in here." Neither Foucault nor Derrida can count on the cumulative effects of his work in leading toward specific kinds of action, since neither aims his work at a developing self-consciousness. The idea of a "developing self-consciousness" will stimulate, I know, knowing nostalgic nods or impulses to irony in theoretically sophisticated poststructuralist readers. However, a pragmatic appropriation of this idea or its translation into the notion of a contingent community or practical solidarity is necessary if cultural criticism is to move beyond irony.

Irony is the trope of sophistication in postmodern talk, and it has become a privileged mode. Under the guise of reflexivity, it can create (or be a recognition of) a comfortable (or painful) distance between the intellectual and the community of which he or she is a member. Of course a blanket condemnation of a rhetorical form is not helpful, and nostalgia for a theoretically totalizing approach to politics will not be the source for a useful way of thinking about cultural criticism and its addressee. But we would do well to recall that irony is not and cannot be justified by contemporary theory; it is a rhetorical stance that is chosen not on theoretical grounds but because of one's moral, political, and aesthetic commitments. One can point out the contingency of these commitments and even remark on their radical instability. But if doing so is not going to be merely an expression of the poverty of posthumanist discourse, this negative attention should be connected to a different set of commitments. In other words, although irony can be an effective style of delegitimation, even this sophisticated mode of discourse does not displace but only expresses moral, political, and aesthetic engagements, however weak they may be.

As Kojève's commitment to revolution dimmed, his irony became overwhelming. But his discourse was still pointed toward the creation of a consciousness that could initiate political action. In the ironist's cage that is part of Kojève's legacy, however, the target of the discourse of cultural criticism has become obscure. It is not irony itself (a form that makes possible important types of criticism, play, and tolerance) but its privileging that has become problematic. Kojève probably exaggerated in saying that the future of the world depended on how one interprets Hegelian texts today. But if cultural criticism no longer has an addressee, then nothing much at all will depend on it. Of course one can be ironic about *that*. To do so would be to accept the end of history and the impossibility of meaningful action not only as the condition of our discourse but as the only announcement that it can endlessly repeat.

NOTES

1. On the reception of Hegel in France from the nineteenth century through the mid-twentieth, see Irving Fetscher, "Hegel in Frankreich," *Antares* 3 (1953): 3–15; Jacques d'Hondt, *Hegel et l'hégélianisme* (Paris: Presses Universitaires de France, 1982); Lawrence Pitkethly, "Hegel in Modern France," Ph.D. diss., London School of Economics, 1975; Roberto Salvadori, *Hegel in Francia: Filosofia e politica nella cultura francese del novecento* (Bari:De Donato, 1974). On the contemporary importance of Hegel in France, see Jean-Michel Besnier, *Le politique de l'impossible* (Paris: Presses Universitaires de France, 1988); Judith Butler, *Subjects of Desire: Hegelian Reflections in Twentieth-Century France* (New York: Columbia University Press, 1987); and Michael S. Roth, *Knowing and History: Appropriations of Hegel in Twentieth-Century France* (Ithaca: Cornell University Press, 1988).

2. A list of those registered for the seminar can be found in Roth, *Knowing and History,* 225–27.

3. "Hegel, Marx et le christianisme," *Critique* 3–4 (1946): 366.

4. Roth, *Knowing and History,* chap. 6.

5. Alexandre Kojève, *Le concept, le temps et le discours* (Paris: Gallimard, 1990), 3–4.

6. On the changing reception of Hegel in France in the early twentieth century, see Roth, *Knowing and History,* 1–15.

7. See Roth, *Knowing and History,* chap. 5. The complete surviving correspondence between Leo Strauss and Alexandre Kojève can be found in the new edition of Leo Strauss, *On Tyranny,* ed. Victor Gourevitch and Michael S. Roth (New York: Free Press, 1991), 214–325.

8. *Introduction à la lecture de Hegel* (Paris: Gallimard, 1967), 436 n.

9. Roth, *Knowing and History,* 142–46.

10. Michael S. Roth, "Foucault's 'History of the Present,' " *History and Theory* 20, no. 1, (1981): 32–46. For a reading of Foucault's last volumes on the history of sexuality as a response to his critics, see Roth, *Knowing and History,* 216–21.

11. "Enfermement, psychiatrie, prison," *Change* 32–33 (1977): 76–110, translated in Michel Foucault, *Politics, Philosophy, Culture,* ed. Lawrence D. Kritzman (New York: Routledge, 1988), 197.

12. Ibid.

13. Richard Rorty, *Contingency, Irony and Solidarity* (New York: Cambridge University Press, 1989), 122–37. See chapter 6 in this collection.

14. Jacques Derrida, *De l'esprit: Heidegger et la question* (Galilée, 1987), 87.

15. This is, I have argued, Foucault's response to Habermas implicit in volumes 2 and 3 of the *History of Sexuality*. See Roth, *Knowing and History*, 216–21. On ethical or political uses of irony more generally, see, for example, Gary J. Handwek, *Irony and Ethic in Narrative: From Schlegel to Lacan* (New Haven: Yale University Press, 1985); John Evan Seery, *Political Returns: Irony in Politics and Theory from Plato to the Anti-Nuclear Movement* (Boulder: Westview, 1990); and Allan Wilde, *Horizons of Assent: Modernism, Post-Modernism, and the Ironic Imagination* (Baltimore: Johns Hopkins University Press, 1981).

• 9 •

The Nostalgic Nest at the End of History

The End of History and the Last Man provides an account of very recent events in the world that have made for "a remarkable consensus concerning the legitimacy of liberal democracy as a system of government." Thus Francis Fukuyama describes how contemporary political and economic developments make sense as the victory of liberal democracy while answering what he describes as "a very old question": "Whether, at the end of the twentieth century, it makes sense for us once again to speak of a coherent and directional History of mankind that will eventually lead the greater part of humanity to liberal democracy?" (xii).

Where is history leading? It is leading to us. And not only is it a good thing that people are becoming more like we are, Fukuyama writes, it is also rational. If a society has not yet arrived at a liberal democracy like that of the United States, it is on the road to it. There are two factors that make this itinerary the only true path: the first has to do with economics and science; the second has to do with "the struggle for recognition." Economics and science show us the way societies must mature in order to compete successfully in the world. The struggle for recognition (a social dynamic that Fukuyama understands by way of Hegel) shows us why a person ("man as man") is motivated to reach maturity.

Before detailing the interplay of these factors, Fukuyama describes modern pessimism about the possibilities for finding a single meaning and direction in history. The traumas of the two world wars and of Stalinism, the destruction of the environment caused by industrialization, and the threat of nuclear annihilation made it all but impossible to claim that historical progress existed on a universal level. Intellectual pessimism seemed appropriate to the Left and Right, based on the historical experience of the first half of the twentieth century. To dispel this focus on negativity, *The End of History* makes a distinction between *history* with a small "h" (events that occur over time) and *History* with a big "H" (the meaning of these events "understood as a single evolutionary process" [xii]). The events of the first half of our century belong to *history,* but the *Historical* experience of the second half of the century should dissolve intellectual pessimism because this period has revealed that the idea of historical progress is capable of explaining much of our history and destiny. "It is possible to speak of historical progress only if one knows where mankind is going" (7), Fukuyama writes. He knows.

Fukuyama knows where History is going because he is already at the destination, assured by Hegel (through his interpreter, Alexandre Kojève) that this present is the final one. In order to remake the Hegelian point profitably, Fukuyama argues that there is a uniform Mechanism that "dictates evolution in a single direction" (71). This Mechanism was provided by "the possibility of mastering nature opened up by modern natural science . . . [which] had to be invented at a certain point in history by certain Europeans" (72). Happily ignoring research in the history of science over the last twenty years (this being little history not relevant to Big History), Fukuyama concludes: "Discovery of the scientific method created a fundamental, non-cyclical division of historical time into periods before and after. And once discovered, the progressive and continuous unfolding of modern science has provided a directional Mechanism for explaining many aspects of subsequent historical development" (73).

The scientific method allowed those who adopted it to improve technology, industrialize, and compete successfully against those societies that failed to adopt the method. Liberal democracies, because of their openness to competition and the freedom of ideas, have a special affinity for the scientific method. Thus liberal democracies develop strong economies and armies, and they survive the struggles that comprise the evolution of world history.

What does Fukuyama mean by a "liberal democracy"? Although he does not make the connection, his "liberal democracy" is much like Karl Popper's "open society" (without any more enemies). Liberalism recognizes freedom from governmental control of person, property, religion, and of those matters that do not plainly affect the welfare of the entire community (43). Democracy is defined formally: a democratic society is one in which people have a set of rights, especially the right "to choose their own government through periodic, secret-ballot, multi-party elections, on the basis of universal and equal adult suffrage" (43). Fukuyama wants his list of liberal and democratic rights to fit the United States. Additional rights that might conflict with one another or with current U.S. practice are simply dismissed. "Formal democracy . . . provides real institutional safeguards against dictatorship, and is much more likely [than substantive democracy] to produce 'substantive' democracy in the end" (43). There is no discussion whatsoever of what "substantive democracy" might be. But remember, we are already at the end.

Those societies that can exploit the scientific method most fully will become stronger than those that do not exploit the scientific method. Eventually, in order to catch up with the major powers in the world, all societies will seek to take advantage of this source of Historical strength. Liberalism (which Fukuyama conflates with capitalism and the scientific method, seeing scientists as entrepreneurs of ideas) will reign in the end of days. And it will reign by providing the members of liberal society with enough toys to play with while providing states with the technological means to defend themselves.

Fukuyama scans the horizon for any possible competition for liberal democracy, but there are "no barbarians at the gates." Those countries that have not yet become rational liberal democracies but that still maintain themselves do so by the luck of having plenty of natural resources (such as oil) or the luck of not having any (their territories being so undesirable that they do not need to defend them) (76). Liberal democracy thrives on competition with nonliberal states. Liberalism wins the universal competition that is World History. But what happens when there are no ideologies left for liberalism to compete with? Fukuyama returns to this question in the last section of his book.

Fukuyama's "Mechanism" accounts for only one side of Universal History:

An economic account of history gets us to the gates of the Promised Land of liberal democracy, but it does not quite deliver us to the other side. . . . this process [of economic modernization] does not explain democracy itself, for if we look more deeply into the process, we find that democracy is almost never chosen for economic reasons. . . . There is no democracy without democrats, that is, without a specifically Democratic Man that desires and shapes democracy even as he is shaped by it. (134–35)

The account to lead us to the Promised Land can be developed by a return to Hegel, who for Fukuyama is not merely the philosopher of the strong state that many have taken him for but the philosopher who defended civil society (60–61). Fukuyama's Hegel is based on his reading of Alexandre Kojève, the provocative and brilliant interpreter of *The Phenomenology of Spirit,* who became known in the United States largely through Leo Strauss and his students. Kojève emphasized a key concept in Hegel and made it the basis of his interpretation of *The Phenomenology* and of human history: the desire for recognition. Kojève used the desire for recognition to define the human in contradistinction to the animal. Here he self-consciously departed from Hegel in order to develop a dualism that separated the historical from the natural. Human desire has as its object another desire and not another thing. Thus an animal desire draws one to the body of another, but a human desire draws one to the desire, the love, or—most generally for Kojève—the recognition that another can provide.[1] Fukuyama believes that the desire for recognition is somehow a noble desire, but for Kojève the distinction between "the animal" and "the human" is not merely an attempt to call "properly human" those desires that are directed at nonmaterial or "higher" things. Anything—no matter how vulgar—becomes desirable in human terms as soon as it is mediated by another's desire: I want that because she wants it. There is nothing particularly noble about this, according to Kojève.

In Kojève's account of Hegel, there is a crucial conflict between our human and our animal desires. The latter are always in the service of preserving the life of the individual, whereas the former are not necessarily attached to objects that contribute to his or her continued existence. The predominance of the human over the animal is the willingness to risk one's life for the sake of some form of recognition, to decide self-consciously that it is preferable to die than to live without the satisfaction that comes from this recognition. The will to risk one's life knowingly is *the* sign of a person's "humanness" for Kojève. Clearly animals other than humans are often in situations where their lives are at stake. Risk itself is not sufficient proof of humanness; the risk has to be in the service of a desire for another desire. Kojève concludes as follows:

> Therefore, to desire the Desire of another is in the final analysis to desire that the value that I am or that I "represent" be the value desired by the other. I want him to "recognize" my value as his value; to "recognize" me as an autonomous value. In other words, all human, anthropogenetic Desire—the Desire that generates Self-Consciousness, the human reality—is, finally, a function of the desire for "recognition." And the risk of life by which the human reality "comes to light" is a risk for the sake of such a Desire. Therefore, to speak of the "origin" of Self-Consciousness is necessarily to speak of a fight to the death for "recognition."
>
> Without this fight to the death for pure prestige, there would never have been human beings on the earth.[2]

This is the version of Hegel that attracts Fukuyama. After all, many find bloody battle and overcoming the fear of death much more exciting than the pursuit of happiness and the right to protect their property. Fukuyama lingers over the "victory of the master" as some sort of moral victory: the triumph of an "indifference to things of this world" (159). Fukuyama feels this moral dimension is missing in our conventional defenses of liberalism's legitimacy. It is as if he thought that if only Hobbes and Locke had considered more deeply the noble desire to own slaves, they would have been able to fill the vacuum at the heart of liberalism with some "positive goals"! (160)

Fukuyama's victorious master has triumphed over nature by risking his life. Kojève, on the other hand, emphasized that the victory of the master was only apparent. True, the slave works to produce what is desired by the master, but that is not what the master risked his life for. The work of the slave satisfies only the animal desires of the master. The recognition that the latter was willing to die for now comes *merely* from a slave, and hence it is not the recognition that will satisfy. The slave's "self" is not made of the same stuff as the master's, and therefore, from the master's perspective, the slave cannot really appreciate him. *Thus the hierarchy established by the struggle for recognition prohibits the satisfaction of properly human desire.* This is a Hegelian point that Fukuyama is aware of but does not pursue, since it is important for him to emphasize that hierarchy is "natural" in human affairs. Never mind that he will also emphasize the humanness of overcoming the merely natural; hierarchy is something in nature he does not want to see overcome. Whereas Fukuyama thinks the Hegelian account honors the master for being really human, Kojève describes the master's position as follows: "But the Master fights as a man (for recognition) and consumes as an animal (without having worked). Such is his inhumanity. Through this he remains a man-of-appetite [*homme de la Begierde*] (which he succeeds to satisfy). He cannot transcend this level because he is idle. He can *die* as a man, but he can only *live* as an animal."[3]

Fukuyama turns away from Kojève-Hegel to add more substance to the glorification of the master's "transcending nature." Plato's concept of *thymos* (spirit) is brought in to provide the "psychological seat of Hegel's desire for recognition." No matter if the *Republic's* discussion of *thymos* has to do with self-worth and does not imply the necessity of an other to recognize that worth. Plato is to be used, like Hegel, to show the superiority of liberal democracies and the capitalism that makes them stronger than communist societies. Fukuyama collapses distinctions between philosophers and among concepts in order to enlist the major thinkers in his effort to recall that communism humiliated people on a regular basis, eroding their self-worth, their dignity, and denying them authentic mutual recognition. And communist regimes could not even provide their subjects with the refrigerators, let alone the VCRs, that in the West helped people forget their regular humiliation and the erosion of their dignity. In passages that show that communism can still play a role in the self-congratulation of Americans even after the Evil Empire's collapse, Fukuyama ignores the moral compromises that have become part of the fabric of life in commercial republics less and less capable of maintaining their imperial power.

Fukuyama's major goal in discussing the desire for recognition and *thymos* is to show that the democratic person does not live by VCRs alone. For him there is something noble in the quest for a liberal society: the quest is not reducible to the pursuit of happiness and the protection of property. However, now that liberal democracies have been established and the struggles to actualize the liberal ideal are over (at least in regard to Big History), what will be the fate of this noble dimension of the liberal project? Here is where the voice of Nietzsche is useful to Fukuyama:

> Nietzsche's well-known doctrine of the "will-to-power" can be understood as the effort to reassert the primacy of *thymos* as against

desire and reason, and so undo the damage that modern liberalism had done to man's pride and self-assertiveness. His work is a celebration of Hegel's aristocratic master and his struggle to the death for pure prestige, and a thunderous condemnation of a modernity that had so fully accepted the morality of the slave that it was not even aware that such a choice had been made.   (189)

A *choice* made by modernity between slave morality and master morality? Even according to Fukuyama's own selective adoption of Kojève's Hegel, there is a *struggle* between competing moralities that results in historical change, not a choice between *Weltanschauungen*. Be that as it may. In Fukuyama's survey of the great thinkers, Nietzsche is not on the side of Hegel's master as a man looking for recognition in ways that are doomed to fail but on the side of a macho, risk-taking tough guy unconcerned for the views of others. Sometimes Fukuyama thinks of this as an unselfish position (for example, 214–15); he always considers it a moral position (such as on 301ff.). Plato, more amazingly still, is also drafted onto this all-star team, since he with his concept of *thymos* also thought about self-worth. Fukuyama makes little of Hegel's insistence that the master is always in the existential impasse of being dependent on his slaves for this consciousness of himself, and he ignores that Nietzsche's noble is indifferent to others in creating value. These contradictions are effaced so that World History can be described in a way that leaves open the possibility that even at the end of history, when risks no longer make a difference, there will be a place for risk taking. There is no place for difference at the end of history.

The point of putting Hegel, Plato, and Nietzsche in the same nest is to show how World History makes sense as the victory of liberalism but that this victory may not leave "man as man" satisfied. Will there be no arena in which people can still struggle for recognition? Without irony, Fukuyama highlights entrepreneurs as risk takers who may not risk their lives (which Kojève saw as essential) but do risk some of their money (or is it other people's money). He says nothing about slaves in this regard. If only Alcibiades had gone into business, he could have been a moral hero! (317). It is natural, says Fukuyama, that "man as man" will never be satisfied with equal recognition: some people will want to be seen as better than those that offer them mutual recognition. If the end of history is going to remain healthy for liberal states, they will have to find domesticated outlets for this desire for what we might call surplus recognition in economic activity, short military conflicts, or sports. In this way Fukuyama tries to "honor" a desire that, according to his own account, History has rendered obsolete and therefore irrational.

Fukuyama takes the idea of the end of history from Kojève's Hegel. He takes the idea of "the last man" from Nietzsche by way of Strauss (and some of his students). Strauss was Kojève's most serious interlocutor and his deepest critic.[4] The two knew each other in Berlin in the 1930s, and after leaving Germany they maintained a correspondence over forty years. Strauss rejected the idea of the end of history because it does not allow for the valuation of specific historical actions.[5] Recognition is not enough, Strauss told Kojève:

> The recognition for which great men of action strive, is admiration. *That* recognition is not necessarily satisfied by the End-State. The fact that great deeds are impossible in the End-State can lead precisely the best to a nihilistic denial of the End-State. . . .
>
> In any case, if not all human beings become wise, then it follows that for almost all human beings the end state is identical with the loss of their humanity . . . and they can therefore not be rationally satisfied with it. The basic difficulty also shows itself in this, that on the one hand the End-State is referred to as the State of warrior-workers (114, 146, 560f.), and on the other hand it is said that there are no more wars, and as little work as possible . . . since nature will have been definitively conquered. . . .
>
> If I had more time than I have, I could state more fully, and presumably more clearly, why I am not convinced that the End-State as you describe it, can be either the rational or the merely factual satisfaction of human beings. For the sake of simplicity I refer today to Nietzsche's "last men."[6]

Fukuyama retains the Kojèvian idea of the end of history while repeating, sometimes through references to Nietzsche, Strauss's objections, now no longer addressed to the *concept* of the "end of history" but redirected to our own historical situation.

The sources of Strauss's objections to Kojève are his rejection of historicism and his insistence that the conflict between philosophy and society is inevitable. There is no political solution to the contradictions of the human condition, and there is no satisfaction in the quest for wisdom: "philosophy as such is nothing but genuine awareness of the problems, i.e., of the fundamental and comprehensive problems."[7] Kojève rejected Strauss's "zetetic" or skeptical understanding of philosophy, for he saw the completion of philosophy through the end of history. The debate between Strauss and Kojève was fundamental and without reconciliation: each man saw himself as arguing for one of the basic alternatives in the history of philosophy. In an effort to quickly package contemporary events and complain about them too, *The End of History* obscures these alternatives.

The fantasy of the end of history allows one to imagine that the real and the ideal will coincide in the world. But what does one do *after* this coincidence has already been achieved?[8] This is Fukuyama's major question and principal worry: now that communism has been defeated and we all want to be (or will want to be) liberals, what will happen to our societies? From the high ground of vulgarized Hegelian historicism, there is little that we must do. The erosion of meaningful democratic political participation, the replacement of mutual recognition by socially sanctioned ethnic and racial strife, the difficulty of reconciling economic liberalism and democracy— none of these count as real historical problems or genuine contradictions. Instead, in a very fin-de-siècle spirit, Fukuyama asks how we will keep ourselves hard after getting what we wanted. That is why Nietzsche is attractive to him as a figure who refused satisfaction. But this is the Gordon Liddy image (the college freshman image) of Nietzsche: "To be true Nietzscheans we would have to harden ourselves in body and spirit. Nietzsche —whose fingers turned blue in winter because he refused to heat his room, and who in the years even before the onset of madness scarcely passed one day without crushing headaches—points to a way of life softened neither by comfort nor peace" (313). It is odd that writing in Washington, D.C., as Fukuyama does, he has to look all the way to Nietzsche for a way of life without comfort or peace. The ambivalent liberal in *The End of History* looks around and sees satisfaction, then worries, American-style, about the dangers of too much satisfaction.

When Kojève first developed his reading of Hegel on the end of history in the 1930s he did so in order to show that equality and mutual recognition were the outcome of historical struggle. When he first wrote of the realization of the realm of freedom, he was claiming only that this reality had been fully described (by Hegel) and the process of its realization mapped out (by Napoleon), not that the final liberation had already taken place. We could know the End of history, but—as Kojève wrote in 1946—the actualization of this End, the ultimate proof of our knowledge, still depended on our action: "In our day, as in the time of Marx, Hegelian philosophy is not a truth in the proper sense of the term: it is less the discursive revelation equivalent to reality than an idea or an ideal, i.e., a 'project' to be realized and therefore proved by action."[9] The interpretation of the Hegelian ideal thus had the status of political propaganda. Kojève in the 1930s and 1940s was a dramatic pragmatist who wanted his flamboyant interpretations to inspire action and to increase the capacity to understand it.

Kojève's early philosophy combined Marx, Hegel, and Heidegger in order to claim the future of the world as the ending of history. By the early 1950s Kojève abandoned this heroic Hegelianism. He now emphasized that the end of history had already arrived as form without content, rituals without faith, and the absence of action, properly so-called. The fantasy of the end of history becomes a nightmare as it is incorporated into a Weberian perspective on the routinization of life. By the early 1950s Kojève saw his work not as a form of propaganda aimed at stimulating a revolutionary self-consciousness but as a commentary on a history that had already run its course. This Hegelian had nothing outside of history to which he could appeal to anchor his criticism of contemporary life, and he refused to project into the future a goal that we were supposedly working toward. He also refused to make the nostalgic appeals to misty notions of master morality and toughness that The End of History depends on. Instead Kojève pointed out how nothing of historical significance had happened since Hegel's day, except perhaps in our becoming more like animals as we had less and less to do with history.

I have argued elsewhere that Kojève's works beginning in the 1950s become increasingly ironic as a result of this valorization of self-consciousness without the possibility of progress.[10] In abandoning dramatic pragmatism he entered the "ironist's cage." The ironist's cage is the condition of the sophisticated cultural critic who no longer has criteria of truth or strategies of legitimation, but who continues to produce criticism. Without belief in self-consciousness or progress, the point of much ironic postmodern social criticism ends up as little more than a parade of sophistication. Fukuyama's alternative to the ironist's cage is the nostalgic nest. In it we can feel proud of our achievements in the present and still glance back on the past from which we have emerged. In the nostalgic nest, Plato, Hegel, Kojève, and Nietzsche can be lumped together in a family romance to show that we were meant to win the struggles of world history, but also that we must be careful always to keep open the possibility for inequality and excellence (for example, capitalist entrepreneurship) in order to remain as worthy of our history as our forebears who made it for us. The nostalgic nest is the place to go to consider the Great Thinkers (all together) and to remind ourselves that the satisfactions of liberal capitalism are not the only things in this world (even if they are the most important). In the nostalgic nest all distinctions are elided. Perhaps this is what Kojève expected when he wrote that the end of history would be the end of philosophy, properly so-called. In the nostalgic nest we can play at master morality and risk with Hegel or watch our fingers go blue and have headaches with Nietzsche. For we know that even their ideas—so different from the ones that guide our daily lives—really lead to us. So, when we are done playing we will still be protected by guarantees of equality; we can turn the heat back on and take aspirins. In the mode of nostalgia, we can express our admiration for the days when men were masters and philosophers really suffered because they were so deep. But in the nostalgic nest we can retain our comfortable confidence that ours is the best of all possible worlds. This nostalgia makes *The End of History* less a serious criticism of the present than a temporary and sentimental withdrawal from it. Have your cake and complain about it too.

NOTES

1. Alexandre Kojève, *Introduction à la lecture de Hegel* [1947] (Paris: Gallimard, 1967), 13. Henceforth, *ILH*.

2. Ibid., 13. Translation, slightly modified, from *Introduction to the Reading of Hegel*, trans. James Nichols (New York: Basic Books, 1969), 7.

3. *ILH*, 55. Compare Fukuyama, 192–93.

4. See Michael S. Roth, *Knowing and History: Appropriations of Hegel in Twentieth-Century France* (Ithaca: Cornell University Press, 1988), 125–46; Victor Gourevitch, "Philosophy and Politics," *Review of Metaphysics* 22, nos. 1–2 (1968): 58–84, 281–328; Victor Gourevitch, "The Problem of Natural Right and the Fundamental Alternatives in *Natural Right and History,*" in *The Crisis of Liberal Democracy,* ed. K. Deutsch and W. Soffer (New York: SUNY Press 1987), 30–47; and Leo Strauss, *On Tyranny,* ed. V. Gourevitch and M. S. Roth (New York: Free Press 1991); and chapter 5 of this collection.

5. Strauss to Kojève in *On Tyranny,* 236–39.

6. Ibid., 238. Page numbers in quotation refer to *ILH*.

7. Ibid., 196.

8. For interesting reflections on this problem see Barry Cooper, *The End of History: An Essay on Modern Hegelianism* (Toronto: University of Toronto Press, 1984).

9. Kojève, "Hegel, Marx et le Christianisme," *Critique* 3–4 (1946): 365. See my *Knowing and History*, 118–19.

10. See my *Knowing and History*, 139–46; Michael S. Roth, "The Ironist's Cage," chapter 8 in this collection.

PART 3

Memory, Trauma, and Mourning

Tradition, Memory, and History: On Edward Shils and Yosef Yerushalmi

One of the common grounds of neoconservatism and an increasingly important current in leftist thought has been their shared doubts about the ideologies of progress and modernization. These doubts have recently taken the form of a defense of tradition against the total insemination of the spirit of capitalism. In the face of the insatiable lust of modernization, one turns not to the self-conscious, playful impotence of modernists and postmodernists but rather to the powerful "grip of the past" on communities and families. The forms in which the past is preserved over time are supposed to show us the sacred limits that bourgeois capitalism and state socialism are out to mystify with the opiate of development. If we only look back to the heart or haven of our modern, routinized world, so it is said, we might find that we already possess one of the key defenses against the inhumanity of progress. Beneath the appearance of incessant change should lie the roots of essential continuity, which nourish our ongoing beliefs and practices.

Both Edward Shils's *Tradition* and Yosef Yerushalmi's *Zakhor: Jewish History and Jewish Memory* attempt to understand the presence of the past in contemporary life.[1] Both are concerned with how we make meaning and direction out of our past, as well as with how our past infuses the present with an aura of signification. Both studies raise some central questions about the rule of modern historical consciousness in regard to tradition, and about the function of this consciousness in regard to the preservation and deepening of memory.

Shils's book is an effort to understand as well as to cultivate the well-springs of continuity that inform our daily lives. He begins by showing how "post-Enlightenment scholarship" has been "insensitive" to traditionality, and goes on to give a detailed account of how objects and practices endure and why traditions change over time. His goal is to show "what difference tradition makes in human life" and to argue that we must protect that difference from rationalization and routinization, the dark sides of historical progress.

The problem for Shils, however, is that rationalization and routinization are also traditions.[2] Both these networks of beliefs and practices thrive, though, by denying their own traditionality while destroying aspects of what Shils calls "substantive" traditions. Once Shils starts to discuss this competition of traditions, however, his criteria for evaluating what is preserved and destroyed over time become vague.[3] He fails to make clear why his favorite survivors from the past are more "deep" or "substantive" than others, and he is ready to dismiss in a cavalier fashion efforts to recover certain traditions that do not immediately excite his antisecular proclivities.[4]

The vagueness of Shils's criteria for evaluating traditions stems from his basic faith that the existence of something is evidence that that something was needed or necessary. For Shils, traditions exist because they serve human needs, and "the fact that a practice or belief has persisted for an extended period of time is an argument for its retention" (328). Of course the author probably does not want us to muster up feelings of sacred awe for some of the most brutal and oppressive of human practices simply because they may have been around for a long time. By failing, however, to give any content to his notion of "human needs," and by completely ignoring the question of whether they should all be treated equally, Shils would escape the problem of choosing among competing traditions. In fact he merely avoids the responsibility of justifying his own choices and evaluations.

The appeal of Shils's book evidently comes from his animosity toward the ideology of progress combined with his willingness to affirm an alternative to this ideology; that is, Shils does not merely criticize modernizers from a reactionary position vis-à-vis technological and social change. Rather, he spends most of his book on those forces—that can be described as popular—which act as inhibitors of these changes. Thus his work has connections with those branches of the social sciences that have focused on the vitality of popular culture, and which have stressed that this vitality has been one of the major forces of resistance to political centralization and the development of capitalism.

Shils's book evinces once again that the appeal by intellectuals to the virtuous forces of popular culture is at best politically ambiguous and can often be intellectually dubious. The discursive appeal to traditions must be made on the basis of a critical historical perspective and can never be made on the basis of tradition itself. In other words, unless one is participating *in* a tradition and developing its significance from the inside, one is left in a critical position vis-à-vis (often competing) traditions. The problem then becomes how to understand (dismiss, make propaganda for) a tradition or group of traditions in relation to others. This problem cannot be avoided by talking about tradition *as such,* as Shils unwittingly demonstrates in his marked—but unsupported—preference for some traditions over others.

Shils's functionalist presupposition leads him to say that "this book about tradition is evidence of the need for tradition" (vii). It seems instead that this book is evidence of the need for understanding the ways in which we choose from what is left to us from the past in order to give sense and direction to the present. One of the chief tasks of historical consciousness has been to discursively legitimate some of these choices, or at least to apprehend the ways in which people have tried to do so; that is, to tell a story in which these choices make sense, have meaning and direction. The call for piety that concludes *Tradition* is yet another technique for avoiding and obscuring this task.

The role of historical consciousness as a vehicle for the discursive legitimation of traditions has often led it into an antagonistic relation with the forces of traditionality. In *Zakhor,* Yerushalmi provocatively discusses this antagonism as one of the major themes of postbiblical Jewish history. Yerushalmi is painting with a large brush in this collection of his four 1980 Stroum Lectures at the University of Washington. He has much to say and little time in which to say it. But the nonspecialist in Jewish history benefits from this form, insofar as it allows the author to raise questions that are central both to the immediate concerns of the historiography of Judaism and to the wider problems involved in the connection between tradition and history.

Yerushalmi shows that in postbiblical Jewish society and culture, up until the nineteenth century, the writing of history had little or no importance, with the exception of the period just following the expulsion of the

Jews from Spain in 1492. This is not to say that the Jews were unconcerned with history; on the contrary, he shows that an intense attachment to the past was a crucial part of everyday life and regular ritual (including the law and celebrations). History, however, was not the "vessel" in which memory was contained. Or rather, the history that was crucial to Jewish life was fully articulated through halakhah (jurisprudence), philosophy, and Kabbalah. The only event that had to be added to that history was its final closing time: the coming of the Messiah. Historiography was unimportant as a way of making sense of the past because it was disconnected from the final redemption to come in the future.

The flowering of historiography in the sixteenth century is for Yerushalmi the exception that proves the rule. In this case the historians, like Azariah de'Rossi, broke little new ground in their methodologies and left a legacy that would be taken up by no one. When faced with the destruction of Europe's most powerful Jewish community, the historians' tools for making sense of suffering in the world seemed weak in comparison with the metahistorical cosmology offered by Lurianic Kabbalah.[5] In their attempt to make meaning out of memory, the historians were all but impotent to preserve a vision of a significant future connected to the horribly difficult present and the glorious past of biblical times. For the successful completion of this task, metahistorical myths (the themes of exile and redemption are most important for Yerushalmi) were much more powerful.

This distinction between metahistorical myth and historiography is of course too neat. All historical visions—even those that have the greatest scientific pretensions—have important metahistorical components.[6] That said, we can, and do, distinguish between historical and mystical visions, if only on the basis of the respective importance of immanence and transcendence to each of them.[7] In any case it is clear that Jews did distinguish between these two ways of making sense of the past, despite the fact that there may be no significant epistemological difference between them. Although Judaism can be regarded as an intensely historical religion (insofar as it places paramount importance on actions in this world), Yerushalmi shows that historiography played little or no role for Jews trying to make sense of their past after the biblical age and before the nineteenth century. Although he does not talk in any detail about the various mystical movements during this long period, it is clear that they had a much more important role in Jewish communities than did any school of historians.

As a historian, then, Yerushalmi uncovers the "at best . . . ancillary role" that historiography played among the Jews before the nineteenth century. In his final lecture he discusses the problems that arise with the growth of Jewish historiography during the last two hundred years; the ways in which history is used as ideology in the wake of emancipation. Emancipation brings with it a new kind of crisis for the Jews: not a crisis—for the moment—of physical survival, but a crisis of memory. Jewish historiography, then, begins at a time of communal disintegration and doubt: "The modern effort to reconstruct the Jewish past begins at a time that witnesses a sharp break in the continuity of Jewish living and hence also an ever-growing decay of Jewish group memory. In this sense, if for no other, history becomes what it had never been before—the faith of fallen Jews. For the first time history, not a sacred text, becomes the arbiter of Judaism. Virtually all 19th-century Jewish ideologies, from Reform to Zionism, would feel a need to appeal to history for validation. Predictably, 'history' yielded the most varied conclusions to the appellants" (86).

The appeal to history for validity has often been noticed as a sign of collective memory's loss of vitality and authority. The mania for commemorative practices in nineteenth-century Europe was not confined to the Jews, of course, and historians have shown how the invention of traditions often accompanied the most extreme stages of modernization.[8] More recently, the use of history writing to shore up the collective identities or memories of groups under enormous economic, social, and cultural pressure signals the fragility of their solidarity. The increased visibility of Afro-Centrism during a period of extraordinary disunity among African Americans and Africans is a case in point. When practices or sentiments that are supposed to "go without saying" are incessantly talked about, those practices and sentiments are in trouble.

Although the response of Jewish historiography to this crisis of memory has been and continues to be great, Yerushalmi is not sanguine about its results. The weakness of historiography as a guardian of memory is revealed by the rejection of all of diaspora history by important components of Israeli society, as well as by the turn to mysticism and simple forgetting by Jews everywhere. The appeal to history has evidently not provided a new faith; as Yerushalmi puts it, the historian has not healed "the wounds of memory," he is only the pathologist who explores them (94).

The phrase "wounds of memory," which Yerushalmi borrows from

Eugen Rosenstock-Huessy, recalls Hegel's discussion of the "wounds of Spirit"; wounds, it will be remembered that "heal and leave no scars behind."[9] For Hegel, the wounds left no scars because they were re-collected by the philosopher, and in this re-collection they were redeemed by their being understood as a part of the development of history as reason. Philosophy made painful memory into the triumph of Spirit, but since there were "no scars left behind," it may be more accurate to say that philosophy negated, even repressed, memory. Re-collection was an essential component of philosophy, but in the completion of history announced by philosophy, the meaning and direction of memory were left behind.

The juxtaposition of Hegel and Yerushalmi in this regard is instructive, insofar as the latter seems ready to acknowledge that the historian cannot replace the philosopher to heal the "wounds of memory." He points out that, "Jewish memory cannot be 'healed' unless the group itself finds healing, unless its wholeness is restored or rejuvenated" (94). Here he is in one sense close to the spirit of Hegel, who also knew that wholeness was not the product of philosophy but of action in the world that was made sense of by philosophy. The important difference between their two perspectives is that Yerushalmi does not see the possibility for a new wholeness in his own time, whereas Hegel was quite sure that *the* final wholeness had been achieved.

Of course few, if any, people look to historiography to create a new wholeness. Although many turn to their personal histories in order to "pull themselves together," professional historiography does not typically see itself in this therapeutic vein. Indeed so much of theoretically minded or self-conscious historiography finds its raison d'être in demystification or critical analysis that it seems fair to say that the writing of history—insofar as it has any practical effect at all—would inhibit the realization of any new form of wholeness, or at least would make it more difficult for us to take our present forms of life as constituting this wholeness.

Are we to conclude, then, that history has no role to play in sustaining the life of a community or nation? If so, it would seem that my earlier comments on Shils's avoidance of history were misguided; that is, I pointed out that Shils's discussion of tradition seemed to be informed by his own prejudices rather than by a sense of history. The implication of this was that an analysis of the role of tradition in modern life would benefit from a historical perspective that would enable us to evaluate the function and significance of a tradition over time. Without such a perspective we are unable to legitimate discursively our preferences or antipathies for particular practices and beliefs from the past; further, we might add now, we can be put at the mercy of those who would like to legitimate through other means particular practices and beliefs as traditional in order to benefit their own private interests.

Yerushalmi's discussion of the role of historiography in relation to Jewish memory reveals the darker side of our own call for a sense of history discursively to legitimate tradition(s). When a traditional way of life is in need of "discursive legitimation," it is no longer traditional in any simple sense of the word. If a tradition is a belief or practice that "goes without saying," then any attempt to justify it through speech or writing will change the very nature of the belief or practice. In other words, a sense of history becomes important only at the moment when group memory is no longer providing the continuity essential to community life. This would not be an occasion for regret or pessimism if historiography were able to compensate for the disintegration of communal memory. The "modern dilemma" that Yerushalmi ends with, however, is that modern historiography, by its very nature, is unable to fulfill that role. As he says: "Nothing has replaced the coherence and meaning with which a powerful messianic faith once imbued both Jewish past and future. Perhaps nothing else can. Indeed, there is a growing skepticism as to whether Jewish history can yield itself to any organizing principle that will command general assent" (95). Historiography will not provide this organizing principle, and it certainly will not develop for us any new traditions or resurrect in usable form any old ones. Does historical consciousness, then, offer us any protection from or critical understanding of the march of modernization?

It does offer this "protection" *through* a critical understanding; that is, in the modern world we have been confronted with an "organizing principle that commands general assent," and it is the ideology of progress and modernization. Historiography, which originally had a crucial role in formulating this ideology, now has assumed the important task of exposing its weaknesses and dangers. If for the Jews emancipation coincided with a general (but certainly not universal) disintegration of messianic faith, it also was paralleled by the increasingly important faith in personal and social progress in this world. This faith became an important "organizing principle" for individual, family, and community life. More generally, the idea of progress and development has become a central tradition with its own rituals and sacred beliefs.

To note this, of course, still leaves us with the problem discussed above: how do we choose between (or simply evaluate) competing forms of traditionality? It seems that what I have been calling the "historical consciousness" merely leaves us with this problem, rather than giving us a solution to it. No such solution, however, *could* be given because the problem is not one of consciousness. In other words, the "choice" between forms of traditionality is a problem of politics, or public life, and not a problem to be solved through discursive means. We may come to understand facets of traditionality through discussion and analysis, but prior to this discussion we participate in or reject traditions that we *must* confront in the present.

We can say, then, that historical consciousness is parasitic on tradition. The appeal to tradition without this critical consciousness is blind, but an appeal only to this consciousness is empty. Historiography, Yerushalmi teaches us, cannot create the bonds of community by reinvigorating memory, but it can help us conceive and care for the possibilities for "a time when men and women think differently than we, be it in the future or the past" (103). This ability is not a substitute for a messianic belief, nor is it the key for rebuilding a meaningful community life. It is, however, essential for us if we are to preserve a past and a future we can live with without having to flee from the present we must live in.

NOTES

1. Edward Shils, *Tradition* (Chicago: University of Chicago Press, 1981), and Yosef Hayim Yerushalmi, *Zakhor: Jewish History and Jewish Memory* (Seattle: University of Washington Press, 1982).

2. I have discussed this theme briefly in "Opening a Dialogue Between Cultural Conservatism and Modernism," *Democracy* 3, no. 4 (Fall 1984): 49–54.

3. Distinctions between substantive, deep, and derivative traditions, as well as between tradition and fashion, are made throughout the book and discussed explicitly on pages 21f., 221f., and 305.

4. The slur against women's studies and black studies is of particular interest insofar as both these disciplines are deeply concerned with cultivating tradition: "Such novelties as 'black studies,' 'women's studies' . . . have become relatively common in colleges and universities without a reputation for intellectual achievement to maintain, or they occur in those parts of superior universities which the more demanding parts of the university have never taken seriously" (183). Evidently, the traditions with which black studies and women's studies are concerned are not deep or substantive enough for Shils.

5. Yerushalmi does not mean to suggest that historiography and Lurianic Kabbalah were in conscious competition with each other, but that by juxtaposing these movements we can learn something about sixteenth-century Jewish mentality.

6. Hayden White's work has been important for showing the ways in which historiography depends on metahistorical structures. See his *Metahistory: The Historical Imagination in Nineteenth-Century Europe* (Baltimore: Johns Hopkins University Press, 1973). See chapter 7 in this collection.

7. See Scholem's distinction between the allegorical and the symbolic in *Major Trends in Jewish Mysticism* (New York: Schocken, 1954), 28ff.

8. In this regard see two fundamental collections: Eric Hobsbawm and Terence Ranger, eds., *The Invention of Tradition* (Cambridge: Cambridge University Press, 1983), and Pierre Nora, ed., *Les Lieux de memoire,* 3 vols. (Paris: Gallimard 1984–1992).

9. G. W. F. Hegel, *The Phenomenology of Mind,* trans. A. V. Miller (Oxford: Oxford University Press 1977), 407.

• 11 •

Freud's Use and Abuse of the Past

The recovery from loss is, in Emerson, as in Freud and in Wittgenstein, a finding of the world, a returning of it, to it. The price is necessarily to give something up, to let go of something, to suffer one's poverty.
—Stanley Cavell, "Finding as Founding"

Some impression of the event must have been left inside me. Where is it now?
—Freud to Wilhelm Fliess, October 15, 1897

I

Let us begin with two sentences from Freud. The first is from his early work with Josef Breuer, *Studies on Hysteria* (1895): "Hysteric patients suffer mainly from reminiscences." The second is from *Three Essays on the Theory of Sexuality* (1905): "The finding of an object is in fact a refinding of it." The difficulties in defining the psychoanalytic use of the past, and its relation to history, can be grasped through an examination of the tension between these two sentences. On the one hand memory can be the core of neurotic pain, and on the other hand pleasure is always sought along routes that carry us through our histories. From Freud's perspective, the past surges up in our memories as the stuff of both pathology and desire. We may abuse the past by turning it against our own lives, by using it as fuel for our suffering. Psychoanalysis would allow us to acknowledge, to claim, a past with which we can live, to grasp our desires in relation to our pasts. Or so I have argued in relation to the key concepts in Freud's oeuvre: psychoanalysis is a form of history.[1]

In *Studies on Hysteria* Breuer and Freud are committed to the view that the reminiscences that cause hysterical suffering are historical in the sense that they are linked to actual traumas in the patient's life. The affect associated with the past trauma cannot be acknowledged, and the amnesia that results means that the force of that affect becomes dammed up. "The injured person's reaction to the trauma only exercises a completely cathartic effect if it is an *adequate* reaction," they wrote.[2] The past that continues to wound is the past that originally found no outlet. Denied an "appropriate" response, the ghost of past experience continues to haunt the hysteric:

> The ideas which have become pathological have persisted with such freshness and affective strength because they have been denied the normal wearing-away process by means of abreaction and reproduction in states of uninhibited association.[3]

Through the uninhibited (free) association of the talking cure, the ghost is laid aside.

Studies on Hysteria belongs to the prehistory of psychoanalysis; that is, the analysis in these case studies was still greatly beholden to the seduction theory which Freud abandoned in 1897. This theory held that a neurotic had passively undergone a sexual experience with an adult, and that this experience became "reactivated" with the onset of puberty. The memory is then charged with libido and confined to the unconscious.[4] Until 1897 Freud was committed to the idea that the traumatic memory referred to a real passive experience that was later sexualized. In other words, he believed the memory that remained charged with affect contained "indications of reality."

As Freud began to emphasize the importance of the unconscious and of infantile sexuality, he abandoned the seduction theory in favor of a science of interpretation that made meaning out of memory in the service of the present.[5] But what of the notion that hysterics suffer from reminiscences? It is interesting that Freud holds to this notion, repeating it in his 1909 lectures at Clark University. The inability to cut oneself off from something in the past was for Freud an important sign of pathology. *"Our hysterical patients suffer from reminiscences,"* he repeated. "Their symptoms are residues and mnemic symbols of particular (traumatic) experiences."[6] Thus, although Freud would change many of his ideas during the course of his life, his fundamental interest in the ways the past can cause pain in the present was a stable component of his psychoanalysis. Why do some of us remain stuck in a way of being that is inappropriate to our present? Why do some of us not use the past in the service of life but instead turn it into a poison from which we persist in seeking nourishment?

In this same lecture at Clark, Freud illustrates neurotic reminiscence in the following way:

But what should we think of a Londoner who paused today in deep melancholy before the memorial of Queen Eleanor's funeral instead of going about his business in the hurry that modern working conditions demand or instead of feeling joy over the youthful queen of his own heart? Or again what should we think of a Londoner who shed tears before the Monument that commemorates the reduction of his beloved metropolis to ashes although it has long since risen again in far greater brilliance? Yet every single hysteric and neurotic behaves like these two unpractical Londoners. Not only do they remember painful experiences of the remote past, but they still cling to them emotionally; they cannot get free of the past and for its sake they neglect what is real and immediate.[7]

Here Freud points to the core of the psychoanalytic conception of neurosis: an unpractical bondage to the past. The emphasis on "practicality" was a deliberate attempt to play to the sympathies of his American auditors. Attention to real and immediate things is practical, and such attention may require the kind of freedom from the past that was at the heart of American culture (especially as seen by Europeans). Psychoanalysis, Freud wanted his New England auditors to know, was on the frontier of science aiming at freedom from the past.

Not all ties to the past are bondage, however; not all painful reminiscences are signs of neurosis. Immediately after this passage in his 1909 Clark Lectures, Freud mentions mourning as a normal fixation to the memory of a dead person. Unlike the example of his Londoners, Anna O.'s "traumas dated from the period when she was nursing her sick father and . . . her symptoms can only be regarded as mnemic signs of his illness and death. Thus they corresponded to a display of mourning," Freud continued, "and there is certainly nothing pathological in being fixated to the memory of a dead person so short a time after his decease; on the contrary, it is a normal emotional process."[8] Mourning is the process through which one disconnects from a painful loss in the recent past. Psychoanalysis is the process through which one disconnects from a painful desire in the distant past. But how are the two related?

2

Freud knew something about taking care of a sick parent, and his comments on Anna O.'s reaction to her father's death should be seen in light of his own experience as a son who witnessed his father's slow decline. In the summer of 1896 the extremely ill Jacob Freud was in the resort of Baden, just outside Vienna. His son feared to leave him for any length of time, knowing that the aged father was near the end. Freud announced the news to his friend Fliess on October 26, 1896: "Yesterday we buried the old man, who died during the night of October 23. He bore himself bravely to the end, just like the altogether unusual man he had been. . . . All of it happened in my critical period, and I am really quite down because of it."[9]

Freud was surprised by the depth of his reaction to his father's death. He was "prepared" for the demise of the elderly patriarch for months: "I don't begrudge him the well-earned rest, as he himself wishes it," Freud wrote.[10] Nevertheless,

> I find it so difficult to write just now that I have put off for a long time thanking you for the moving words in your letter. By one of those dark pathways behind the official consciousness the old man's death affected me deeply. . . . By the time he died, his life had long been over, but in my inner self the whole past has been reawakened by this event.
>
> I now feel quite uprooted.[11]

After having revealed his feelings and his lack of control over them to his good friend, Freud immediately tries to find something else to discuss. "Otherwise," he begins to try to change the subject (as if there were something else worthy of inclusion in the letter), and he does say something about his research, about his practice, about his desire to talk with Fliess. But he speaks only his own feeling of isolation, of aloneness, and of being misunderstood. His father is dead. At the end of the letter, he returns to the only subject there can be for him at that moment, an absent subject:

> I must tell you about a nice dream I had the night after the funeral. I found myself in a shop where there was a notice saying:
>
> YOU ARE REQUESTED
> TO CLOSE THE EYES.
>
> I recognized the place as the barbershop I visit every day. On the day of the funeral I was kept waiting and therefore arrived a little late at the house of mourning. At that time my family was displeased with me because I had arranged for the funeral to be quiet and simple,

which they later agreed was quite justified. They were also somewhat offended by my lateness. The sentence on the sign has a double
meaning: one should do one's duty to the dead (an apology as though
I had not done it and were in need of leniency), and the actual duty
itself. The dream thus stems from the inclination to self-reproach
that regularly sets in among the survivors.[12]

Freud reports the dream to Fliess on November 2, eight days after the
funeral. Freud is a latecomer, someone who gets stuck in one of his ritual
habits and fails to arrive on time. We can see here one of his obsessions
from this period of his life: that he had failed to *arrive,* that his professional
ambitions were coming to naught. This picture of himself is connected to
an episode in his childhood involving his father that was to become a
source for several dreams. Freud reports that as a child he had "disre-
garded the rules which modesty lays down and obeyed the calls of nature
in [his] parents' bedroom." His father spoke the foreboding words, "The
boy will come to nothing."[13] In 1896 these words find deep echoes in the
forty-year-old neurologist who feels at best ignored by the world, and at
worst persecuted as one who practices "gruesome, horrible, old wives' psychiatry."[14] Freud is responsible for the funeral arrangements; the final duty
to the old man is his. But he is late (again?); the family must close its eyes to
his performance, even as he manages to fulfill his obligations.

The same dream is reported in *The Interpretation of Dreams* as an example
of an either-or dilemma in interpretation. I quote the report in full in order
to show its differences from the earlier version:

> During the night before my father's funeral I had a dream of a
> printed notice, placard or poster—rather like the notices forbidding
> one to smoke in railway waiting rooms—on which appeared either
>   "You are requested to close the eyes"
>   or, "You are requested to close an eye."
> I usually write this in the form:
>   the
>   "You are requested to close   eye(s)."
>   an
> Each of these two versions had a meaning of its own and led in a
> different direction when the dream was interpreted. I had chosen

the simplest possible ritual for the funeral, for I knew my father's own views on such ceremonies. But some other members of the family were not sympathetic to such puritanical simplicity and thought we would be disgraced in the eyes of those who attended the funeral. Hence one of the versions: "You are requested to close an eye," i.e., to "wink at" or "overlook." Here it is particularly easy to see the meaning of the vagueness expressed by "either—or." The dreamwork failed to establish a unified wording for the dream-thoughts which could at the same time be ambiguous, and the two main lines of thought consequently began to diverge even in the manifest content of the dream.[15]

In this report the problem of being the latecomer drops out. It is perhaps for this reason that Freud now remembers having the dream *before* the funeral. He is anticipating the reaction of his family members, not provoking it by his failure to arrive (on time). And the dream is, as Freud now reports it, clearly expressing a wish: that his puritanical arrangements will be overlooked by those family members wanting to put on a show.

In his letter to Fliess the dream begins with a notice in the very familiar barber shop, and ends with the funeral. In *The Interpretation of Dreams* it begins and ends with the notice. We are no longer in a barber shop, however; we are in a place "like those railway waiting rooms." And the notice has the authority of a command: *Rauchen Verboten!* although it has the syntax of a request. Freud does not discuss this aspect of the dream; he stays at the level of "winking" and "overlooking." But what has *he* overlooked?

He has overlooked the filial piety expressed in his letter and in his dream as reported to Fliess. He has also closed an eye to the connection between that piety and the guilt of one who comes too late, of one who continues to live after the father. When first reporting the dream, Freud is expressing his pain, his isolation, and his frustration to his close friend. Despite these feelings, or perhaps because of them, he also recognizes the guilt of continuing to live (and to feel these things) after such an important loss. When Freud wrote his friend after the funeral, the past stirred within him, he was torn up by the roots. From whence did the new relationship to the past and to this dream emerge?

Freud began systematic self-analysis sometime in the late spring or early summer of 1897, that is, less than a year after the death of his father. The sustained self-analysis was not undertaken for theoretical purposes only; he was afflicted with neurotic conflicts resulting in painful symptoms. In the 1890s Freud suffered from important mood swings, migraines, anxiety attacks, and phobias.[16] Given the theory he was developing at the time, in order to alleviate these symptoms he had to discover their roots, their development, and hence their significance. But how much self-scrutiny is "appropriate," or "practical"? Feeling oneself "torn up by the roots" might be a normal facet of mourning, of disconnecting from the past that one feels stirring within. Why consider this in relation to other conflicts? How to know if intensive self-scrutiny is not merely a delay from real work, an obstacle sought out by perennial latecomers, or an addiction, like smoking, which can prove most intense just when it is forbidden?

The only way to answer these questions was to risk the analysis. There was no knowing before the work was through. Mourning became work for Freud, as his reactions to his father's death became the substance of his understanding of desire, guilt, and the use and abuse of the past generally. In a manuscript draft sent with a letter to Fliess on May 31, 1897 (a letter in which he describes, in an aside, a presentiment that he is about to discover the source of morality!), Freud writes as follows:

> Hostile impulses against parents (a wish that they should die) are also an integrating constituent of neuroses. . . . These impulses are repressed at periods when compassion for the parents is aroused—at times of their illness or death. On such occasions it is a manifestation of mourning to reproach oneself for their death (so-called melancholia) or to punish oneself in a hysterical fashion, through the medium of the idea of retribution, with the same states [of illness] that they have had. The identification which occurs here is, as can be seen, nothing other than a mode of thinking and does not make the search for the motive superfluous.[17]

The discovery of these "hostile impulses" helped Freud decide to give up his seduction theory. He announces this to Fliess in the fall of 1897, after an extended summer vacation. It was following the summer of 1896 that his father had fallen ill for the last time. Now, at the end of the traditional year-long mourning period for Jews, Freud unveils not only his refusal to believe that fathers, including his own, sexually molested their children *as a rule,* but also his exploration of sexual fantasies and desires that children develop about their parents. About a week before the first anniversary of his father's death, Freud announced to Fliess the "single idea of general value" that had occurred to him: "I have found, in my own case, too, [the phenomenon of] being in love with my mother and jealous of my father, and I now consider it a universal event in early childhood."[18]

The "motive" for the hostile impulses was now clear, even if it had been repressed in Freud's own period "in which compassion for the parents was aroused." This role of repression in disguising the expression of these impulses was also part of the unveiling. The master theory of seduction by fathers would not work. Fame, wealth, and travel would all have to wait now that the key to all of hysteria clearly would not fit.[19] Yet Freud did not feel shame, or depression at having to give up what he had seen as his great insight into psychopathology, but "more the feeling of a victory than a defeat."[20] The exploration of dreams had assumed crucial importance, and Freud remained confident that he was onto something. The dream book would make clear the shift away from an emphasis on a trauma's "adequate reaction," and to the psychoanalytic focus on desire as that which enables us to understand our connections with our past.

The Interpretation of Dreams is, as Freud himself noted in the preface to the 1908 edition of the book, a reaction to his father's death. He also noted that he only realized this once he had completed the book; that is, only once he had completed the work of mourning was he able to disclose to himself what would count as a reaction to "the most important event, the most poignant loss, of a man's life."[21] The book bore the marks of his process of disconnecting from the past, and of his reconnection to the present via an acknowledgment of the past. The discovery of Oedipal impulses and of the fundamental nature of ambivalence changed the way he viewed his own past, and the way he understood how we make meaning and direction from our histories or how we deny them. We are not only the victims of our pasts, nor are we simply their (guilty) survivors. We do not only undergo trauma, we are capable of making meaning and direction out of our past. As we acknowledge desires over time, we come to see how we make (and can remake) our histories; how we create the pain of guilt, and how we can work our way out from under it. An interpretation of the signs of the past still legible in the present helps us to achieve this. In its "final" form the "Close the Eyes" dream no longer expressed guilt, nor a fear of being (yet again) a latecomer. In closing the father's eyes Freud turned his own gaze inward. He (or was it only his train?) had arrived.

3

Anna O.'s persistent symptoms were "mnemic signs" of her father's illness and death. What made this display of mourning pathological was not the attachment to the dead man it expressed, but her inability to recognize the signs *as* part of her reaction to loss and her inability to feel she was the author of these signs. This was not the case with the unpractical Londoners: they knew very well that they were in mourning; indeed they worked to maintain their attachment to the past. Their sorrow had become their pleasure. For Freud, however, the work of mourning consisted in the progressive detachment from the past. He came to see *The Interpretation of Dreams* as just such a work. It helped him to close the eyes.

Freud discussed the connections between normal grief and neurosis in some of his earliest writings. In 1895 he describes melancholia as "consist[ing] in mourning over loss of libido."[22] We have seen how in his evaluation of his own feelings following the death of his father he came to examine the role of the repression of "hostile impulses" in grief and in neurosis. How does the process of mourning succeed in channeling these impulses into ways of loving and working without merely repressing them (and thus making them potentially pathogenic)? How to understand the psychological dynamics of mourning when it is unsuccessful, when it leads to a disabling self-punishment under the guise of grief and fidelity to the past?

These are some of the questions Freud had in mind when he wrote "Mourning and Melancholia." This is one of the surviving papers from his excursions into metapsychology in 1915 to 1917, a time in which much of psychoanalytic theory was in flux, and in which Freud was moving death and aggression to the center of his understanding of desire. Of course death and aggression were all around Freud and the rest of Europe at this time, and much of his writing in this period and through the publication of *Beyond the Pleasure Principle* (1920) should be understood in relation to the enormous destruction of the war, to Freud's fears about his own death and about the deaths of those close to him.[23]

The paper begins with the idea that just as dreams have aided in the understanding of narcissistic mental disorders, the "normal emotion of grief" and its expression in mourning might "throw some light on the nature of melancholia."[24] Melancholia has many of the same characteristics as grief, although it also involves a "loss of self-regard" or self-persecution not characteristic of the mourning process (244). Freud considers mourning to be work, a process through which the libido "shall be withdrawn from its attachments to this [the loved] object" (244). This withdrawal requires labor because "people never willingly abandon a libidinal position, not even, indeed, when a substitute is already beckoning to them" (244). The beloved is sought for but is no more; in response to the longing of the survivor, reality is firm, its orders are clear: Your desire is for nothing here, turn away. The work of mourning reveals a plethora of forms of this turning away; this too I must learn to live without . . . and this, and this. The confrontation with and turning away from absence in mourning is a repetitive task, and thus "the existence of the lost object is prolonged" (245).

> Each single one of the memories and expectations in which the libido is bound to the object is brought up and hypercathected, and detachment of the libido is accomplished in respect of it. Why this compromise by which the command of reality is carried out piecemeal should be so extraordinarily painful is not at all easy to explain in terms of economics. It is remarkable that this painful unpleasure is taken as a matter of course by us. The fact is, however, that when the work of mourning is completed the ego becomes free and uninhibited again. (245)

How is the work of melancholy different from mourning so described? Although there is a loss of some kind behind the grief, the loss is unconscious for the melancholic: he or she experiences the absence and the longing but is not aware of what has been lost. The mourner looks at the present world and sees it as "poor and empty," like an abandoned house; the melancholic tells us instead that he or she is empty, worthless, and, often, abandoned. Thus the mourner has lost something in the world; we might even say that the world has become lost to the person. She or he then gives up the world as it had been known, and gives it up piece by piece, slowly and painfully, until a connection with the world as it can be known is established as the period of mourning ends. The person in melancholy is lost to himself or herself; the work of melancholy is to preserve oneself *as* lost, as not worthy of being found. How does this happen?

The "key to the clinical picture" is that the self-degradation of melancholics, the reproaches that they aim at themselves, are those that were aimed at a loved object and shifted to the person's own ego (248). A mild or at least temporary state akin to this is found in the guilt feelings that often accompany mourning. Melancholics would like to rail against the world that deprives them of love; they would like to revolt against a present reality that "orders" them to give up hopes of satisfaction, of happiness. But through a process of identification with precisely those aspects of reality which deny satisfaction, which refuse to return love, the melancholic now finds the object of revolt within. The revolt against reality becomes a revolt against oneself in the "crushed state of melancholia" (248).

Freud had already confronted this revolt against oneself during his own period of grief following his father's death. In trying to understand the "obscure routes behind the official consciousness" through which this loss affected him, he was led to examine the "hostile impulses against parents (a wish that they should die)." As we saw above, in 1897 he wrote that "it is a manifestation of mourning to reproach oneself for their death . . . or to punish oneself in a hysterical fashion, through the medium of the idea of retribution, with the same states [of illness] that they have had." This is exactly the process of pathological identification that he details in "Mourning and Melancholia." "The shadow of the object fell on the ego," he wrote in 1917, with the result that in the now split ego one part persecuted the other. The lost object is "saved" through introjection; the past is retained but at great cost, because the past becomes that which enables the present to be seen as something that is never good enough, always missing that which is essential: "The complex of melancholia behaves like an open wound, drawing to itself cathectic energies . . . from all directions, and emptying the ego until it is totally impoverished" (253). The lost object-saved-within makes the external world seem like an empty place, even as it provides the satisfaction of always being superior to the present in which one is condemned to live. But essentially melancholics are always already latecomers, and they have an internal schedule according to which they can always condemn themselves.[25]

4

In 1973 Carl Schorske published an extremely influential article on Freud's *The Interpretation of Dreams*.[26] Schorske examined what he called "the counterpolitical ingredient in the origins of psychoanalysis."[27] Faced with the intractable Viennese establishment, Freud retreated from overt political activity into a world of subversive intellection. The famous epigraph to

The Interpretation of Dreams puts it this way: "If I cannot shake the higher powers, I will stir up the depths." Freud gave up on the dream of a political career, and through his psychoanalytic work made politics itself epiphenomenal. "Having exhumed his own political past through dream analysis, he had overcome it by identifying his political obligations and impulses with his father, explaining them away as attributes of his father's ghost."[28] This "explaining away" is Freud's letting go of his past and the public desires that had helped to define it. Psychoanalysis here is seen as part of a more general modernist retreat from history, as "Freud gave his fellow liberals an a-historical theory of man and society that could make bearable a political world spun out of orbit and beyond control."[29]

Psychoanalysis in this view is compensation for political impotence. In its displacement of more concrete political problems, the science of the depths is conformist in relation to the status quo. Moreover, there is a political wish at the beginnings of psychoanalysis, but that wish is given up in the face of reality. How to find this originating desire? Schorske employs the tools of psychoanalysis itself to find the wish concealed in Freud's own dreams. Nothing is lost to the unconscious, and the traces of political wishes remain in Freud's accounts of his own dreams. Even when one abandons a quest, the longing remains. But how does one give up on something? What is the process through which a person lets go of an ambition, a desire, a goal?

We are perhaps now in a better position to understand the centrality of these questions for Freud. Throughout his corpus, the process of mourning —its work—figures for him as an extraordinary, but not a morbid, means available to us of letting go of the past without denying it. Anna O.'s symptoms, the signs (for us, but not for her) of her father's death, were her way of retaining a past that was dead. The cost of this retention was self-persecution, conflict, and pain which became a misery that was its own reward. The Londoners who stopped each day before the monument were not only unpractical; from Freud's perspective in "Mourning and Melancholia" they were cultivating their pain as a vehicle for deprecating the present.

Is psychoanalysis itself, however, only an elaborate mnemic sign of the death of Freud's and his fellow liberals' political ambitions? Is the decision to ignore the "higher powers" in favor of the depths an extraordinary deprecation of the human and a failure to confront the loss of political, moral, and aesthetic values in modernity? How close are the dynamics of psycho-analysis and melancholia?

The relationship between melancholia and mourning is one of the cru-cial figures for Freud's thinking about the ways we can turn the past into fuel for our self-abuse, or use the past for our love and work. How to trans-form painful reminiscence into memory and desire that can be put in the service of the pursuit of satisfaction? In his own period of mourning for the death of his father he discovered how difficult it was even to tell the differ-ence between these two modes of relating to the past. This difficulty was the core of his self-analysis, which led him to an acknowledgment of the fundamental ambivalence—the contradiction of desires—in all impor-tant human relationships. This ambivalence, when unconscious, can lead to strategies of repetitive denial and self-denigration like those found in melancholia. Confined to those "obscure pathways behind the official con-sciousness," conflicts of desire that keep us lost to the world remain split off from us, and we remain alien to ourselves. When unveiled, the ambiva-lence does not disappear; it becomes that out of which we can make our histories so as to create the possibilities for change. Recognition of the ambivalence at the heart of Freud's relation to the "old man" was decisive for the creation of *The Interpretation of Dreams,* as he was able to acknowl-edge only retrospectively; that is, he turned the process of mourning and the work that came out of it (or was a large part of it) into a history—meaningful memory—with which he could live.

The possibility remains that "the history with which Freud could live" was a liberal lullaby meant to console those whose political dreams ended in disaster or desperation. But lullabies, like dreams, have more than one meaning, and they can, like history, be used or abused. Psychoanalytic ac-knowledging and freedom can help us apprehend the connections and conflicts between personal history and the demands of the groups to which we belong or that claim us. To grasp these connections and conflicts pro-vides only some preconditions for change for some people with particular resources; not more than that. But it can facilitate transforming melan-cholic abuse of the past, and thus of our present, into grief, and then into work and love. There is much to mourn, and psychoanalysis unveils the pain of a past unconsciously bound up in the present. Perhaps when the depths of this pain can be grasped and not merely suffered, we will not find it necessary to turn away from acknowledgment, negation, and freedom.

As Freud noted, the "Close the Eyes" dream had more than one meaning. In this dream that expressed his mourning and was used to overcome it, he closed his father's eyes, not his own. In so doing he began to make history, not only to retreat from it.

NOTES

1. Michael S. Roth, *Psycho-Analysis as History: Negation and Freedom in Freud* (Ithaca: Cornell University Press, 1987).

2. Sigmund Freud and Josef Breuer, *Studies on Hysteria*, in *The Standard Edition of the Complete Psychological Works of Sigmund Freud*, trans. and ed. James Strachey, 24 vols. (London: Hogarth Press, 1953–74), 2:8.

3. Ibid., 11. The passage appears in italics in the *Standard Edition*.

4. Ibid., 133–34, 173.

5. For a detailed account of Freud's complex motivations for abandoning the seduction theory see William McGrath, *Freud's Discovery of Psychoanalysis: The Politics of Hysteria* (Ithaca: Cornell University Press, 1986), chaps. 4–6.

6. *Five Lectures on Psycho-Analysis, Standard Edition*, 11:16.

7. Ibid., 16–17.

8. Ibid., 17. Freud had briefly discussed Anna O.'s case in this first lecture at Clark. See also *Studies on Hysteria, Standard Edition*, 2:21–47.

9. *The Complete Letters of Sigmund Freud to Wilhelm Fliess, 1887–1904*, trans. and ed. Jeffrey Moussaieff Masson (Cambridge, Mass.: Harvard University Press, 1985), 201. Originals are published in *Sigmund Freud Briefe an Wilhelm Fliess, 1887–1904: Ungekürzte Ausgabe*, ed. J. M. Masson (Frankfurt: S. Fischer Verlag, 1985).

10. Ibid., 195. See also Peter Gay, *Freud: A Life for Our Times* (New York: Norton, 1988), 88.

11. Masson, *Freud to Fliess*, 202. The last sentence in the original reads: "Ich habe nun ein recht entwurzeltes Gefühl."

12. Ibid., 202.

13. Freud, *The Interpretation of Dreams, Standard Edition*, 4:216.

14. These were, Freud reported to Fliess, "some of the things that were said" about his early "incursion" into psychiatry (Masson, *Freud to Fliess*, November 2, 1896, 202).

15. Freud, *Interpretation of Dreams*, 317–18.

16. The letters to Fliess are full of references to Freud's physical and mental problems. See also Max Schur, *Freud: Living and Dying* (New York: International Universities Press, 1972), 71–73, 97–110.

17. Freud, "Draft N," May 31, 1897; Masson, *Freud to Fliess*, 250.

18. Ibid., 272 (October 15, 1897).

19. Ibid., 265–66 (September 21, 1897).

20. Ibid.

21. Freud, *Interpretation of Dreams*, xxvi.

22. Masson, *Freud to Fliess*, 99. On the same page he writes the following: "The affect corresponding to melancholia is that of mourning or—that is, longing for something lost."

23. On Freud's suspicions about his own approaching death see Ernest Jones, *The Life and Work of Sigmund Freud* (New York: International Universities Press, 1955), 194; Schur, *Freud: Living and Dying,* 185–89, 231–33. These sources also discuss his anxiety about his two soldier sons. Both would survive the fighting, but his youngest daughter Sophie fell to influenza in January 1920. The death of her younger son, Heinele, in 1923 completely stunned Freud: "I am taking this loss so badly, I believe that I have never experienced anything harder" (see Gay, *Freud,* 421–22). On World War I see "Thoughts for the Time on War and Death" (1915), *Standard Edition,* 14:275–300, and *Introductory Lectures on Psycho-Analysis, Standard Edition,* 15:146. On the war and mourning see the brief "On Transience," *Standard Edition,* 15:305–7.

24. Freud, "Mourning and Melancholia," *Standard Edition,* 14:243. The page numbers of subsequent references to the essay will be given in parentheses in the text.

25. See Julia Kristeva, *Soleil Noir: Dépression et Mélancolie* (Paris: Gallimard, 1988), especially 13–41; and Eric L. Santner, *Stranded Objects: Mourning, Memory and Film in Postwar Germany* (Ithaca: Cornell University Press, 1990), especially 1–13.

26. The essay first appeared in the *American Historical Review* 78 (1973): 328–47. The page references in the notes refer to the republication in Carl E. Schorske, *Fin-de-siècle Vienna: Politics and Culture* (New York: Knopf, 1980), 181–207.

27. Ibid., 183.

28. Ibid., 202.

29. Ibid., 203.

• 12 •

You Must Remember This: History, Memory, and Trauma in *Hiroshima Mon Amour*

My interest in the ways film affects our understanding of the construction of a past has developed in two different but related ways. On the one hand I have been working for some time on questions in the philosophy of history, questions that ask not so much whether history is a science or an art as what *kind* of a science and what *kind* of an art the writing of history is. What do we mean when we say that we know something historically?[1] On the other hand, over the last several years I have been engaged in a study of how the criteria for the *normal* connection between present and past are established through a medical, literary, and philosophical exploration of memory disorders, especially in nineteenth-century France.[2] These areas of research have led me to examine how different cultures (and specific groups within a culture) treat the following questions: *What is the point of having a past, and why try to recollect it? What desires are satisfied by this recollection?* In thinking about these questions in cultural history and the theory of history, I became interested in how photography and film set up criteria for a normal memory, and also in how they explore what it means to have knowledge about the past. *What can film teach us about historical knowing? What can historical knowing teach us about film?* Different film genres have different modes of configuring these questions and thus of proposing answers to them. As I have explored some of these genres and the directors who work in them, the films of Alain Resnais have stood out as an extraordinarily rich body of reflection on the connections among history, memory, and trauma. Resnais's *Hiroshima Mon Amour* (1959), written by Marguerite Duras, is an important exploration of the possibility of living with the past and of living without it. In charting some of the vicissitudes of writing history as a problem of memory, *Hiroshima Mon Amour* forces the viewer to confront some of the crucial problems concerning the construction of a past with which one can live, especially in regard to our (limited) capacities for representing that past to another.

In the early 1950s Alain Resnais was asked to make a film to mark the tenth anniversary of the liberation of the concentration camps. The result was *Nuit et Bouillard,* a short film whose powerful images of mutilated bodies are juxtaposed with a text warning viewers of the omnipresent threat of the *mentalité concentrationaire. Night and Fog* remains one of the most startling, powerful films made about the Nazi period. When the charges of crimes against humanity were first dropped in the case of Paul Touvier, Minister of Culture Jack Lang asked French television channels to show *Night and Fog.* Its visual, musical, and verbal languages are aggressive in the extreme. There is no place to hide from its assault. In writing about *Night and Fog,* Robert Benayoun recalls Paul Strand's film *Heart of Spain,* in which we are shown a nurse dressing a horrible wound as the voice over tell us: "You must not look away."[3] The events that were obscured by the night and fog are to be revealed by the piercing gaze of the camera. We get to see the camps *en pleine lumiere* as a warning against the politics and culture that made them possible.

Resnais seems to think that he can burn his lesson into the minds of his viewers. He was asked to commemorate the liberation of the camps, but what would count as a "proper" memory of these places? What are the appropriate images with which to mark this past and our present relation to it? Resnais insisted that he work together on this project with a deportee, because he himself had no authority to speak on this subject. Thus the text is written by Jean Cayrol, who had been imprisoned at Oranienburg.[4] The authors of the film aim to make not a memorial to the dead but rather "a warning signal." Intolerance and racist militarism were no strangers to France in the mid-1950s, and Resnais means to remind his viewers about the dangers of the culture of totalitarianism.

The connection of horror and memory has recently been given much attention, and what I want to suggest here is that already in *Night and Fog* Resnais is problematizing that connection. He does so by acknowledging and exploring the impossibility of adequately representing the reality of the camps. And if the camps cannot be represented, what does that say about our capacity to remember them? How does memory depend on representation? I quote from the film's text:

> How to discover the reality of these camps, when it was despised by those who made them and eluded those who suffered here? These wooden blocks, these tiny beds where one slept three, these burrows where people hid, where they ate furtively and where even sleep was a threat? No description or shot can restore their true dimension, that of an uninterrupted fear. One would have to have the very mattresses where they slept, the blanket which was fought over. Only the husk and shade remain of this brick dormitory.

We are shown the "husk and shade," we are shown the skeletons, but we are ceaselessly reminded that we are seeing nothing of the reality of the camps. In the language that Duras would use so successfully in *Hiroshima Mon Amour:* You have seen nothing of the camps. And we are told this as we see on the screen pictures that are almost impossible to look at. For Resnais, the history that is written in *Night and Fog* does not capture the past, but it can provoke us into an awareness of present dangers.

Hiroshima Mon Amour begins where *Nuit et Bouillard* concludes. Resnais was asked to make a documentary about the dropping of the atomic bomb: Hiroshima twelve years later. He decided he could not do it and that in *Nuit et Bouillard* he had already explored why documentary knowledge was impossible. Film offered the temptation to make good on the Rankean claim to provide a representation of the past *as it really was,* and Resnais had already refused (and illuminated) that temptation. The film he would make in Hiroshima would explore what other kinds of connection to the past could be established and maintained in both the most extreme and the most ordinary conditions.

We begin in the banality of a hotel room, where two strangers have spent the night: this could be Paris, New York—almost anywhere. But this is Hiroshima, and there is a friction (Duras calls it a sacrilege) in having the banality of the affair rubbed up against this city whose name is equivalent to horror. The friction is intensified in the early part of the film as we see newsreel film footage of victims of the atomic blast as well as clips from Japanese films made about Hiroshima. She (viewers of the movie will recall the principal characters are not given personal names) claims to have seen Hiroshima, to have recollected its horror, while her lover repeats, "Tu n'as rien vu à Hiroshima" (You have seen nothing in Hiroshima). He is insisting that there is no way of seeing Hiroshima because there is no way of re-membering it adequately. He is correct, of course, but only in the superficial sense that has come to be all too familiar to us through contemporary theory; that is, he is correct in the adolescent way that the theorist is correct in saying that there is no interesting issue about history writing representing the past, because as a form of *writing* history is always already inadequate to history as experience or even as memory. He is a theorist of memory defending against someone who he thinks believes she has the presence of the past during her trip to Hiroshima. But he is completely wrong about her. She is no simple empiricist eager to get the past right. The woman who is with him knows that recollection is about the confrontation with absence and forgetting, and that is what she has seen in Hiroshima and everywhere else. She tells him, "So as in love this illusion exists, this illusion to be able never to forget, so too I have had the illusion facing Hiroshima that I would never forget."[5] He is worried about positivist illusions and eagerly wants to deconstruct them. She is already on a different level: seeking an *illusion* of the unforgettable, knowing full well that its illusory qualities are not the only secret to its power. As a sophisticated sufferer, he does not at first want to accept her claim to be "*douée de mémoire,*" gifted with memory, but he comes to realize that she understands that to be so gifted means to face up to the force of forgetting.

> ELLE: Like you, I too, tried to struggle with all my might against forgetting. Like you, I forgot. Like you, I desired to have an inconsolable memory, a memory of shadows and of stone. (32)

She remembers her forgetting but knows this is no reason to deny the "evident necessity of memory" (33). This makes all the difference.

In *Nuit et Bouillard* Resnais was struggling with commemorating a history that resisted representation, and he filmed the limits and the possibility of meaningful memory about this past. In *Hiroshima Mon Amour* he has the even more difficult task of projecting forgetting onto the screen—first, the forgetting of historical memory, the withdrawal of the destroyed Hiroshima from our consciousness; second, the forgetting of personal memory, the evaporation of the traumatic memory of love for the woman in the film; and third, the connection between forgetting and narration.

"Tu n'as rien vu à Hiroshima." She has not seen Hiroshima for the same simple reason that he could not have been there for the event. *There is no Hiroshima to see.* What we can see are its traces, in film, in flesh, in stories, and, most graphically, in the stones that have "photographed" the objects that were burned into them. But traces are dangerous for the Japanese man because they can give us the idea that we have seem something of the Hiroshima *of that day.* That day is beyond reach, and coming to Hiroshima a decade later brings us no closer to it.

Now this might seem like a rather trivial point to make. After all, *any* moment in the past is beyond reach, so why is Hiroshima of special significance in this regard? The significance stems from Hiroshima's status as trauma: as a trauma it draws one to it even as it demands acknowledgment that one can never comprehend what happened there. A trauma is a part of one's past that seems to demand inclusion in any narrative of the development of the present but that makes any narrative seem painfully inadequate. As B. A. van der Kolk and Onno van der Hart make clear, "Traumatic memories are the unassimilated scraps of overwhelming experiences, which need to be integrated with existing mental schemes, and be transformed into narrative language."[6] The "need" for integration stems from the claims that the traumatic past can still make on the person in the present: flashbacks, reenactments, severe anxiety. But there is also a *threat* of integration, stemming from the possibility that the horrific past may, after all, be distilled through "existing mental schemes." The successful integration would necessarily relativize this past in relation to the rest of one's life. The Japanese man discovers that his lover has grasped these lessons of trauma: she makes this clear in her description of her knowing of Hiroshima, and she suggests it in her remarks about her own past when they part on that first morning. He had asked her to describe her episode of madness: "Madness is like intelligence, you know. It can't be explained. Just like intelligence. It hits you; it fills you up, and then you understand it. But when it goes, you can no longer understand it at all" (58). Trauma too fills you up, but when it leaves there remain traces that resist any meaningful description. This is the aspect of latency that Cathy Caruth has emphasized as a part of all trauma: "The [traumatic] event is not assimilated or experienced fully at the time, but only belatedly, in its repeated *possession* of the one who experiences it. To be traumatized is precisely to be possessed by an image or an event."[7] One is "filled up" by the flashback or reenactment of the traumatic past, but one cannot explain or even describe this belated expe-

rience to oneself or another. When the past does not entirely possess the
traumatized person, it is inaccessible to him or her. This inaccessibility is
closely related to patterns of repetition that Sharon Willis sees at the core
of *Hiroshima.*[8] How to live with this past, which refuses to find a home in
the present?

He is an architect, and much of the film shows us the new Hiroshima. It
is not a pretty sight. Apart, perhaps, from his home, the new city vacillates
between being a tragic tourist spot and a mere denial of any past at all. We
can wince at the atomic gift shops and the Hotel New Hiroshima, but what
kind of buildings could possibly cover the scars of the past without being
scars themselves? What kind of life can be built from a past that refuses
translation or assimilation into the present but that will not be forgotten?

She has carried her own trauma in silence for twelve years. In the village
of Nevers, the young woman fell in love with a German soldier. The occu-
pier, the enemy, would be shot by snipers as the Germans fled the forces of
liberation. And the good citizens of Nevers who had abided this occupa-
tion can now turn on those who had forgotten who their enemies were.
She speaks to no one about this first, wartime love. It is only in Hiroshima,
when faced with this man in this context, that her story emerges. And it is
when she tells her story that she fully realizes that the past, this past, cannot be told because it cannot be maintained in recollection. She had experienced an absolute fidelity to the past just after the Liberation. This was
her madness, her refusal to live in the present. Then she became *raisonable;*
that is, she began to "emerge from her eternity." When she returned to the
world of time—to the world where her hair grew back, where the bells of
St. Etienne rang the hours, where the seasons changed, where her lover
was dead and she was not—then she accepted living with the memory of
her lover. And to live with the memory of something (to be "gifted with
memory") is to live with forgetting. But she keeps the process of forgetting
(and hence memory) at a distance by never bringing this past to mind—at
least, never forming it into words uttered to another. Until Hiroshima.

How does one live with forgetting? She has left her bitterness behind.
No madwoman here; she has a career, children, and lovers. She is, in her
own way, an architect, a builder. But perhaps the most important way in
which she lives with her forgetting is by not exposing it to anyone else. And
when he first asks about her wartime love in Nevers, she seems startled.
How can he be on to this?

ELLE: Why talk about him instead of others?

LUI: Why not?

ELLE: No. Why?

LUI: Because of Nevers, I can only begin to know you. And among the thou-
        sands and thousands of things in your life, I choose Nevers.

ELLE: Like anything else?

LUI: Yes.

        *Can one see that he is lying? Surely. She, she becomes almost violent, and trying to
        discover what she could say (slightly crazy moment).*

ELLE: No. It's not an accident. (*Some time passes.*) It's you who must tell me
        why.[9]

How can he be on to this? How can he be on to the importance of this past? After an afternoon in his house—which looks nothing like any of the other interiors we see in the film—they have sixteen hours before her plane leaves for Paris where no one knows the importance of Nevers. Time enough to recount the past? To make one's past count for another?

As he draws her story out in a Hiroshima bar, she feels herself losing not only the past but also the present; that is, she knows that even the most intense of experiences, even the traumas that seem to call out for recollection, will evaporate from one's consciousness once they are remembered in a form that can be shared, unlike the madness that invaded her as France was liberated, unlike the flashbacks of moments with her German lover that rush into her consciousness without warning. We are not stones that photograph the things burned into us. She faces this as she recounts her past, and he understands in knowing that her story is a tale of what he calls the "horror of forgetting."

But that is not the only horror here for her. Speaking about the trauma, which is the translation of memory into history, is a violation of the sacred relation to this past that she had maintained for a dozen years. She, of a *moralité douteuse,* had cultivated piety for the preservation of the trauma as something that could never be represented or shared. She had not "integrated" her life into a "coherent whole" because there were events in it that for her belonged apart; when they were lived they filled one up, but they were joined with nothing else. She was not the person who experienced these events; she was subject to them. That is why they could suddenly appear in flashbacks and other forms of possession. Psychiatrists would pretend to offer cures for this phenomenon:

In the case of complete recovery, the person does not suffer anymore from the reappearance of traumatic memories in the form of flashbacks, behavioral reenactments, etc. Instead the story can be told, the person can look back at what happened; he has given it a place in his life history, his autobiography, and thereby his whole personality. Many traumatized persons, however, experience long periods of time in which they live, as it were, in two different worlds: the realm of the trauma and the realm of their current, ordinary life.[10]

She lives in these two worlds and finds it enormously threatening to consider "integrating" them, assimilating that early wound to the rest. When she is finally able to speak her past, when she is able to turn the trauma into a narrative success, success, to quote an old song, is failure and failure is no success at all. To the extent that she is able to tell her story to him she robs it of its uniqueness; she destroys its aura.[11] We can see that for him to the extent that she is able to do this she gives their own connection a unique status; she creates a new aura. The successful narrative means that the trauma is not the trauma one thought it was. It can be told. It can then be lost. Narrative memory can be forgotten, unlike hallucinations and automatic memories, such as one finds in madness and in flashbacks where the past takes over, and the "pastness" of what one is conscious of evaporates.

> You were not completely dead.
> I told our story.
> I betrayed you tonight with this stranger.
> I told our story.
> It was, you see, tellable.
> I haven't rediscovered for fourteen years . . . the taste for an
>   impossible love.
> Since Nevers.
> Look how I forget you.
> —Look how I have forgotten you.
> Look at me.[12]

The scandal of *Hiroshima Mon Amour* is that nothing is unforgettable and that, on the level of both collective memory and personal memory, to make the past into a narrative is to confront the past with the forces of forgetting. If something is unforgettable, this is, paradoxically, because it could not be remembered or recounted.

Narrative memory integrates specific events into existing mental schemes. In so doing the specific events are decharged, rendered less potent as they assume a place *in relation* to other parts of the past. This is a process closely akin to what Stephen Heath describes as "narrativization" in film: "Narrativization is the mode . . . of a continuous memory, the spectator as though "remembered" in position, in subject unity, throughout the film."[13] "The final time of film as narrative," Heath writes, "is that of identity, centre perspective, oneness, the vision of the unified and unifying subject, the reflection of that."[14] Heath seems to be thinking of only the most simple of narratives, or simplifying all narratives for polemical purposes. Even one of the most conservative forms of narrative exposition, history writing, allows for more than "centre perspective" and "oneness." But there is an important point here about the integrative function of narrative. Historical writing, for example, necessarily configures the past—any past—into something that can be told. And this configuration has important consequences. As Carl E. Schorske has noted, historians "reconstitute the past by relativizing the particulars to the concepts and the concepts to the particulars, doing full justice to neither, yet binding them into an integrated life as an account under the ordinance of time."[15] Sometimes "doing full justice to neither" can be accepted as a fact of life (or at least of looking back at life). As Robert Dawidoff has noted, however, sometimes the capacity of history to integrate elements into a "meaningful whole" is enormously threatening to those who care for the particulars *as* particulars.[16] Claude Lanzmann raises a similar set of issues in regard to the representation of the Holocaust on film: "It is enough to formulate the question in the simplest terms, to ask: 'Why were the Jews killed?' The question immediately reveals its obscenity. There is really an absolute obscenity in the project of understanding. Not to understand was my iron law during all the years of the elaboration and the production of *Shoah*."[17] This obscenity of understanding is what Hans Kellner has called the beautification of the sublime. The explanatory or merely domesticating power of historical discourse "hides the 'primitive terror' behind us, obscuring the possibility that a 'non-sense' lurks behind all 'sense.'"[18] This primitive terror explodes in trauma and is at the heart of trauma's relation to historical representation. Insofar as that representation is tied to narrative, the very quality that makes an experience traumatic (that we cannot take it in through the mental schemes available to us) is lost in the telling. This "loss" can be felt as a cure and as a betrayal, a sacrilege.

In *Hiroshima Mon Amour* Resnais and Duras explore the question of how one can be fully alive under the burden of a history that is not a stranger to trauma but that has not fully domesticated the traumatic. Insofar as they provide an answer to this question, they suggest that it is through an acknowledgment of the powers of forgetting that one can live with (and with losing) the past. This means that history writing can be fully understood only when one grasps that the writing is a sign of the process of forgetting. Neither the accuracy of science nor the expressiveness of art will in any way allow one to escape losing the past, and the necessary "failure" to prevent this loss remains an important sign of our impoverishment.

From a perspective we might associate with Nietzsche and some of his contemporary postmodern fans, we might think that this is a false, perhaps even a sentimental problem. From this perspective there would be no *problem* of losing the past unless one started with some naive assumption that the past somehow needed to be retained for action (or inspiration) in the present. To be free from the burden of memory as history would not then be a problem of mourning but a promise of liberation. This perspective, coherent and powerful on many levels, is foreign to *Hiroshima Mon Amour* because the perspective denies the power and perhaps even the possibility of trauma. In other words, it denies that parts of one's past remain necessarily and effectively unassimilated to one's present; it denies that parts of the past resist representation and yet pressure our capacity to act in the present. It is within this resistance and pressure that *Hiroshima Mon Amour* takes place.

After wandering through the new Hiroshima, our characters take separate cabs to an all-night café in the city. The name of the bar is the *Casablanca,* hence the title of this essay. The reader will remember Bogart's character in *Casablanca* as a man with a past—a screamingly silent past until Elsa walks into his gin joint with Victor Laslow one fateful evening and orders two champagne cocktails. It is only then that Bogart's Rick can let the song be played: if she can take it, he can. "You must remember this . . ."

Now, I am aware that in many ways a comparison between these two films could turn out to be downright silly. But the wink to *Casablanca* that Resnais gives us near the end of his film should not be neglected. But not because one can imagine Emmanuelle Riva or Elji Okada saying, "We'll always have Hiroshima"; no, we are given the allusion to *Casablanca* precisely because they see that this powerful romantic claim is (perhaps like all powerful romantic claims) impossible. What these two lovers find themselves sharing is the acknowledgment of the powers of forgetting that their encounter has thrust upon them. Of course in the film we are shown only the confrontation with forgetting. What it might mean to share in this acknowledgment is left completely obscure or open.

What is the point of having a past, and why try to recollect it? It is crucial to see that *Hiroshima Mon Amour* asks precisely these fundamental questions in the philosophy of history on both a personal level and a collective one. It asks, in other words, why one retains a construction of the past in the face of the relentless pressure of temporal erasure. It acknowledges that this pressure "wins," that there is no way to defeat the power of forgetting. The most powerful form of forgetting is narrative memory itself, for it is narrative memory that assimilates (filters, reconfigures) the past into a form that can be "integrated" into the present. Narrative memory, which is at the core of historical representation both on paper and on film, *transforms* the past as a condition of retaining the past. *Hiroshima Mon Amour* examines the costs of this transformation, this forgetting, and of the remembering that tries to preserve identity, love, and fidelity with full self-consciousness of the inevitability of loss. The injunction from *Casablanca*'s theme melody, "As Time Goes By," still applies: "You must remember this." Only in the effort to remember can one acknowledge the losses in one's personal and political life. I have claimed in much of my other work, and can only suggest here, that this acknowledgment of the past in the present is a necessary ingredient of modern historical consciousness and hence of modern freedom. *Hiroshima Mon Amour* shows us that the acknowledgment of trauma and forgetting is also a condition of piety, of the caring attention one can provide to parts of one's past. Whether history is written for accuracy or for expressivity, it is always written against forgetting and perhaps ultimately for either freedom or piety. *Hiroshima Mon Amour* is *douée de mémoire* because it is a film that remembers forgetting.

NOTES

1. See, for example, the other chapters in this collection. An earlier version of this paper was written for a session of the 1991 Twentieth-Century Literature Association's annual meeting entitled "The Writing of History: Science or Art."

2. Parts of this project have been published as the following: "Remembering Forgetting: Maladies de la Mémoire in Nineteenth-Century France," *Representations* 26 (1989): 49–68; "Dying of the Past: Medical Studies of Nostalgia in Nineteenth-Century France,"

History and Memory 3, no. 1 (1991): 5–29; and "The Time of Nostalgia," *Time and Society* 1, no. 1 (1992): 271–86.

3. Robert Benayoun, *Alain Resnais, arpenteur de l'imaginaire: De Hiroshima à Mélo* (Paris: Stock, 1980), 52.

4. Ibid.

5. Marguerite Duras, *Hiroshima Mon Amour* (Paris: Gallimard, 1960), 28. Unless otherwise indicated, translations are my own. Henceforth, references to the screenplay will be given in the text.

De même que dans l'amour cette illusion existe, cette illusion de pouvoir ne jamais oublier, de même j'ai eu l'illusion devant Hiroshima que jamais je n'oublierai.

6. B. A. van der Kolk and Onno van der Hart, "The Intrusive Past: The Flexibility of Memory and the Engraving of Trauma," *American Imago* 48, no. 4 (1991): 447.

7. Cathy Caruth, "Introduction," *American Imago* 48, no. 1 (1991): 3.

8. Sharon Willis, *Marguerite Duras: Writing on the Body* (Urbana: University of Illinois Press, 1987), 33–62, 24. Willis's interesting reading of the screenplay depends heavily on Lacan's notion that the "real appears under the form of trauma" (39). Although such a notion has the virtue of dramatizing everything one concentrates on as *always already traumatic,* it makes distinguishing trauma from other forms of experience (or from experience, properly so-called) impossible. Since *Hiroshima Mon Amour* is crucially concerned with the connections between trauma and experience and their connections with memory and forgetting, Lacan's formulation is particularly unfortunate. If the real is always already traumatic, one cannot question how particular traumas exist in painful tension with other elements of one's reality or memory of the real.

9. ELLE: Pourquoi parler de lui plutôt que d'autres?

    LUI: Pourquoi pas?

    ELLE: Non. Pourquoi?

    LUI: A cause de Nevers, je peux seulement commencer à te connaître. Et, entre les milliers et les milliers de choses de ta vie, je choisis Nevers.

    ELLE: Comme autre chose?

    LUI: Oui.

    Est-ce qu'on voit qu'il ment? On s'en doute. Elle, elle devient presque violente, et, cherchant elle-même ce qu'elle pourrait dire (moment un peu fou).

    ELLE: Non. Ce n'est pas un hasard. (*Un temps.*) C'est toi qui dois me dire pourquoi. (80–81)

10. van der Kolk and van der Hart, "The Intrusive Past," 448. On the "cure" produced through mourning (but not available in Duras) see Carol Hofmann, *Forgetting and Marguerite Duras* (Nitwot: University Press of Colorado, 1991), 86–100.

11. In this regard see Sanford Scribner Ames, "Edging the Shadow: Duras from Hiroshima to Beaubourg," in *Remains to Be Seen: Essays on Marguerite Duras,* ed. Sanford Scribner Ames (New York: Peter Lang, 1988), 17.

12. Tu n'étais pas tout à fait mort.

    J'ai raconté notre histoire.

Je t'ai trompé ce soir avec cet inconnu.

J'ai raconté notre histoire.

Elle était, vois-tu, racontable.

Quatorze ans que je n'avais pas retrouvé . . . le goût d'un amour impossible.

Depuis Nevers.

Regarde comme je t'oublie . . .

—Regarde comme je t'ai oublié.

Regarde-moi.

13. Stephen Heath, *Questions of Cinema* (Bloomington: Indiana University Press, 1981), 123.

14. Ibid., 122.

15. Carl E. Schorske, "History and the Study of Culture," in *History and . . . : Histories Within the Human Sciences,* ed. Ralph Cohen and Michael S. Roth (Charlottesville: University of Virginia Press, 1995), 383–84.

16. Robert Dawidoff, "History . . . but," ibid., 370–81.

17. Claude Lanzmann, "Hier ist kein Warum," in *Au sujet de Shoah: le film de Claude Lanzmann* (Paris: Belin 1990), 279.

18. Hans Kellner, "Beautifying the Nightmare: The Aesthetics of Post-Modern History," *Strategies* 4, no. 5 (1991): 292–93.

• 13 •

Shoah as Shivah

I had no concept; I had obsessions, which is different . . .

—Claude Lanzmann

The room was not a holy place, no Torah, no prayer books, no candles. We may have called it an auditorium, but it resembled a basement playroom, or a place where socials—not quite dances—could take place when the school hours were finished. There may have been an American flag in one corner, an Israeli flag in the other; but perhaps I am condensing rooms here to lend the scene of this memory more sociological specificity than it had, as a room, at the time. Religious school on suburban Long Island. Reform. Assimilated. I now know how hard it is for communities to perpetuate a sense of their collective identities without rituals of some kind, without a dogma that goes without saying. Then, I just liked going to Temple for religious school. At age sixteen it had become a place to see other Jews, friends with whom I felt something in common. There were very few Jews in my large high school, and at Temple there was some undefined sense of commonality. Where did this commonality come from? Was it simply the case that I knew my parents had *only* Jewish friends, and so I adopted their feelings of connection ("we are more *comfortable* with Jews, that's all") despite my protests about them? Or was there something else that not only set me and the kids at this school apart but also bound us together? (I knew I was set apart; my Gentile friends gently—and not so gently—and frequently reminded me.) We had all by this time completed the rudimentary education that allowed us to perform the bar and bat mitzvah rituals. We had that much. But what connected us with one another? What made us Jews? Why, at least for me at this time, did being a Jew have to do with being connected with (tied to?) other Jews?

The room was not a holy place, no Torah, no prayer books, no candles.

We gathered there sometimes to sing, to hear talks about the attractions of Israel, or about the dangers of the conspiratorial Jews-for-Jesus, or simply to "get together." That night there would be a film. I remember no other specific occasion of our gathering in this room; indeed I have no other memory of religious school as powerful as my memory of this film. I imagine that we sat talking, flirting, fooling around just before the projector began to flash. But then I remember (that's right, I don't imagine, I remember) the tears of rage, of sadness, of impotent anger, that burned my eyes in that darkness. What to do with this film?

Alain Resnais's *Night and Fog* remained locked in my memory as a fixed point of Jewish consciousness, of consciousness of what it meant for me to be Jewish. The mountains of eyeglasses, of shoes, of hair; these were Jewish glasses (they were mine), these were Jewish shoes (they were mine), this was Jewish hair (it was mine). *That's* what it meant to be a Jew—to have some connection to the people (were they still people?) whose skeletons were being shoveled into pits; whose empty eyes stared out from behind the barbed-wire fences. An adolescent response, to be sure; an identification that was totally "unearned." And yes, I know there was surely an ideological function to this identification. I was being shown that I belonged to the Jewish people, and the Jewish people could be constituted by its enemies (at any time) and annihilated. One does not have to be Sartre to see that. The moral was clear. Vigilance! Never Again! Assimilation was not protection. Look at the screen! What made us, in this banal room, so like any other social hall, Jews? We could be *them*. Look at the screen! Now, when I look at this film on the screen, when I discuss it with my students, I also screen this memory of that room in the basement of the synagogue. But what does this memory screen? Look at the screen.

Although Alain Resnais's montage and rhetoric does provoke fear, *Night and Fog* concludes with the impossibility of a history adequate to these places and events of the horrific past. Even while admitting the impossibility of an adequate representation of these events, Resnais suggests that a sense of the past may still be necessary for an effective politics in the present. When work began on *Night and Fog*, the cold war dominated the international scene, and French intellectuals felt trapped between the sparring superpowers. The threat of massive confrontation was real, and politics offered little to be hopeful about. France was in the midst of the violent struggle of decolonization. What had changed since the Second World War? Had the world learned anything from this experience? How *could* one learn from it, if this past experience could not be represented?

But I cared nothing about the problems of representation, nor even about French decolonization when I first saw this film. These thoughts came much later, when I tried to understand (publicly) Resnais's achievement, and when I tried to come to terms (privately) with my memory of the film. I recall the film as imposing my Jewishness on me. "So, this is what it means to be a Jew," I thought, "and yes, this is what I am." Jews are those who must remember these events. Jews are those who must carry this loss with them, to abide this loss. This is not quite an identification with the victims. No, it even prohibits such an identification. The burden of living with this loss, of bearing it but not suffering it, was the task I took from *Night and Fog,* and it is a task I have been trying to acknowledge and understand ever since.

Until very recently there seemed to me nothing particularly Jewish about this task; or rather, I had not yet come to think about it in relation to my being a Jew. As my intellectual interests began to form, they centered on problems that were shared by philosophy, psychology, and history. These problems all concerned the status of the abnormal, and the ways in which one's past could make one sick or could provide one with the capacities for change. My first book (which I began as my senior thesis project in college), *Psycho-Analysis as History: Negation and Freedom in Freud,* is an attempt to read Freud's work as a theory of history that aims at freedom through a self-consciousness of the presentness of the past. In retrospect I can see that I had two agendas in undertaking this study. The first was clear and somewhat familiar: to show that Freud's work was compatible with radical politics—that it led not only to accommodation but to a self-consciousness that could initiate fundamental change. The second was to insist that radical change carried the past along with it. Freedom could be found only in acknowledging the scars of one's history, not in escaping from it. In Freud I had found (and constructed) a thinker who rejected reconciliation, redemption, and forgiveness: "the dialectic [in psycho-analysis] is not resolved; knowing is not resolution.[1] The thinker I'd found (and constructed) allowed me to retain a hope in and commitment to change without having to abandon the effort to dwell with loss, to sustain the memory of loss. *Jews are those who must remember these events. Jews are those who must carry this loss with them, to abide it.* The Freud I found (and constructed) transformed living with loss into "creating a past with which one could live":

> The reading of Freud presented here forecloses any escape from our histories and our desires, and instead aims to make a clearing in which the acknowledging and creation of a meaningful past will enable us to find the effects of our freedom in the present.[2]

Hegel was the philosopher I set off against Freud. Hegel, who wrote "the wounds of Spirit heal, and leave no scars behind," insisted that some things were just too painful to be preserved, worked through, negated. The great miracle of Spirit (a miracle that could be apprehended by the dialectical philosopher, who in all other respects insisted on the presentness of the past) was the "reconciling affirmation" that redeemed the past—the appearance of God on earth, the disappearance of senseless suffering from consciousness. Those things that were just too traumatic to be integrated into a coherent whole could be let go without trace, without scars. The Hegel of increasingly unfashionable totality, the philosopher of hyper-narrative coherence (which for me meant living with loss, living with what Hegel called the pain of the negative), was the other thinker who most attracted me. The philosopher's description of the disappearance of wounds was for me the disappearance of loss—a failure of nerve, a giving in to (Christian) redemption. Freud corrected this. He made his territory the scars that did not heal; only by dwelling within this territory could real change occur. Or so I argued. And it is an argument I would return to at length in my next book, *Knowing and History: Appropriations of Hegel in Twentieth-Century France.*

Why was this landscape so important to me? It was, I think, the same place where *Night and Fog* led me, a place where redemption seemed obscene, but where authentic representation was impossible. Freud called this place the unconscious, and although he usually thought of it in individual terms, one can also consider it on a historical level. The unconscious does not disappear through Enlightenment or revelation. Psychoanalysis aims only at transforming misery into unhappiness, and makes no claim that the interpretations offered are authentic representations of what really occurred in the past. Instead Freud insisted on the importance of acknowledging ineradicable ambivalence, and creating possibilities for change out of the meanings one finds in the past in relation to one's desires in the present. This was a Freud who thought through the dialectics of fundamental change without leaving the past behind:

> Negation through acknowledgment and action is not an escape from the past, but like all negations, a form of preservation as well. This hard fact of dialectical awareness must be an essential part of any self-conscious effort at change.[3]

Is there anything Jewish about this "hard fact of dialectical awareness?" Or perhaps the better question is the following: Is there anything about my life as a Jew that made this question important to me?

Only one ritual was observed without fail in my family. My mother would buy the little drinking glasses with candles in them well in advance. She would light them silently, I think; at any event, without ceremony. The candle would be set on top of the refrigerator, and I would see its flickering light if I came out of my room at night. I remember this flickering light, and I knew that one candle was for my grandfather and that one was for my brother, both of whom died not long before I was born. I knew many stories about my grandfather, but very little about my brother, whose sudden death at five years old cut a wedge through my parents' life. The balm for this pain was pregnancy: and I was born about a year after Neil's death. I was to fill the void left by this loss; or was I to create a place for myself and my family to put alongside this loss? I was "given" a special role: to be both the hero who would set the family right again, who would heal the wounds caused by the death of that beautiful little boy whose pictures still haunt my memories; and to be the sign of those wounds, their trace.

Perhaps my own relation to loss, to the preservation of a sign of loss and the refusal to think this sign an adequate representation of what is absent, is part of what lies behind the screen of my reaction to *Night and Fog.* The film's refusal to function as a documentary, and the insistence nonetheless on the political importance of remembering, has continued to resonate with me as I pursue my investigations of how people make sense of, live with, and deny their pasts. I only began to connect this work with themes in Judaism when I wrote a review essay on Josef Yerushalmi's brilliant book, *Zakhor: Jewish History and Jewish Memory.*[4] Yerushalmi shows that although an intense attachment to the past was a crucial part of daily life for premodern European Jewry, historiography played little or no role for

premodern European Jewry, historiography played little or no role for
Jews trying to make sense of their past after the biblical age and until the
nineteenth century. History writing only gained importance with emancipation and assimilation, that is, when the lived memory of the past was in
crisis. And history was a weak substitute for daily rituals and faith, which
had been the vessels that perpetuated the past in the present. How can the
past of a community be carried over into the present, especially when that
past is a trauma?

Claude Lanzmann's *Shoah* is an attempt to speak to this problem of
memory, its transmission, and what he calls its incarnation. The film seeks
to portray this living with loss, and at times to perform this mode of life as
well. But to "perform this mode of life" means somehow to convey a silence, an absence, at the heart of these events:

> The Holocaust is first of all unique in that it constructs a circle of
> flames around itself, the limit not to be broken because a certain
> absolute horror is not transmittable: to pretend to do so, on the oth-
> er hand, is to become guilty of the most serious transgression. One
> must speak and be silent at the same time, to know that here silence
> is the most authentic mode of speech, to maintain, as in the eye of
> the cyclone, a protected, preserved region in which nothing must
> ever enter.[5]

The problem is to screen loss, to make present in the film the absence of
the dead, yet without representing this lost object, the world destroyed
with the murdered Jews.

"I began precisely with the impossibility of telling this story," Lanzmann
told the *Cahiers du Cinema* (295). His view of this impossibility is very different from Resnais's in *Night and Fog*. Resnais took powerful, arresting archival images and juxtaposed them with a voice-off which told us, "even this
is not enough . . . even this is just husk and shade of a reality which remains inaccessible to us." Lanzmann shows us no archival material, he presents us with no gruesome images from the past. He aims at the silence and
the absence:

> That convoy—there was no way of knowing that it was the first
> earmarked for extermination. Besides, one couldn't have known that
> Sobibor would be used for the mass extermination of the Jewish

people. The next morning when I came here to work, the station was absolutely silent, and we realized, after talking with the other railway men who worked at the station here, that something utterly incomprehensible had happened. First of all, when the camp was being built, there were orders shouted in German, there were screams, Jews were working at a run, there were shots, and here there was silence, no work crews, a really total silence. Forty cars had arrived, and then . . .nothing. It was all very strange.

It was the silence that tipped them off?

That's right.

Can he describe that silence?

It was a silence . . . a standstill in the camp. You heard and saw nothing; nothing moved. So then they began to wonder, "Where have they put those Jews?"[6]

Shoah must create that silence in order to open a clearing in which the past can become present. The past must *be* in the present. As Anny Dayan-Rosenman has said, the silence created in the film allows the past to emerge now, for us:

> Above all we needed silence.
> To create in us a hole, to distance us from the exterior world, to separate the words of Shoah from other everyday, profane, words.
>   (188)

For Lanzmann this does not mean that the past is represented in the present, but that the past is incarnated in the present. He insists that this is neither a problem of history nor of memory.

> The film was not made with memories, I knew it immediately. Memory horrifies me: memory is weak. The film is the destruction of all distance between past and present, I relived this history in the present.   (301)

> It is not a historical film: it is a kind of originary event since I filmed it in the present, since I was obliged myself, to construct it with the traces of traces, with that which was strong in what I had filmed.
>   (303–4)

The traces of traces had to be put together in just such a way as to open the clearing in which the past could emerge. There are times when Lanzmann insists that he is responsible for these occasions: he is the director, the *auteur* who does not find past material in the archives but creates it in front of the camera:

> There is much *mise en scène* in the film. It is not a documentary. The locomotive, at Treblinka, it is *my* locomotive, I rented it at the Polish Railways, which was not simple, as it was not simple to insert it into the traffic.   (298)

Even in what is probably the film's most emotional scene and the one that seems the most spontaneous—the interview with the barber, Abraham Bomba—the director insists on his role:

> This is the reason why I rented the barber shop. I tried to create a setting where something could happen. I was not sure. You have to understand me, I did not know what would happen during the scene. But I knew what I wanted from him, what he had to say.[7]

In a moving essay on *Shoah,* Shoshana Felman underlines how Lanzmann's function is to be a silent narrator, even as he creates possibilities for narration as an interviewer and an inquirer:

> It is only in this way, by this abstinence of the narrator, that the film can in fact be a narrative of testimony: a narrative of that, precisely, which can neither be reported nor narrated, by another. The narrative is thus essentially a narrative of silence, the story of the filmmaker's *listening.*[8]

By assembling the conditions for this kind of listening, by opening this clearing in which the past can be embodied in voices in the present, Lanzmann has created the conditions for shivah.

Shivah, the Jewish ritual observed for seven days after the burial of the mourned person, seemed to me as I grew up to be a strange, powerful sign of Jewishness. In the assimilated, almost areligious context of my childhood, shivah was still observed in my family and among the Jews that I knew. I was struck by what seemed to me to be the injunction to talk about the dead. Was this because my brother's brief life was thereafter to be guarded in silence? Was this because of my own fear of breaking this silence with my parents or older brother? I imagined shivah, and perceived it when I participated in the ritual, as an incessant talking about the deceased. In religious school this was given a psychological explanation: by talking about the mourned, the mourners work through their own feelings of loss. The point is not simply, however, to dissipate these feelings but to heighten and share them. The absence is made present for the community of mourners through a ritual that brings the dead to mind, to voice.

Lanzmann's film creates the conditions for this experience of loss, as we become the witnesses of the losses of those talking on the screen. We sit with them (there is nothing we can do) as they describe the horrors of *not* dying with their brethren; we sit with them (there is nothing we can do) as they describe watching their loved ones go to their deaths; we sit with them (there is nothing we can do) as their torturers explain in gruesome detail the mechanics of murder, the technical problem of killing so many so quickly without leaving too many traces. But there are traces, and they speak to us; they are made to speak to us, and we must force ourselves to stay, seated with them. Often throughout the nine and one-half hours of the film we want to turn away, walk away, stop the talking. It is, after all, very repetitive: the cold, the screams, the cold, the beatings, the trains, the trains. . . . But we stay seated with them. There is nothing we can do. The absence is made present for the community of mourners through a ritual that brings the dead to mind, to voice.

How different this message is from that delivered by Resnais's film! Although *Night and Fog* was made as a "warning signal," we should be clear that the warning is not what Jews have in mind with the deceptive phrase "Never Again!" There is no attention to Jews as such in *Night and Fog,* and this is one of the curiosities about its becoming *the* Holocaust film for American religious schools. The word *Jew* does not occur in the film, although we do see people with stars of David sewn on their clothes. Resnais's film is to remind us of the dangers of racist fascism; the *esprit concentrationnaire* can return. As the narrative of the film proclaims, "War nods but has one eye open. The skill shown by the Nazis would be child's play today." It also tells us to beware:

> Who is on the lookout from this strange observation post for the new executioners? Are their faces really different from ours? Somewhere among us lucky kapos survive.

There are those who look sincerely at these ruins as if the old concentration camp monster was dead underneath them. Those who hope as the image fades that we have been healed of the old *concentrationnaire* plague, who pretend that all this happened only one time and in one country, who do not think to look around us, who are deaf to the endless deafening cry.

By awakening us to this cry, *Night and Fog* puts its viewers on alert, in a position to defend themselves against any revivals of the spirit that made the camps possible.

Shoah does not put us into a position of alert. Its goal is to allow us to assume a posture of receptivity. We must become ready to listen to the past emerge from the people on the screen; we must become ready to see the past become present. How do we become ready? We are silent before all this testimony, as the film itself opens with silence—written paragraphs on the screen to be read silently by the viewers and not spoken by any narrator. The *Shulhan 'Aruk* tells us in the laws of mourning: "The comforters are not permitted to open [conversation] until the mourner opens first." No one speaks to Job before he begins to tell of his misery. They await his words. Thus the film attempts to put its viewers in proper relation to the past being (re)experienced by the people on the screen. It presents the past on film but a past manifested in the present. The events of the Shoah happened thirty-five years before the interviews were done, and yet under the persistence of Lanzmann's questioning the people being interviewed at times seem to be right *there* with the past. And this is why Lanzmann insists that the distance between past and present is abolished in the film, a claim that is at the heart of a historian's effort not merely to represent the past but to *bring it back*. Michelet called his nineteenth-century histories "resurrections."

Resnais's film has the problem of trying to confront us with an exceptional experience—an experience of ultimate horror and absolute evil—so as to remind us of what human beings are capable. The difficulty here is that in showing us something exceptional he may so distance us from the event as to make it almost irrelevant for us. Lanzmann's film, on the contrary, gives us small, recognizably ordinary human beings: people with whom you can identify, people whom you can hate. Lanzmann's interviews—on the farm, in a living room, in a barber shop or a restaurant—are *everyday;* they are scenes we are to imagine as taking place right next door. Both films use shots of the train lines, but in *Shoah* the railway track is a commuter line; we should imagine ourselves going down it; or at least traveling down the track of memory until we get to the black hole of the camps. The track in Resnais's film is of a very different order. He is taking us to another planet; or at least that is part of what he wants us to feel. It is true that there are areas of the other planet that we can recognize: it has its orphanage, its home for the handicapped, its hospital, and its prison. It is the world, perhaps, of our nightmares, a landscape both foreign and familiar. We are to feel not the small steps that led the old gentleman to being a sadistic beast but the leap into a world of total fear. We are to be afraid of what we see. Now, one of the responses we have to fear is flight. We may view these images and mentally leave the theater or physically close our eyes. This is *too much;* is there any real possibility of relating to the mountain of hair, or to the skin and soap? Resnais's gamble is that we will not turn away mentally or physically, but that instead we will have the other response to fear: we will want to fight. Fight against what? Not just Nazi war criminals or collaborators but against the human propensity for evil that is nakedly displayed in the film. This propensity is usually hidden beneath the cover of night and fog. Lanzmann has a very different agenda. He takes us slowly into this night—or at least into the darkness of his subjects' memories. He is willing to navigate in the fog. Resnais, on the other hand, shines his light into this obscure evil. Look at it, he says, and beware!

The dilemma for both filmmakers is a problem with all historical representation. Let me call that problem the dialectic between connection and otherness. All historical representation must indicate that the subjects being referred to are of another time; they are not simply *just like us.* This is clear if you study the history of a culture not your own, but it is always the case insofar as the time you study is not your own. Historical representation, properly so-called, must communicate this distance, this otherness. At the same time, the representation cannot be confined to difference or otherness. All history is history of the present, and a successful representation must convey something of the way we connect to this otherness. When Lanzmann is carried away by the fantasy of obliterating the distance between present and past, he neglects an important quality of his own achievement. This fantasy helped him make his extraordinary film, and the desire to unite with the past lends the work enormous energy. I think I recognize this fantasy and can acknowledge the energy it sometimes provides. But uniting with the past, taking the place of the dead or even being in their place, is only a fantasy.

Lanzmann's interviews show us *the distance* the survivors must travel to have the past return to them; we witness them making the connection to the past. Lanzmann is also at times fascinated by this distance, by the difference between those things that stay the same and those that have changed (and thus have a past different from the present). "But the tracks? I show them to him, I ask him: 'Are these the same ones?' 'Yes,' he tells me, 'absolutely the same.' I needed that: a permanence of iron, of steel. I needed to attach myself to it" (290). Lanzmann struggles to find the line dividing the world of the camp from the rest of the world, and he wants to record the ramp over which the Jews passed from one to the other. Here is the series of questions the director poses to Jan Piwonski at the Sobibor Station:

> The station building, the rails, the platforms are just as they were in 1942? Nothing's changed?
> Exactly where did the camp begin?
> So I'm standing inside the camp perimeter, right?
> Where I am now is fifty feet from the station, and I'm already outside the camp.
> This is the Polish part, and over there is death.[9]

You can see some of the people he interviews cross that line, and struggle against doing so. The distance between present and past cannot be obliterated for the survivors. They can cross over, but neither they nor we are anywhere but in the present. This is something we must learn from *Shoah,* and from shivah. Mourning, or the historical consciousness that results from it, is not a reparation; it is not replacing the dead but making a place for something else to be in relation to the past. This is a crucial part of the pain of surviving the dead, of consciously coming after them. It is a lesson Lanzmann continues to wrestle with:

> The idea which was always the most painful for me, it was that all these people died alone. [. . .] When I say that they died alone, it is in relation to me that this phrase has meaning. For me, the most profound and at the same time most incomprehensible meaning of the film, is in a way . . . to resuscitate these people, and to kill them a second time, with me; in accompanying them.   (291)

This is the language of mourning, of shivah. In accompanying these people, in passing with them through the past, Lanzmann performs what Jewish law calls a "highly meritorious act." He comes to dwell with those who suffer loss, and with some who are lost in their suffering. The absence is to be made present for the community of mourners through a ritual that brings the dead to mind, to voice.

The community helps one to make a connection to loss, to cross the line from the past and return to the present. *Shoah,* like shivah, is an act of piety. The point of the repetitive details of the film, of all those hours sitting with the people on the screen and in the theater, is not just to understand the past correctly (although that is part of the project); nor is it just to arm people against future outbursts of racism (although that too may be a result); but to dwell with loss, to suffer one's poverty, to be linked together in the presence of those absent and to give them, as Lanzmann quotes from Isaiah, an everlasting name.

Shivah reminds us in the midst of our pain that we are not alone. Two of Lanzmann's survivors related to him that as they struggled to stay alive each had the fantasy that he was the last Jew or the last person in the world. *Shoah* reminds us that they and the survivors of the Holocaust were not and are not alone. But one does not have to identify with them—to assume their place—to be connected to them. The painful work of mourning enables one to find one's own place, to find a way of living with the dead as the past in the present. During shivah we bring the past to the present, we allow ourselves to experience what we have lost, and also what we are—that we are—despite this loss. Neither *Shoah* nor shivah attempts to replace the past, to offer compensations for loss. They allow us to incarnate the past, to name it, and to remain in the present. They are acts of connection and of otherness. Acts of piety.

In my life, such acts recall me to my Jewishness.

NOTES

1. Michael S. Roth, *Psycho-Analysis as History: Negation and Freedom in Freud* (Ithaca: Cornell University Press, 1987), 132.

2. Ibid., 189.

3. Ibid., 133.

4. See chapter 10 in this collection.

5. *Au sujet de Shoah: le film de Claude Lanzmann* (Paris: Belin, 1990), 310. Subsequent references to this book will be given parenthetically in the text.

6. Claude Lanzmann, *Shoah: An Oral History of the Holocaust* (New York: Pantheon, 1985), 67.

7. Claude Lanzmann, "Seminar on *Shoah,*" *Yale French Studies* 79 (1991): 95.

8. Shoshana Felman and Dori Laub, *Testimony: Crises of Witnessing in Literature, Psychoanalysis and History* (New York: Routledge, 1992), 218.

9. Claude Lanzmann, *Shoah: An Oral History of the Holocaust,* 38–39.

Index

on, 28; of philosophers, 103–4; post-
modern apartness versus paths to
community, 115–16; private versus
public concerns, 115–19, 128; problem of evaluating change, 83, 84–85,
87, 88; relation to history and meaning, 143–44; retreat from, 51–52, 60;
Schorske's investigations, 48–49, 50,
55
The Political Philosophy of Hobbes, 97
"The Politics of Historical Interpretation:
Discipline and Desublimation," 143
Postmodernism, 58, 65, 126, 150
Poststructuralism, 56, 57, 71, 142
Prisons, Foucault's studies of, 80, 122, 155
Progress: from accidental coincidence,
118–19; of freedom, 3; ideology of,
110; Jewish faith in, 183–84; loss of
faith in, 54, 105, 164, 172, 177
Proust, M., 126
Psychoanalysis: as compensation for political impotence, 197; as creation of viable connections with painful past, 12–
13, 186; as form of history, 186, 216–
18; and problems of emigrant psychoanalysts, 38; Schorske's probing of limitations of, 50–51, 55
*Psycho-Analysis as History: Negation and Free-
dom in Freud*, 216

Racism, 27, 28, 30, 226
Ranke, L. von, 22, 139
"Realism," 139, 141, 143, 145
Recognition, man's desire for, 166–67
Reflexivity: in Foucault, 73–74, 77; in
Foucault's Nietzsche, 73; irony in guise
of, 160; in Rorty, 116; in Schorske, 48,
59, 61, 64
Relativism: as failure of moral systems,
25–26, 35–36; predicament of, 119–
20; recognition of, 24–25
Religion, 125
Resnais, A., 201, 202, 219, 224

Rhetoric: importance for creating realities, 14, 56, 142–43; irony as device
for contingency, 160; relativization of
ideas for transparency, 41, 42, 43;
White's examination of use of, 139–40
Ricoeur, P., 145
Robinson, J. H., 24
Rorty, R.: on Davidson, 117–18; on Derrida, 157–58; distinguishing private
from public concerns, 115–19, 128;
emphasis on solidarity, 10–11; on
Freud, 118–19; history as contingent,
118–19, 130; history as legitimating
stories, 5; on irony of Foucault, 122–
23; liberalism of, 114, 115, 119, 120,
121, 122, 123, 124, 128; on Nietzsche
and Heidegger, 126, 127–28; praise
for, 113; on Proust and Derrida, 126–
27, 128; questioning idea of genuine
knowledge, 7, 8; silent on sexism, 136;
on universalism with diversity, 125;
view of liberal utopia, 119–21
Rwanda, 11

Saar, F. von, 52
Sartre, J., 34–35
Schiele, E., 60
Schnitzler, A., 48, 49
Schoenberg, A., 53, 60
Schönerer: G., 50, 53
Schorske, C. E.: comparison to Hughes,
60–61; on costs of political resignation, 60, 62; criticisms of, 61–63; fragmentation as antihistoricism, 4; on
Freud, 196, 197; historians as synthe-
sizers of isolated discourses, 4, 209; on
Klimt, 52, 55; reflexivity, 48, 59, 61,
64; solutions to fragmentation, 3; use
of narrative, 59, 64–65
Science: for legitimation of history writing, 22, 26, 55, 138; scientific method,
120, 164; White on historians' antiquated conceptions of, 138

Credits

The essays in this book appeared in different versions in a variety of books and periodicals. I gratefully acknowledge permission to reprint the essays here.

1. "Unsettling the Past: Objectivity, Irony, and History"
   Annals of Scholarship (1992), 171–78. Reprinted by permission of Wayne State University Press.
2. "Narrative as Enclosure: The Contextual Histories of H. Stuart Hughes"
   Journal of the History of Ideas 51, no. 3 (1990): 505–15.
3. "Performing History: Modernist Contextualism in Carl E. Schorske's *Fin-de-siècle Vienna*"
   American Historical Review 99, no. 3 (1994): 729–45.
4. "Foucault on Discourse and History: A Style of Delegitimation"
   The Philosophy of Discourse, vol. 2, ed. Chip Sills and George H. Jensen (Portsmouth, N.H.: Heinemann, 1991), 102–124.
5. "Natural Right and the End of History: Leo Strauss and Alexandre Kojève"
   Revue de Metaphysique et de Morale 96, no. 3 (1991): 407–22.
6. "Thin Description: Richard Rorty's Use of History"
   History and Theory 29, no. 3 (1990): 339–57. Reprinted by permission of Wesleyan University Press.
7. "Cultural Criticism and Political Theory: Hayden White's Rhetorics of History"
   Political Theory 16, no. 4 (1988): 636–46. Reprinted by permission of Sage Publications.

8. "The Ironist's Cage"

   Political Theory 19, no. 3 (1991): 419–32. Reprinted by permission of Sage Publications.

9. "The Nostalgic Nest at the End of History"

   History and Theory 32, no. 2, (1993): 188–96. Reprinted by permission of Wesleyan University Press.

10. "Tradition, Memory, and History: On Edward Shils and Yosef Yerushalmi"

    "Review essay on Edward Shils, *Tradition,* and Yosef Yerushalmi, *Zakhor: Jewish History and Modern Memory,*" *Telos* 62 (1984–1985): 218–22.

11. "Freud's Use and Abuse of the Past"

    Rediscovering History: History, Politics, and the Psyche, ed. Michael S. Roth, 336–48, by permission of the publishers, Stanford University Press. Copyright 1994 by the Board of Trustees of the Leland Stanford Junior University.

12. "You Must Remember This: History, Memory, and Trauma in *Hiroshima Mon Amour*"

    Revisioning History: Film and the Construction of the Past, ed. Robert Rosenstone (1995), 91–101. Reprinted by permission of Princeton University Press.

13. "*Shoah* as Shivah"

    Wrestling with the Angel: Jewish Identity in the Academy (Madison: Wisconsin University Press, 1996).